Paris

France

This guide offers a selection of Paris's hotels, restaurants and stores hand-picked from the thousands the city has to offer.

EVERYMAN
CITY GUIDES

EVERYMAN CITY GUIDES

ISBN 1-84159-017-7

First published April 1998
Revised and updated April 1999
Revised and updated April 2000

Originally published in France by Nouveaux Loisirs, a subsidiary of Gallimard, Paris 1997, and in Italy by Touring Editore, Srl., Milano 1997

SERIES EDITORS
Seymourina Cruse/Marisa Bassi
PARIS EDITION: Seymourina Cruse, Sophie Lenormand *with* Lionel Monéger
GRAPHICS
Élizabeth Cohat, Yann Le Duc
LAYOUT: Gérard Dumas, Olivier Lauga, Yann Le Duc
AIRPORT MAPS
Kristoff Chemineau
MINI-MAPS, AROUND PARIS MAPS:
Édigraphie
STREET MAPS:
Touring Club Italiano
PRODUCTION
Catherine Bourrabier

Translated by Wendy Allatson

Edited and typeset by First Edition Translations Ltd, Cambridge, UK

Printed in Italy by Editoriale Lloyd

Authors and editors
PARIS

Things you need to know:
Lionel Monéger (1)
Historian Lionel Monéger has worked on travel guides for Éditions Autrement and Gallimard.

Where to stay: François Simon (2)
François Simon is a journalist who learned his trade with the regional daily *Presse-Océan* and *Gault Millau*. He has written books on Paris hotels and restaurants and was editor-in-chief of *Figaroscope* until 1997.

Where to eat:
Jean-Claude Ribaut (3)
Jean-Claude Ribaut has been writing the gourmet column of the French national newspaper *Le Monde* since 1989. He has collaborated on several gourmet publications and co-edited *Jardin des épices* (Du May, 1992). His architectural training and long-standing friendship with the French chef, Jacques Manière, have helped to make him an astute critic of gourmet cuisine.

After dark: Anne-Isabelle Jolly (4)
Anne-Isabelle Jolly is editor-in-chief of several works on the theater, a frequent contributor to the 'Sortir' column of *Femme* magazine and daily theater reviewer on French radio (FM 88.2).

What to see/Further afield:
René Maurice (5)
René Maurice is the author of several historical works on Paris and the Île-de-France and an enthusiast for the more unusual aspects of Paris.

Where to shop:
Evelyne Vermorel (6)
Journalist Evelyne Vermorel writes for *Le Point*, *Le Figaro* and *Vogue Homme* magazines. In 1981, she founded the 'Beauté' column of the *Madame Figaro* magazine and since 1994 has been director of international editions of *Madame Figaro*, and contributing to the Italian publication *Madame 'Class' Figaro*.

Note from the publisher:
To keep the price of this guide as low as possible we decided on a common edition for the UK and US, which has meant American spelling.

Symbols

- telephone
- fax
- price or price range
- opening hours
- credit cards accepted
- credit cards not accepted
- toll-free number
- e-mail/website address
- ★ tips and recommendations

Access

- subway stations
- bus (or tram)
- private parking
- parking attendant
- no facilities for the disabled
- train
- car
- boat

Hotels

- telephone in room
- fax in room on request
- minibar
- television in room
- air-conditioned rooms
- 24-hour room service
- caretaker
- babysitting
- meeting room(s)
- no pets
- breakfast
- open for tea/coffee
- restaurant
- live music
- disco
- garden, patio or terrace
- gym, fitness club
- swimming pool, sauna

Restaurants

- vegetarian food
- view
- formal dress required
- smoking area
- bar

Museums and galleries

- on-site store(s)
- guided tours
- café

Stores

- branches, outlets

The Insider's Guide is made up of **8 sections** each indicated by a different color.

Things you need to know (mauve)
Where to stay (blue)
Where to eat (red)
After dark (pink)
What to see (green)
Further afield (orang
Where to shop (yello
Finding your way (purple)

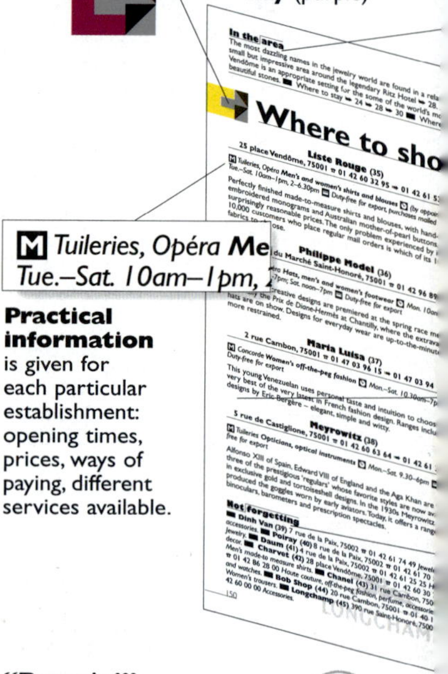

Practical information is given for each particular establishment: opening times, prices, ways of paying, different services available.

"Bargain!"
This star marks good value hotels and restaurants.

How to use this guide

In the area
The most dazzling names in the je
small but impressive area around
eat ➥ 62 ➥ 64 ➥ 74
■ After dark ➥ 88 ➥
■ What to see ➥ 10

The section **"In the area"** refers you (➥ 00) to other establishments that are covered in a different section of the guide but found in the same area of the city.

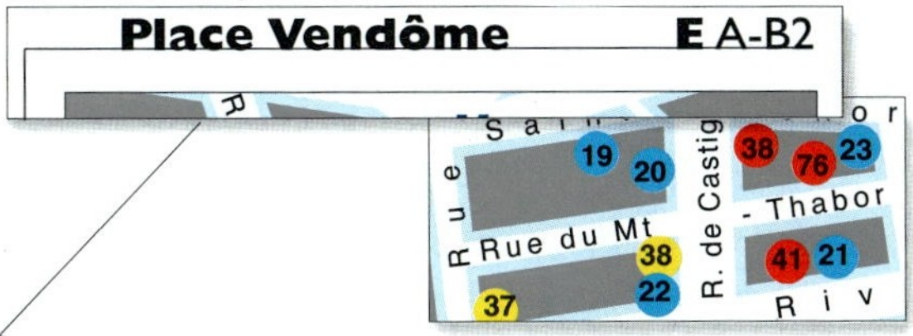

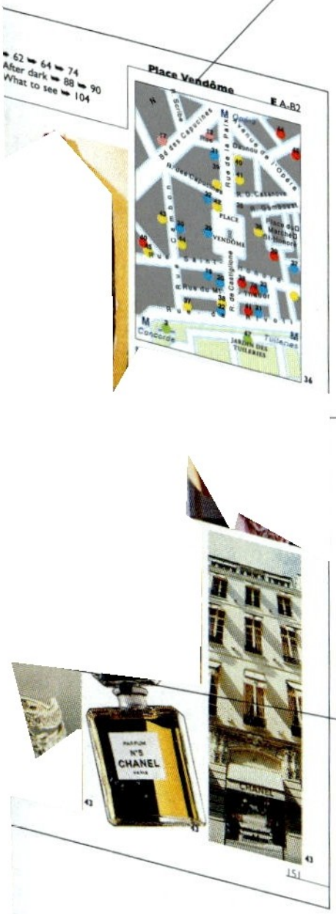

The small map shows all the establishments mentioned and others described elsewhere but found "in the area", by the color of the section.

The name of the district is given above the map. A grid reference (**A** B-C 2) enables you to find it in the section on Maps at the end of the book.

numbers ending in 4 – e.g. 'Ronsard' (no. 14) and
54) – overlook the street. ★ 'Balzac' (no. 56) is a

Hot tips, indicated by a star ★, contains advice from the author: the best rooms, recommended dishes, views not to be missed...

Not forgetting
■ **Dinh Van (39)** 7 rue de la Paix
accessories. ■ **Poiray (40)** 8 rue d

The section "Not forgetting" lists other useful addresses in the same area.

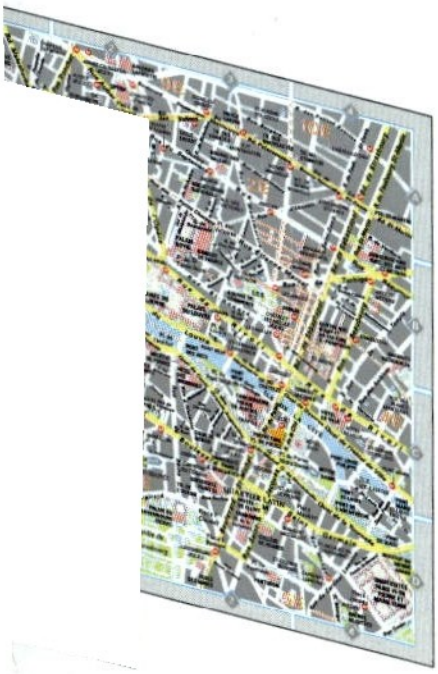

The opening page to each section contains an index ordered alphabetically (Getting there), by subject or by district (After dark) as well as useful addresses and advice.

The section "Things you need to know" covers information on getting to Paris and day-to-day life in the city.

Theme pages introduce a selection of establishments on a given topic.

The "Maps" section of this guide contains 9 street plans of Paris followed by a detailed index.

Time difference
France is one hour ahead of Greenwich Mean Time (GMT). For example, when it is 6pm in Paris, it is 5pm in London and noon in New York.

Getting around

Electrical appliances
Electrical appliances in France operate on 220 volts and use 2-pin plugs ➥ 15.

Paris for all seasons
Spring: flowering chestnut trees and pleasant weather, but watch out for April showers!
Summer: pleasant weather (67°F 20°C, average), free parking in August.
Autumn: generally fine weather; the Paris trade fair season is at its peak in September.
Winter: low average temperatures (46°F 7–8°C,) but a full cultural calendar.

Changing money on arrival

Take French currency (French francs) with you if you are going to arrive in Paris late at night or if you don't want to waste time. The bureaux de change at Roissy and Orly airports are open daily from 6.30am–11.30pm, and in the mainline stations from 7–8am and 8–10.30pm. Alternatively, you can withdraw money from cash machines with an international credit card.

50 Things you need to Know

Passport

EU nationals can stay in France for up to six months if they have a national identity card, and for an indefinite period if they have a valid passport. US and Canadian tourists visiting France for up to three months do not currently require a visa. Others should enquire about visa requirements before departure.

Health

EU nationals are covered for urgent medical treatment and should take form E111 with them ➡ 14. Non-EU nationals are not covered and are therefore advised to take out adequate medical insurance before departure.

Driving

Drivers must carry their driver's license, car registration documents and certificate of insurance. Seat belt must be worn on all roads.

INDEX

- Departure lounge
- Public area
- Airline desks
- Shops
- Check in
- Bus
- Taxis
- Car for hire
- TGV
- RER-Orlyval
- Informations A
- Bureau de Change
- Post office
- Business center
- Hotels

Getting there

Useful numbers

Flight times
☎ *01 49 75 15 15*

Information
Orly
☎ *01 49 75 52 52*
CDG
☎ *01 48 62 22 80*

Police
Orly
☎ *01 49 75 43 04*
CDG
☎ *01 48 62 31 22*

Customs
Orly
☎ *01 49 75 84 00*
CDG
☎ *01 48 62 35 43*

Medical center
Orly
☎ *01 49 75 48 09*
CDG Terminal 1
☎ *01 48 62 28 00*
CDG Terminal 2
☎ *01 48 62 53 32*

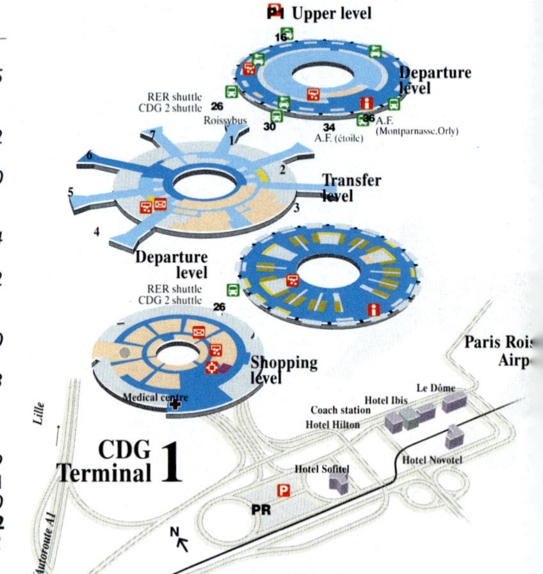

Business

Business center
ORY ☎ *01 49 75 12 33*
CDG ☎ *01 48 62 22 90*

Mobile phone hire
SFR-Ellinas
☎ (courtesy) *01 48 16 10 99*

Links from CDG

CDG to Paris
RER B
to Gare du Nord and Chatelet-Les-Halles
(35–45 mins)
daily 4.55am–11.55pm ● *F45*
Taxi *(45 mins)*
● *F250 (approx.)*
Bus Air France
to Porte-Maillot and Étoile
(40 mins)
daily 5.40am–11pm ● *F55*
to Montparnasse
(50 mins)
daily 7am–9pm
● *F65*
Roissybus to Opéra *(45 mins)*
daily 5am–11pm ● *F40*

Roissy to Orly
RER B, Orlyval
(70 mins)
Mon.–Sat. 6am–10.30pm; Sun. 7am–10.55pm ● *F97*
Taxi *(60 mins)*
● *F300 (approx.)*
Bus Air France
(75 mins) ● *F70*

Links from Orly

Between west and south terminals
Orlyval
(2 mins) ● *free*

Orly to Paris
Orlyval
to Châtelet
(35 mins)
Mon.–Sat. 6am–10.30pm; Sun. 7am–11pm
● *F57*
to La Défense
(45 mins)
● *F62*
Orlyrail
to Austerlitz
(35 mins)
daily 6.30am–11.30pm ● *F30*
Taxi *(45 mins)*
● *F155 (approx.)*
Orlybus
to Denfert-Rochereau
(25 mins)
daily 6am–11pm ● *F30*
Bus Air France
to Invalides
(45 mins)
daily 5.50am–11pm ● *F45*

Paris has two airports: Orly to the south and Roissy-Charles-de-Gaulle (CDG) to the north.

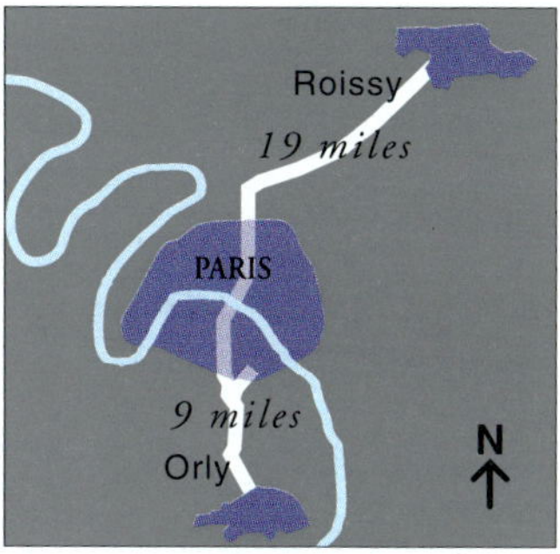

Hotels

At CDG
Cocoon
☎ 01 48 62 06 16
➟ 01 48 62 56 97
Ibis
☎ 01 49 19 19 19
➟ 01 49 19 19 21
Novotel
☎ 01 49 19 27 27
➟ 01 49 19 27 99
Sofitel
☎ 01 49 19 29 29
➟ 01 49 19 29 00
Hilton
☎ 01 49 19 77 77
➟ 01 49 19 77 78
Sheraton
☎ 01 49 19 70 70
➟ 01 49 19 70 71

At Orly
Mercure
☎ 01 46 87 23 37
➟ 01 46 87 71 92
Hilton
☎ 01 45 12 45 12
➟ 01 45 12 45 00
Ibis
☎ 01 56 70 50 50
➟ 01 46 87 29 92

Aéroports de Paris

Rendezvous points

These are located near the Aéroports de Paris (ADP) desks.

Car hire

Avis
☎ 0802 05 05 05
Budget
☎ 08 00 10 00 01
Europcar
☎ 0803 352 352
Hertz
☎ 01 39 38 38 38
National-Citer
☎ 01 44 38 61 61
Sixt
☎ 01 44 38 55 55
Inter-touring Service
♿ Manual gearbox
☎ 01 45 88 52 37

CDG

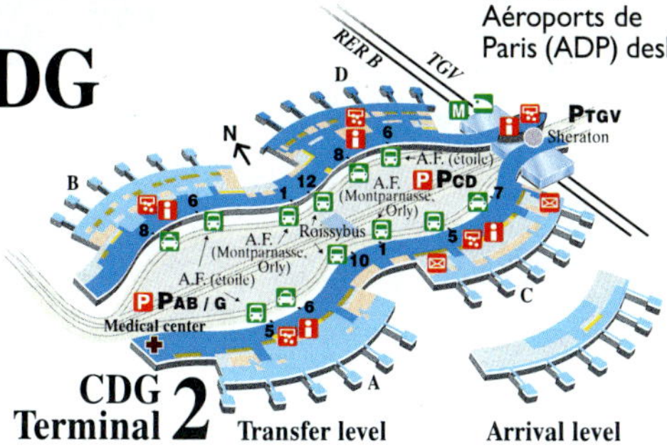

Airline companies

Air France ☎ Paris 08 02 80 28 02 **British Airways** ☎ Paris 01 47 78 14 14 ☎ US 800-433-7300 ☎ UK 0345 789 789 **Delta** ☎ Paris 01 47 68 92 92 US ☎ 800-241-4141 ☎ UK 0800 414 767 **Virgin** ☎ US 800-862-8621 ☎ UK (01293) 747 747

ORY

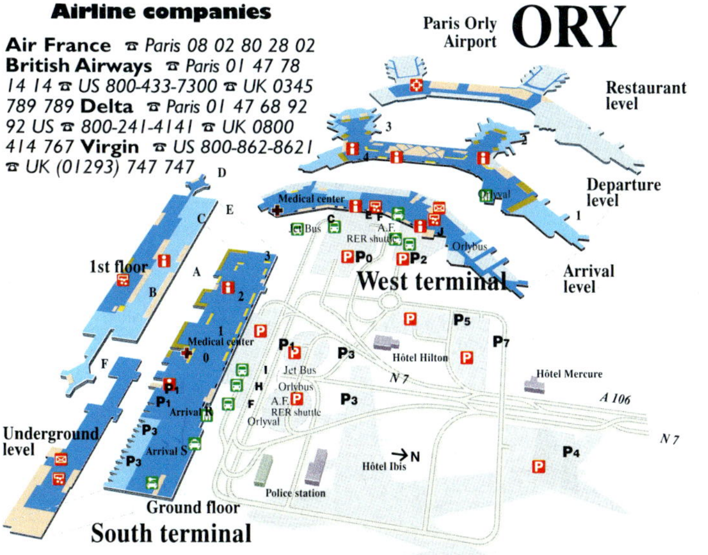

Basic facts

Paris, located in the center of western Europe, is also at the center of the French motorway and rail networks. TGV (1), Thalys (2) and Eurostar (3) trains travel from London, Amsterdam and Brussels to the Gare du Nord in Paris in record time. Paris has major parking problems

Getting there

4 3 2 1

By train

The city's six main-line stations are linked to the subway and bus networks. Métro map ➥ 172. Gare du Nord and Gare de Lyon are also linked to the RER (suburban express) network.

Main lines
There is one phone number for all the main-line stations. It deals with train times and ticket reservations.
☎ *08 36 35 35 35*

Île-de-France
Information:
☎ *01 53 90 20 20*

Travelers with disabilities
☎ *0800 15 47 53*

Euraffaire
A business area and lounge is available for first-class passengers:
Gare Montparnasse
☎ *01 40 48 11 72*
Gare de Lyon
☎ *01 53 33 16 56*
Gare de l'Est
☎ *01 40 18 60 62*

Stations

Gare du Nord
Services the northern French regions, the United Kingdom, Benelux countries and northern Germany.

Gare de l'Est
Services northeastern France, Switzerland, Austria and southern Germany.

Gare de Lyon
Services south-eastern France, Switzerland and Italy.
🍴 *Le Train Bleu* ➥ *66*

Gare d'Austerlitz
Services central and southwestern France, Spain and Portugal.

Gare Montparnasse
Services western and southwestern France and Spain.

Gare Saint-Lazare
Services Normandy and the United Kingdom via the ports of Normandy.

Le Thalys

This high-speed train operates a daily service between Belgium/ the Netherlands and Paris.

Information/ reservations
☎ *08 36 35 35 36*

Brussels–Paris
Gare de Bruxelles-Midi (Brussels) to Gare du Nord (Paris), 1hr 25 mins (17 departures daily). ● *F320-521 roundtrip.*

Amsterdam–Paris
Amsterdam CS to Gare du Nord (Paris), 4 hrs 47 mins (4 departures daily). ● *F446-892 roundtrip.*

Thalys Entreprises
☎ *01 47 16 27 37*
🕘 *9am–6pm*

(5) and drivers are advised to use the city's parking lots (6).

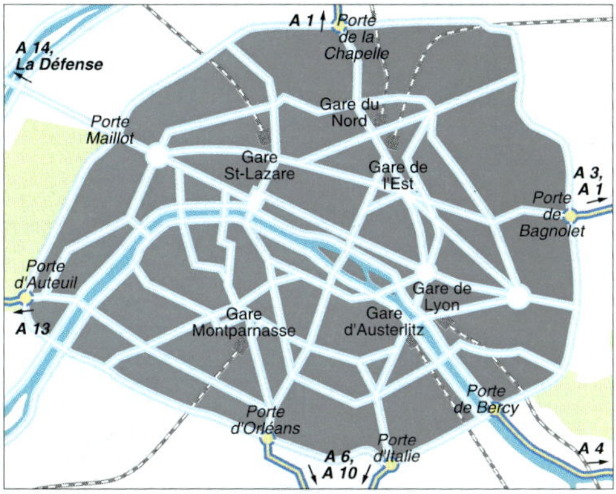

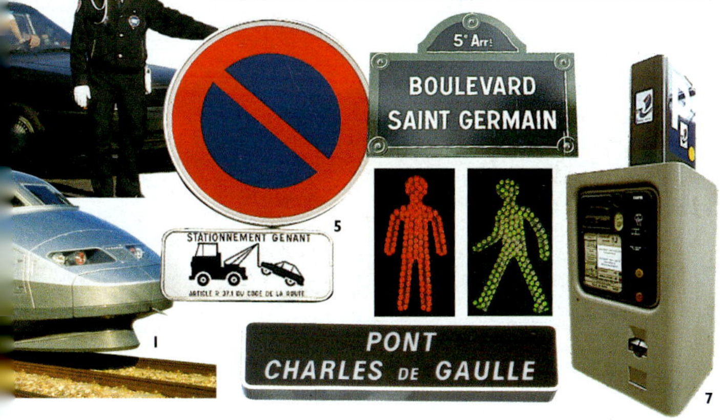

6 5 1 7

Eurostar

Reservations
☎ *UK 0990 186 186* ☎ *France 08 36 35 35 39*

London–Paris
Eurostar high-speed train service between London (Waterloo Station) and Paris (Gare du Nord) via the Channel Tunnel in 3 hrs. Departures every hour during the week.
From London:
🕒 *daily 5.15am–7.53pm*
From Paris:
🕒 *daily 6.37am–9.13pm*

Train and car
SNCF and Avis offer a car rental service in every railroad station in Paris. Make a reservation when buying your train ticket.

By bus

International buses to the Paris-Galliéni international bus station at Porte de Bagnolet.

Eurolines
Daily departures to Paris from major European cities.
☎ *08 36 69 52 52*
🕒 *8am–8pm*

By car

Travel information
Drivers can obtain information from the regional travel information center:
☎ *01 48 99 33 33*
Information in French on short wave:
FIP *90.4 MHz* during the day.
France Info *105.5 MHz* in the evening.

Driving in Paris
There is a speed limit of 30mph (50kph) except on the *périphérique* (Paris ring road). Although driving in Paris does not present any particular problems, the same cannot be said for parking.

Parking
Pay and display
Mon.–Sat., 9am–7pm
Charges vary according to districts.
● *F5–F15 per hour.*
Tickets can be obtained from ticket machines using coins or parking cards available from tobacconists.
● *F100 and F200.*

Free parking
Sundays and public holidays and through August.

Car pound
It is quite common for cars to be towed away for obstruction. You can get the address of the local car pound from the nearest police station or the Préfecture de Paris.
☎ *01 53 71 53 71*

Basic facts

Paris is served by a comprehensive public transport system. Buy a 'carnet' (book) of tickets for use on both the bus and metro systems. On the bus you must stamp your ticket to validate it. Métro map ➥ 172.

Getting around

Public transport

The transport network is divided into 5 zones: 1 and 2 for the city of Paris, 3 to 5 for the suburbs. There is a standard fare for zones 1 and 2.

RATP Information

☎ *08 36 68 77 14*

Tickets

RER (suburban express) and bus tickets available from ticket offices, machines in stations, and some tobacconists.

● *F8 each; F52 for a book of ten.*

Travel cards

'Carte Paris Visite'

Entitles you to unlimited journeys by subway, RER, bus and train within the Île-de-France (Paris region). ● *3 zones: F55 (1 day); F90 (2 days); F120 (3 days); F175 (5 days)* ● *5 zones: F110 (1 day) F175 (2days); F245 (3 days); F300 (5 days)*

Mobilis

One-day travel card

● *3 zones: F40; 1–5 zones: F70.*

Métro

Map ➥ 172

With 15 lines and some 300 stations, the métro is the most compact subway network in the world. It has connections with the RER and SNCF (main-line) networks.

🕒 *5.30–12.30am*

RER

Map ➥ 172

Four suburban express lines (A, B, C, D) link Paris with the Île-de-France. Line C2 runs to Orly, C5 to Versailles and B3 to Roissy-Charles-de-Gaulle. Practical for quick trips across Paris.

🕒 *5.30–12.30am*

Bus

During the week, services operate on the 60 or so bus routes from 5.30am–8.30pm. Some run until 12.30am and on Sundays and public holidays. Few buses run after 1am.

Balabus

Runs between Grande Arche de la Défense and Gare de Lyon (50 mins).

🕒 *Apr. - Sep. Sun.*

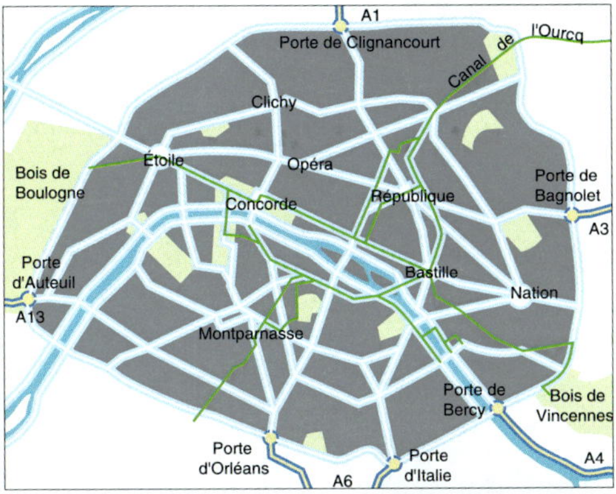

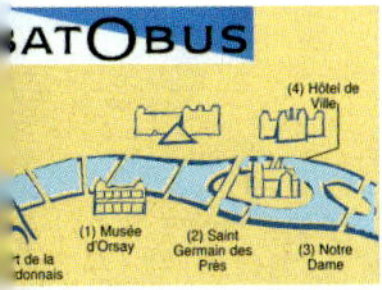

and public holidays 12.30–8pm

Batobus

The Batobus (boat-bus) offers a five-stop tour of the center of Paris (see map). It leaves from the Eiffel Tower (port de la Bourdonnais): *Musée d'Orsay* (Solférino); *Saint-Germain-des-Prés* (Quai Malaquais); *Notre-Dame* (Quai Montebello); *Hôtel de Ville* (town hall); *Louvre* (Quai du Louvre).
🕒 *Apr. - May, Sep.- Nov.. 10am-7pm; June.-Aug. 10am-9pm* ● *Inclusive: F60 (1 day) or F20 on departure and F10 per step.*
☎ *01 44 11 33 44*

Taxis

Paris has 14,500 taxis. Unlike London and New York, taxis need not stop if hailed. Find one of the 460 taxi stands. A taxi is free when the Taxi sign is lit up, occupied when there is an orange light showing.

Charges
The pick-up charge is F13, and there is a surcharge for a fourth passenger or bulky luggage. Tips are not compulsory but it is customary to give 10%.

Complaints
In the event of difficulties, phone the Préfecture de Police:
☎ *01 45 31 14 80*

Taxi companies
Alpha Taxi
☎ *01 45 85 85 85*
Artaxi
☎ *01 42 03 50 50*
Taxis Bleu
☎ *01 49 36 10 10*
Taxi Étoile
☎ *01 41 27 27 27*
Taxis G7
☎ *01 47 39 47 39*

Cycling

Paris has 30 miles of cycle tracks, including two major routes: from Bois de Vincennes to Bois de Boulogne, and from Porte de Pantin to Porte de Vanves (see map). The quays along the Seine are reserved for the use of pedestrians and cyclists only on Sundays.

Cycle hire
● *F80 per day*
Paris à Vélo
37 bd. Bourdon, 75004
☎ *01 48 87 60 01*
Paris Vélo
2 rue du Fer-à-Moulin, 75005
☎ *01 43 37 59 22*

Basic facts

The Office du Tourisme (1) on the Champs-Élysées will make reservations and provide information on events in Paris and the Île-de-France region. For lost property, go to the Objets Trouvés (2), and the Poste du Louvre (3) is open all night if you have urgent mail to send.

Getting by

Tourist Office

Office du Tourisme, 127 avenue des Champs-Élysées, 75008
☎ *08 36 68 31 12*
🕒 *9am–8pm*
Ⓜ *Charles-de-Gaulle-Étoile*

Money

Coins/notes
The French unit of currency is the *franc* (F). There are 100 centimes (cts) to the franc. Coins: cts5, 10, 20 and 50; F1, 2, 5, 10 and 20. Notes: F20, 50, 100, 200 and 500.

Exchange
To change cash, traveler's checks and Eurocheques you will need to present your passport or other proof of identity.

Banks
🕒 *Mon.–Fri. 9am–4.30pm. Most bureaux de change are open Sat. 9am–noon (some are open until 5pm).*

Approved bureaux de change

Chèque Point
150 avenue des Champs-Élysées, 75008
☎ *01 49 53 02 51*
🕒 *open 24 hours*

Thomas Cook
52 avenue des Champs-Élysées, 75008
☎ *01 42 89 80 32*
🕒 *8.30am–10.30pm*

Bank transfers

American Express
11 rue Scribe, 75009
☎ *01 47 14 50 00*
🕒 *9am–6.30pm*

Press

Dailies
Le Monde; Le Figaro; Libération; Le Parisien.

Weeklies
L'Événement du Jeudi; Le Nouvel Observateur; Le Point; L'Express.

International press kiosk
Corner of the avenue Matignon and the Champs-Élysées, 75008
🕒 *open 24 hours*

English-language bookstores

Paris has a number of located English-language bookstores.

Brentano's
37 avenue de l'Opéra, 75002
☎ *01 42 61 52 50*

Galignani
224 rue de Rivoli, 75001
☎ *01 42 60 76 07*

W. H. Smith
248 rue de Rivoli, 75001
☎ *01 44 77 88 99*

Phone calls

Phone numbers
To call abroad from Paris, dial 00 followed by the national code (e.g. Australia 61; Great Britain 44; New Zealand 64; USA and Canada 1) followed by the number you are calling. To call Paris from abroad, dial 00 33 from the UK or 011 33 from the USA, then the 9 figures of the number omitting the initial 0.

Public phones
Most public call boxes take phone cards, which are available from France Télécom agencies, tobacconists and RATP ticket offices.

Paris has a diversity of places of worship: the Orthodox Church (4), the Mosque (5) and the Synagogue (6).

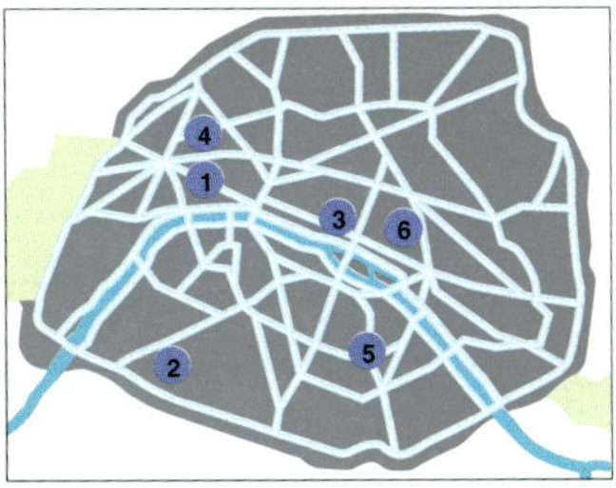

Information
National: *12*
International: *00 33 12* + national no.

Mail

Main post office
52 rue du Louvre, 75001
🕑 *open 24 hours*
☎ *01 40 28 20 00*

Express mail
Chronopost
3–5 avenue Gallieni, 94257 Gentilly cedex
☎ *01 49 69 86 86*
🕑 *Mon.–Fri. 8.30am–6.30pm; Sat. 8am–1pm.*

DHL
59 avenue d'Iéna, 75016
☎ *01 45 01 91 00*
🕑 *Mon.–Fri. 9am–8pm; Sat. 9am–5pm.*

Religious services

Catholic
Notre-Dame
Île de la Cité, 75004
☎ *01 42 34 56 10*

Protestant
Oratoire du Louvre
145 rue Saint-Honoré, 75001
☎ *01 42 60 21 64*

Orthodox
Saint-Alexandre-de-la-Neva
12 rue Daru, 75008
☎ *01 42 27 37 34*

Jewish
Synagogue Nazareth
15 rue Notre-Dame-de-Nazareth, 75003
☎ *01 42 78 00 30*

Muslim
Grande Mosquée de Paris
place du Puits-de-l'Ermite, 75005
☎ *01 45 35 97 33*

Embassies

American Embassy
2, avenue Gabriel 75008 Paris
☎ *01 43 12 22 22*

British Embassy
35, rue du Faubourg St-Honoré 75008 Paris
☎ *01 44 51 31 00*

Canadian Embassy
35, avenue Montaigne 75008 Paris
☎ *01 44 43 29 00*

Irish Embassy
4, rue Rude 75116 Paris
☎ *01 44 17 67 00*

Lost property

Possessions
Objets trouvés
36 rue des Morillons, 75015
☎ *01 55 76 20 20*
🕑 *Mon., Wed., Fri. 8.30am–5pm; Tue., Thu. 8.30am–8pm.*

Credit cards
If your credit card is lost or stolen, contact:
Visa
☎ *08 36 69 08 80*
Eurocard
☎ *01 45 67 53 53*

Passports
Register the loss or theft of your passport immediately at the nearest police station and your national embassy. It is advisable to keep a separate record of the number of your passport and date and place of issue.

Emergencies

Emergency medical service Samu
☎ *15*
Police ☎ *17*
Fire service
☎ *18*
Medical emergency
☎ *01 43 37 77 77*
Dental emergency
☎ *01 43 37 51 00*
Anti-poison Center
☎ *01 40 37 04 04*
Pharmacy
Derhy
84 avenue des Champs- Élysées, 75008
☎ *01 45 62 02 41*
🕑 *daily, open 24 hours*
Ⓜ *Franklin-D.-Roosevelt*

Vacating your room

Rooms are usually vacated by 11.30am. After a long stay, most managers are more flexible and may even offer to keep your luggage until the evening. However, they are perfectly within their rights to charge you for half a day.

Where to stay

Telephone

There is usually a surcharge on calls made from hotels. Use a phonecard ➥ 14 or your mobile phone to avoid unpleasant surprises.

Leading hotel restaurants

Alain Ducasse ➥ 56
Les Ambassadeurs ➥ 62
L'Astor ➥ 60
Bertie's ➥ 74
Élysées du Vernet ➥ 52
Le Meurice ➥ 62
Le Paris ➥ 78

Good value hotels

Well situated, these clean and functional hotels offer double rooms at less than F350. Friendly welcome.
Hôtel de Lille, 8 rue du Pelican, 75001 ☎ 01 42 33 33 42 ● F240
Gay Lussac, 29 rue Gay-Lussac, 75005 ☎ 01 43 54 23 96 ● F320
Marigan, 13 rue du Sommerard, 75005 ☎ 01 43 25 31 03 ● F330

77 Hotels

THE INSIDER'S FAVORITES

Prices

For each hotel listed: the number of rooms and their price range; the number of suites whether breakfast is included in the price of the room or is extra. The prices are all inclusive of service and taxes. Preferential rates depending on number of people, the season and the length of stay.
The hotels below are indexed in ascending order of price.

LIST OF HOTELS

5 PRICE RANGES
● under F800 for a double room
●● F800–F1100
●●● F1100–F1500
●●●● F1500–F2000
●●●●● over F2000

In the area

Twelve avenues converge on the place Charles de Gaulle, known as l'Étoile (the star), with the Arc de Triomphe at its center. This area combines quiet residential districts and busy avenues full of restaurants and luxury shops. ■ Where to eat ➥ 52 ➥ 54 ➥ 74 ■ After dark

Where to stay

Hôtel Mercédès (1)

128 avenue de Wagram, 75017 ☎ 01 42 27 77 82 ➠ 01 40 53 09 89

M *Wagram* ***35 rooms*** *(and 2 suites)* ● *extra*

The Hôtel Mercédès comes as a pleasant surprise in the Étoile district. Its furniture and general design are in 1930s style with occasional authentic details such as the Gruber windows. The private rooms are decorated in pastel shades and there is one spectacular split-level suite (no. 720).

Hôtel Pergolèse (2)

3 rue Pergolèse, 75016 ☎ 01 53 64 04 04 ➠ 01 45 00 12 11/01 53 64 04 40

M *Argentine* ***40 rooms*** ●●● *extra* *safe*

The Pergolèse is designed in resolutely contemporary style by Rena Dumas. It opts for elegance in its choice of materials (leather, white marble, oak) and names (MacConnico and Stark). A delightfully restful interior.

Libertel Argentine (3)

1 rue d'Argentine, 75116 ☎ 01 45 02 76 76 ➠ 01 45 02 76 00

M *Argentine* ***40 rooms*** ●●● *extra* *7am–11pm* *safe*

Situated in a quiet, narrow street, only a stone's throw from the Arc de Triomphe and the Champs-Élysées, the Hôtel d'Argentine offers the comfort of a private residence and personal, friendly service. The designer, F. Méchiche, took great care with the refurbishment of this neoclassical residence. The mahogany furniture and commemorative plaque, presented by the ambassador of Argentina, may well be an attempt to escape from the more traditional Empire style, with extensive use of imitation marble and Greek-style plaster. The private rooms echo the same themes on a more modest scale, while bathrooms are luxuriously marbled.

Hôtel Raphaël (4)

17 avenue Kléber, 75116 ☎ 01 44 28 00 28 ➠ 01 45 01 21 50

M *Kléber* P ***90 rooms*** *(and 35 suites)* ●●●●● *extra* *Dining room* *Bar* ➥ *86*

Among the leading Paris hotels on account of its unique atmosphere, and the studied authenticity of its Louis XV decor, Persian carpets and stylish elegance. A chic, well-groomed clientele adds to its typically Parisian charm. The luxurious private rooms offer extensive views across Paris. Dine in the restaurant to complete the experience.

Not forgetting

■ **Hôtel Étoile-Péreire (5)** 146 boulevard Péreire, 75017 ☎ 01 42 67 60 00 ➠ 01 42 67 02 90 ●●

■ **Hôtel Élysée Ceramic (6)** 34 avenue de Wagram, 75008 ☎ 01 42 27 20 30 ➠ 01 46 22 95 83 ●●

➥ 86 ➥ 88 ➥ 100
■ What to see
➥ 106

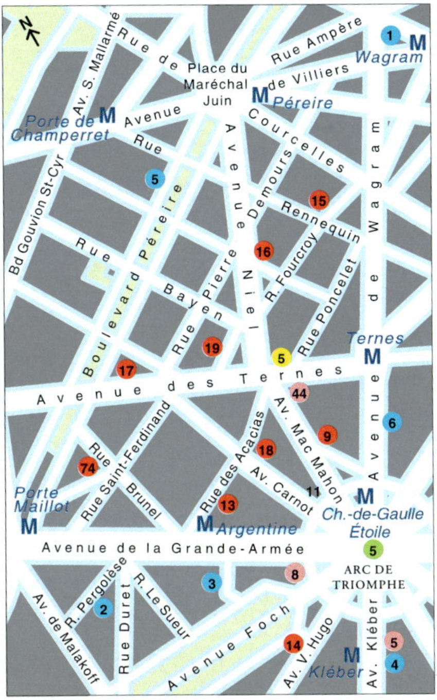

Close to the place Charles de Gaulle-Étoile, the façade of the Élysée Ceramic (1904) is an example of Parisian Art Nouveau.

6

2

2

4

5

In the area

This largely residential, wealthy area contains some of the city's finest restaurants as well as the Musée Marmottan and the Musée Guimet.
■ Where to eat ➡ 56 ➡ 74 ■ What to see ➡ 106 ■ After dark ➡ 90

Where to stay

Hôtel Baltimore (7)

88bis avenue Kléber, 75016 ☎ 01 44 34 54 54 ➠ 01 44 34 54 44

M *Boissière* ***105 rooms*** *(and 1 suite)* ●●●●● *extra* *Le Bertie's* ➡ *74* *Le Bertie's Bar* *reception rooms* *baltimore@cie.fr*

Built in 1892, the hotel claims to have been at least partly designed by Gustave Eiffel. The impressive dimensions of its particularly spectacular entrance are enhanced by marble and by elaborate architectural decoration. The same theme is echoed less ostentatiously in its private rooms, where the emphasis is on modern comfort (the hotel was restored in 1991).

Hôtel Le Parc (8)

55–57 avenue Raymond-Poincaré, 75016
☎ 01 44 05 66 66 ➠ 01 44 05 66 00

M *Victor-Hugo, Trocadéro* P ***116 rooms*** *(and 20 junior suites)* ●●●●● *extra* *safe* *Alain Ducasse* ➡ *56, Le Relais du Parc* *0800 908 567*

One of the most successful modern luxury hotels in recent years. It occupies a former mansion (1912) and offers an exceptional menu under the direction of the master chef, Alain Ducasse. The rooms have been designed by top names (Nina Campbell, David Linley) with an eye to the type of comfort befitting one of the best Paris hotels. A clientele consisting of the international elite and the gourmet jet set.

K. Palace (9)

81 avenue Kléber, 75016 ☎ 01 44 05 75 75 ➠ 01 44 05 74 74

M *Trocadéro* ***83 rooms*** *(and 15 suites)* ●●●●● *extra* *Kpalace@Wanadoo.fr*

This 1990s luxury hotel was designed by Ricardo Bofill. Its modern decor combines leather and chrome enhanced by blond wood. It is no surprise then that its rooms are often reserved by fashion magazines so that top models can pose in a sophisticated modern setting.

Hôtel Massenet (10)

5bis rue Massenet, 75116 ☎ 01 45 24 43 03 ➠ 01 45 24 41 39

M *Passy, La Muette* ***41 rooms*** ● *extra*

A family residence converted into a delightful hotel. A successful combination of Louis XV furnishings, modern decor and tradition (the Mathieu family has been running the hotel for three generations).
★ The Massenet offers some spectacular views, including that of the familiar outline of the Eiffel Tower visible from the terrace.

Not forgetting

■ **Hôtel Garden Élysées (11)** 12 rue Saint-Didier, 75116
☎ 01 47 55 01 11 ➠ 01 47 27 79 24 ●●●●

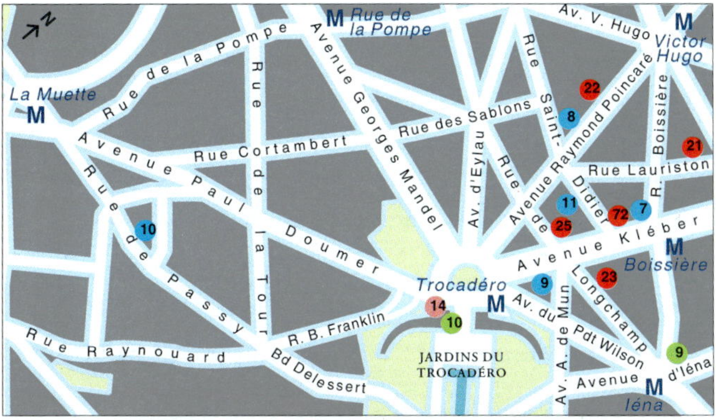

7

11

11

8

The quiet, flower-filled gardens of the Hôtel Le Parc are an ideal setting in which to enjoy the cuisine of the Relais du Parc.

9

9

In the area

Despite large investment and some improvement, the famous broad avenue of the Champs Élysées, lined with shops and restaurants, has not altogether recovered the charm and elegance of the 19th century.
■ Where to eat ➥ 48 ➥ 52 ➥ 56 ➥ 60 ➥ 66 ➥ 74 ■ After dark

Where to stay

Hôtel de Vigny (12)

9–11 rue Balzac, 75008 ☎ 01 42 99 80 80 ➟ 01 42 99 80 40

M *George-V* ***37 rooms*** *(and 11 suites)* ●●●●● *extra*

Only a stone's throw from the Champs-Élysée, this hotel, listed by Relais et Châteaux, is a haven of peace and quiet. It combines charm and excellence with decor designed by Nina Campbell in 19th-century English style (antiques, four-poster beds).

Hôtel Vernet (13)

25 rue Vernet, 75008 ☎ 01 44 31 98 00 ➟ 01 44 31 85 69

M *Charles-de-Gaulle-Étoile* ***57 rooms*** *(and 3 suites)* ●●●●● *extra* *Élysées du Vernet* ➥ 52

A small, old-fashioned hotel located in a quiet street off the Champs-Élysées, with its excellent cuisine served in an exquisite dining room with an Edwardian glass roof. Open fires in its bar and lounges and live piano music make afternoon tea or an aperitif very appealing. The comfortable private rooms are decorated in neoclassical style. Peace, elegance and excellent service.

Plaza-Athénée (14)

25 avenue Montaigne, 75008 ☎ 01 53 67 66 65 ➟ 01 53 67 66 66

M *Alma-Marceau* ***196 rooms*** *(and 42 suites)* ●●●●● *extra* *Le Régence, Relais Plaza, La Cour Jardin* *Le Montaigne* *reception rooms* *hairdresser*

This exceptional hotel is situated in the heart of the haute couture and jewelry district of Paris. Opened in 1897 and still considered one of the best hotels in the world, it boasts Louis XV, Louis XVI and Regency furniture and a highly sophisticated international clientele. Excellent cuisine and a very pleasant patio garden.

San Regis (15)

12 rue Jean-Goujon, 78008 ☎ 01 44 95 16 16 ➟ 01 45 61 05 48

M *Franklin-Roosevelt, Champs-Élysées* ***33 rooms*** *(and 11 suites)* ●●●●● *extra* @ *hotel-sanregis.fr*

A former 19th-century mansion with a magnificent neoclassical façade. Its very 'English' decor is a blend of Empire, Chippendale, Regency and Queen Anne, while it is furnished in 18th- and 19th-century style. It has a lounge opening onto a winter garden and a lovely restaurant. The suites with balconies enjoy a superb view of Paris and the Eiffel Tower.

Not forgetting

■ **Bradford Élysées (16)** 10 rue Saint-Philippe-du-Roule, 75008 ☎ 01 45 63 20 20 ➟ 01 45 63 20 07 ●●●

■ **Châteaubriand (17)** 6 rue d'Artois, 75008 ☎ 01 40 76 00 50 ➟ 01 40 76 09 22 ●●●●

➡ 86 ➡ 92 ➡ 96 ■ What to see ➡ 106 ■ Where to shop ➡ 142 ➡ 144

4

12

14

Luxury settings – wood paneling, gilt and stylish furniture – reflect the aristocratic elegance of the so-called 'Golden Triangle'.

15

In the area

Place de la Concorde lies between the Louvre and the Arc de Triomphe, like a clearing in the Parisian landscape. It offers some splendid views of the city and is within easy reach of a number of museums. ■ Where to eat ➡ 62 ➡ 66 ➡ 74 ■ What to see ➡ 104

Where to stay

Hôtel de Crillon (18)

10 Place de la Concorde, 75008 ☎ 01 44 71 15 00 ➡ 01 44 71 15 02

M *Concorde* *120 rooms* *(and 43 suites)* ●●●●● *extra* *Les Ambassadeurs* ➡ *62, L'Obélisque*

The Hôtel de Crillon, the most majestic of the luxury hotels in Paris, is located in one of the world's most beautiful squares. It occupies an 18th-century palace and boasts an exquisite gold and marble façade. The rooms and suites are elegant and spacious, and some – such as the Leonard Bernstein suite overlooking place de la Concorde – are truly exceptional. Anticipate or prolong the experience by sampling the cuisine of Dominique Bouchet in Les Ambassadeurs restaurant.

Hôtel Costes (19)

239 rue Saint-Honoré, 75001 ☎ 01 42 44 50 00 ➡ 01 42 44 50 01

M *Tuileries* *83 rooms* *(and 3 suites)* ●●●●● *extra*

Beyond the main courtyard lies a small Italian-style *palazzo*. Jean-Louis Costes called upon interior designer Jacques Garcia to create the hotel of his dreams. Garcia mixed styles, superimposed periods and combined the classic with the extravagant. The result is both stunning and familiar. Spacious rooms and unique decor make this a truly delightful place to stay.

Lotti (20)

7 rue de Castiglione, 75001 ☎ 01 42 60 37 34 ➡ 01 40 15 93 56

M *Tuileries* *130 rooms* *(and 2 suites)* ●●●●● *extra* *7am–midnight* *Le Lotti* *0800 258 021*

The smallest of the grand hotels has preserved its early 20th-century club atmosphere, where members were only accepted on recommendation. The tradition has been maintained and now celebrities such as Paul McCartney, Paul Newman and Jane Fonda enjoy its discreet and personal service.

Hôtel Meurice (21)

228 rue de Rivoli, 75001 ☎ 01 44 58 10 10 ➡ 01 44 58 10 78

M *Tuileries* *160 rooms* *(and 25 suites and 11 junior suites)* ●●●●● *extra* *Le Manège* ➡ *62* *reception rooms*

The Meurice, designed at the turn of the century, became known as the *Hôtel des Rois* (Hotel of Kings) for its regal welcome. Its magnificent marble interior sparkles with chandeliers, and is furnished with antiques, sculptures and old master paintings. Part of the hotel's appeal is that, for all its tradition and elegance, the service is attentive and friendly.

Not forgetting

■ **Hôtel Intercontinental (22)** 3 rue de Castiglione, 75001
☎ 01 44 77 11 11 ➡ 01 44 77 14 60 ●●●●●

■ **Royal Saint-Honoré (23)** 221 rue Saint-Honoré, 75001
☎ 01 42 60 32 79 ➡ 01 42 60 47 44 ●●●●

Where to shop
➥ 146 ➥ 150

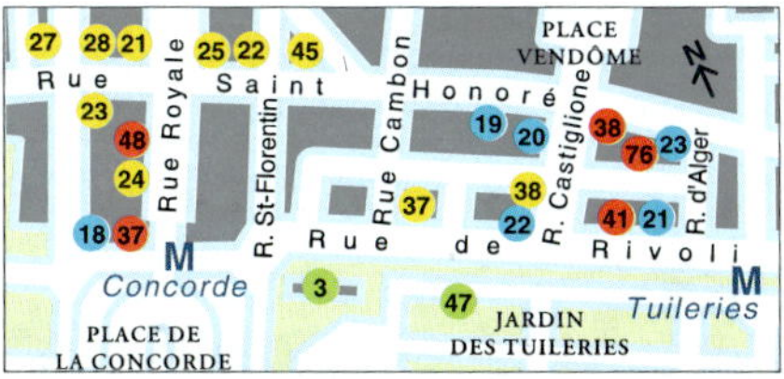

19

23

The Hôtel Meurice offers guests a unique view of the Jardin des Tuileries and the Eiffel Tower while they enjoy a traditional breakfast.

1

21

8

18

In the area
Place de la Madeleine, famous for its bustling flower market since 1834, is a pleasant place to stay. Situated in a continually changing district, it has become one of the gourmet centers of Paris and boasts specialist delicatessens, and some of the city's top restaurants.

Where to stay

Concortel (24)
19–21 rue Pasquier, 75008 ☎ 01 42 65 45 44 ➡ 01 42 65 18 33

M *Madeleine, Saint-Augustin* ***34 rooms*** *(and 12 junior suites)* ●● *extra*

The Concortel occupies a 19th-century building conveniently located near the district's main department stores. Decorated in a combination of ancient and modern styles, it provides a high level of modern comfort and attracts a regular clientele who appreciate its location. Attentive and discreet service and a quiet, flower-filled garden are two of its key strengths.

Astor Westin Demeure Hôtel (25)
11 rue d'Astorg, 75008 ☎ 01 53 05 05 05 ➡ 01 53 05 05 30

M *Saint-Augustin, Madeleine* P ***134 rooms*** *(and 5 suites)* ●●●●● *extra* *L'Astor* ➡ *60*

This newly built hotel has attracted attention not only for the very real comfort of its brand new premises (classic 1930s decor) but also for a menu that marks the unexpected comeback of Joël Robuchon. The famous chef is acting only in a consultative capacity, but a corner of the menu is reserved for his best-known dishes, including the famous purée that gourmets thought had disappeared forever. Rooms at higher levels offer a spectacular view of Paris.

Hôtel Beau Manoir (26)
6 rue de l'Arcarde, 75008 ☎ 01 42 66 03 07 ➡ 01 42 68 03 00

M *Madeleine* ***29 rooms*** *(and 3 suites)* ●●● *included* @ *bm@paris-hotels.charm.com*

The Hôtel Beau Manoir, already extremely pleasant before it was renovated, has since moved up the league table of the district's top hotels. The 18th-century decor includes wood paneling, handmade walnut furniture, Burgundy stone and beautiful Aubusson tapestries. Coordinated cotton prints, sofas, wing chairs, and Moustier earthenware lamps add to the sophistication of its spacious private rooms, most of which have their own lounge area. A calm and elegant place to stay.

Alison (27)
21 rue de Surène, 75008 ☎ 01 42 65 54 00 ➡ 01 42 65 08 17

M *Madeleine* ***35 rooms*** ● *extra*

This recently renovated hotel occupies a 19th-century building in a busy part of the district. Its clientele reflects its location, which is ideal for business people and tourists alike. It has a small central courtyard and offers practical, modern comfort in a surprisingly peaceful setting.

Not forgetting
■ **Lido Hôtel (28)** 4 passage de la Madeleine, 75008 ☎ 01 42 66 27 37 ➡ 01 42 66 61 23 ●●●

■ Where to eat ➥ 60 ➥ 62
■ Where to shop ➥ 140 ➥ 148

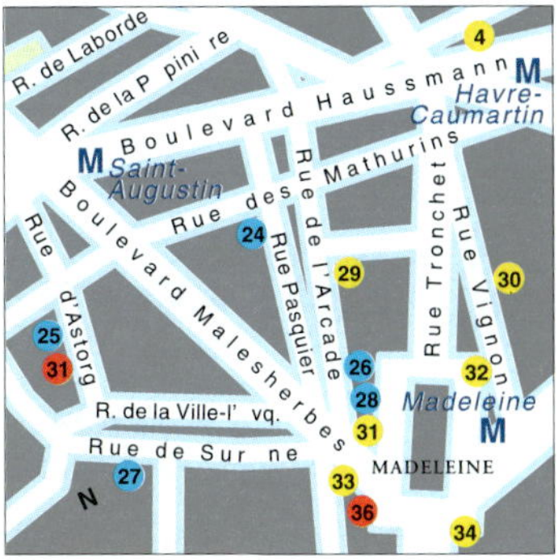

24

26

A sophisticated breakfast in a sophisticated setting: the Hôtel Beau Manoir.

26

25

In the area

Since the end of the 19th century, place Vendôme has been considered the most successful expression of classical architecture in Paris. It provides a beautiful setting for world-famous jewelers', the major fashion houses and the city's luxury hotels.

Where to stay

Ritz (29)

15 place Vendôme, 75001 ☎ 01 43 16 30 30 ➠ 01 43 16 31 78

Opéra **175 rooms** *(and 42 suites)* ●●●●● *extra* *L'Espadon, Bar Vendôme, Ritz Club* *Hemingway* *reception rooms* *beauty salon* *Ritz Club*

Since it opened in June 1898, the Ritz has been the very epitome of luxury. The first Paris hotel to have electricity, it enjoys a unique location in the elegant place Vendôme. Mohammed Al-Fayed, who bought the hotel in 1979, has ensured that the Ritz both retains its traditions (including splendid afternoon tea and its cookery school, the École Ritz-Escoffier) and offers modern facilities such as a fitness center and swimming pool. Every room is different, with decor varying between Louis XV and Louis XVI. Fabulous restaurant.

Hôtel Castille (30)

33 rue Cambon, 75001 ☎ 01 44 58 44 58 ➠ 01 44 58 44 00

Opéra, Madeleine **107 rooms** *(and 8 suites)* ●●●●● *extra* *safe* *Il Cortile* *reception rooms*

The Hôtel Castille stands next to the famous fashion house of Coco Chanel in what was once the Ritz Annex. Its style is both Parisian (decor by Jacques Grange in 20 of its rooms) and Venetian, with 87 rooms graced with marble, engraved glass, painted wood furniture and lamps. Ask for one of the rooms that overlook the beautiful central courtyard with its sculpted fountain.

Westminster (31)

13 rue de la Paix, 75002 ☎ 01 42 61 57 46 ➠ 01 42 60 30 66

Opéra **83 rooms** *(and 18 suites)* ●●●●● *extra* *safe* *Le Céladon* *Les Chenets* *reception rooms* *0800 463 441* *resa.westminster@warwickhotel.com*

Two hundred years ago, the Westminster was a convent. During the reign of Napoleon III, it was a post house. In 1900, it was given a stone façade and, in 1981, it was bought by the Warwick chain. Today, this luxury English-style hotel offers modern comfort and convenience in period surroundings. The rooms have been entirely redecorated. Guests can enjoy an aperitif in the intimate atmosphere of the piano-bar on the ground floor and the excellent cuisine of its restaurant: Le Céladon.

Hôtel Mansart (32)

5 rue des Capucines, 75001 ☎ 01 42 61 50 28 ➠ 01 49 27 97 44

Opéra **51 rooms** *(and 6 junior suites)* ●●● *extra*

This former private residence is located 'next door' to the Ritz, on the corner of the place Vendôme and the rue des Capucines. It enjoys a privileged position and a unique view, especially from the Suite Mansart. The rest of the hotel is a successful blend of classic – Regency and Baroque – styles.

■ After dark ➥ 88 ➥ 90 ➥ 82
■ Where to shop ➥ 150

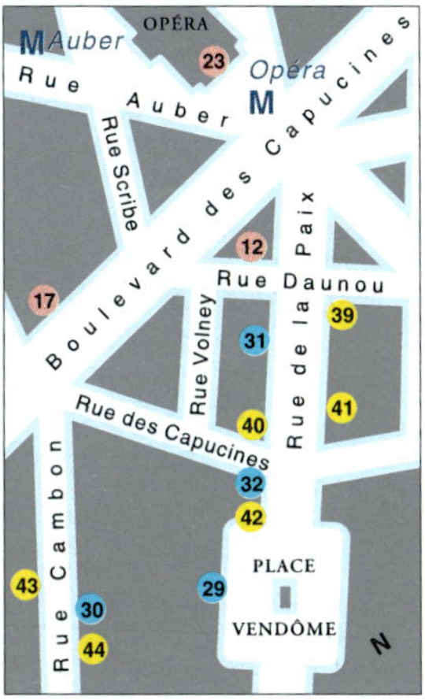

29

The hotels in the vicinity of place Vendôme combine traditional elegance with the facilities of modern luxury hotels.

30

32

29

In the area

The hotels in this area are set against the magnificent backdrop of the Palais du Louvre ➡ 104 and the Jardin des Tuileries ➡ 122. ■ Where to eat ➡ 48 ➡ 50 ➡ 62 ■ After dark ➡ 90 ■ What to see ➡ 104 ■ Where to shop ➡ 140 ➡ 150 ➡ 152 ➡ 154 ➡ 160

Where to stay

Hôtel Régina (33)

2 place des Pyramides, 75001 ☎ 01 42 60 31 10 ➡ 01 40 15 95 16

M *Tuileries, Pyramides* ***116 rooms*** *(and 14 suites)* ●●●●● *extra* *reception rooms*

Movie directors often choose to film against the backdrop of this Second-Empire hotel, with its vast entrance hall and lounges pervaded by the scent of wax polish. Its *fin de siècle* atmosphere is enhanced by its art nouveau decor and Louis XV- and Louis XVI-style furniture. An English bar and a restaurant with a beautiful open fireplace (1900) add a pleasantly cozy touch. Last and by no means least, the Régina is located in the heart of historic Paris and enjoys spectacular views of the Louvre ➡ 104 and the Jardin des Tuileries ➡ 122.

Louvre Saint-Honoré (34)

141 rue Saint-Honoré, 75001 ☎ 01 42 96 23 23 ➡ 01 42 96 21 61

M *Louvre, Palais-Royal* ***40 rooms*** ●● *F75* *safe*

The Louvre Saint-Honoré combines classic (in its private rooms) and modern (in its public rooms) styles. In the modern vein, a glass pyramid links the hotel's two buildings. It is ideally located for shopping: near Les Halles and only a stone's throw from the rue Montorgueil and its famous market, and the designer boutiques of the place des Victoires ➡ 154.

Tonic Hôtel (35)

12–14 rue du Roule, 75001 ☎ 01 42 33 00 71 ➡ 01 40 26 06 86

M *Châtelet* ***34 rooms*** *(and 1 split-level suite)* ●● *extra*

One of the main advantages of this modern hotel is undoubtedly its location: between the church of Saint-Eustache, Les Halles and rue de Rivoli, and very close to the Louvre. Functional rooms, some of which have been recently renovated with jacuzzis and saunas.

Hôtel de la place du Louvre (36)

21 rue des Prêtres-Saint-Germain-l'Auxerrois, 75001
☎ 01 42 33 78 68 ➡ 01 42 33 09 95

M *Louvre, Rivoli, Pont-Neuf* ***18 rooms*** *(2 split-level suites)* ● *extra* @ *123France.com/hotlouv.htm*

This old building was successfully renovated in 1989. The vaulted breakfast room, known as the *Salle des Mousquetaires* (Musketeers' Room), used to be linked to the Louvre. A key attraction is its spectacular view of the colonnaded façade of the Louvre and the church of Saint-Germain-de-l'Auxerrois, the parish church of the French kings.

Not forgetting

■ **Tuileries (37)** 10 rue Sainte-Hyacinthe, 75001 ☎ 01 42 61 04 17 ➡ 01 49 27 91 56 ●●

■ **Relais du Louvre (38)** 19 rue des Prêtres-Saint-Germain-de-l'Auxerrois, 75001 ☎ 01 40 41 96 42 ➡ 01 40 41 96 44 ●●

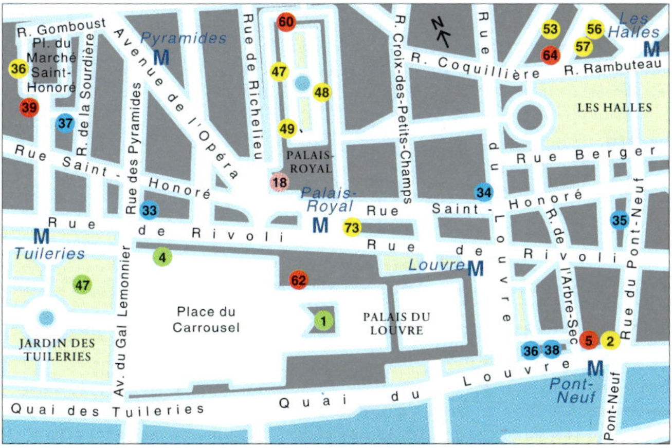

37

33

The staircase in the Tuileries, the former residence of Marie-Antoinette's first lady-in-waiting.

33

36

In the area

The Marais district lies on the north bank of the Seine near the Île Saint-Louis. One of the most historic districts of Paris, its charm is heightened by its many small squares and gardens. ■ Where to eat ➡ 72 ■ After dark ➡ 92 ■ What to see ➡ 110 ■ Where to shop ➡ 160

Where to stay

Pavillon de la Reine (39)

28 place des Vosges, 75003 ☎ 01 40 29 19 19 ➡ 01 40 29 19 20

M *Saint-Paul, Bastille* ***35 rooms** (and 20 suites)* ●●●● *extra*

Set back from the place des Vosges, built by Henri IV in 1609, and close to Musée Carnavalet, the Pavillon de la Reine is one of the most delightful hotels in Paris. Liberty prints and beautiful stonework create an atmosphere of great charm.

Pavillon Bastille (40)

65 rue de Lyon, 75012 ☎ 01 43 43 65 65 ➡ 01 43 43 96 52

M *Bastille* ***24 rooms** (and 1 suite)* ●● *extra*
@ *hotel-pavillon@akamail.com; www.France-Paris.com*

Opened in 1991, the Pavillon Bastille is favored by singers from the nearby Opéra-Bastille. Its discreet, muted atmosphere combines magnificent modern decor – by Jean-Pierre Heim – with the soft yellows and blues of the private rooms. ★ A delightful Italian garden with an 18th-century fountain.

Hôtel des Deux Îles (41)

59 rue St-Louis-en-l'Île, 75004 ☎ 01 43 26 13 35 ➡ 01 43 29 60 25

M *Pont-Marie, Cité* P ***17 rooms*** ●● *extra* *7am–8pm* *safe*

A 17th-century building with unusual decor: wooden blinds, cane chairs, bamboo furniture painted blue and yellow, a cellar-bar with an open fireplace and a flower-filled patio with a murmuring fountain.

Hôtel du Jeu de Paume (42)

54 rue St-Louis-en-l'Île, 75004 ☎ 01 43 26 14 18 ➡ 01 40 46 02 76

M *Pont-Marie* P ***30 rooms** (and 1 junior suite)* ●●● *extra*

This leading hotel stands on the site of the royal tennis court (1634) which was converted into a private mansion. It has a particularly skilful blend of contemporary and 17th-century styles, and the sophisticated elegance of its atmosphere is enhanced by the fabrics of Pierre Frey ➡ 148, exposed beams and limed oak. Most rooms overlook the small patio and well-lit garden.

Not forgetting

■ **Hôtel Saint-Merry (43)** 78 rue de la Verrerie, 75004 ☎ 01 42 78 14 15 ➡ 01 40 29 06 82 ●

■ **Hôtel Saint-Paul-le-Marais (44)** 8 rue de Sévigné, 75004 ☎ 01 48 04 97 27 ➡ 01 48 87 37 04 ●

■ **Hôtel de Lutèce (45)** 65 rue Saint-Louis-en-l'Île, 75004 ☎ 01 43 26 23 52 ➡ 01 43 29 60 25 ●●

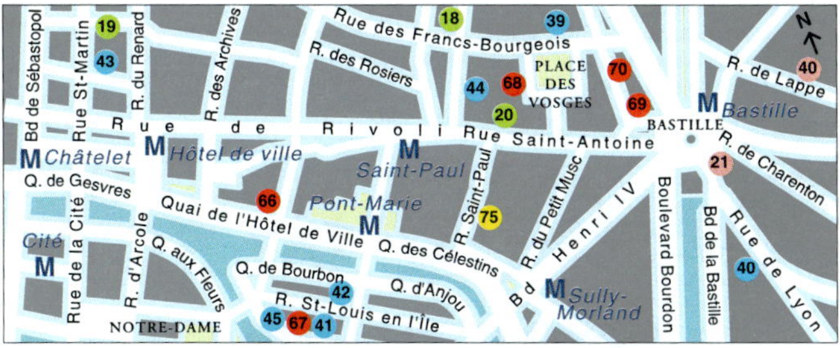

44

40

42

40

42

The 17th- and 18th-century buildings of the Marais and Île St-Louis contrast with the modern architecture of the Bastille district.

42

42

43

In the area
The Latin Quarter is the district of the famous Paris universities (*Sorbonne, Beaux Arts, Sciences Politiques*) where the young student population combine the serious business of study with enjoyment and relaxation.

Where to stay

Relais Hôtel Vieux Paris (46)

9 rue Gît-le-Cœur, 75006 ☎ 01 44 32 15 90 ➟ 01 43 26 00 15

M *Saint-Michel* P ***13 rooms** (and 7 suites)* ●●● *extra* *vieuxpar@worldnet.fr*

This beautiful Directory-style hotel occupies a timbered, freestone building dating from 1480. Its more recent guests have included members of the beat generation – Allen Ginsberg, William Burroughs, Jack Kerouac – who have all sat on the flower-filled terrace overlooking the roofs of Paris and the Sainte-Chapelle.

Hôtel Esméralda (47)

4 rue St-Julien-le-Pauvre, 75005 ☎ 01 43 54 19 20 ➟ 01 40 51 00 68

M *Saint-Michel, Maubert-Mutualité* ***19 rooms*** ● *extra*

Sophia Loren has often stayed in this small hotel opposite Notre-Dame. The beams and old stone of the 17th-century building combine with art nouveau decor to create the blend of bohemian and Vieux Paris styles appreciated by its regular clientele. Don't miss the tiny church of St Julien-le-Pauvre (rebuilt 1165) in square Viviani, which has the oldest tree in Paris, a false acacia planted in 1620.

Relais Médicis (48)

23 rue Racine, 75006 ☎ 01 43 26 00 60 ➟ 01 40 46 83 39

M *Saint-Michel* P ***16 rooms*** ●●● *included* *7am-6pm* *safe*

A consistently popular style of hotel. It uses all the tricks of the trade and combines all the latest fashions in contemporary decoration and design: Italy, Provence, mixed marble floors and smart fabrics. The overall effect is skillfully managed, giving a cheerful and bright atmosphere that ensures the success of this 18th-century hotel.

Select Hôtel (49)

1 place de la Sorbonne, 75005 ☎ 01 46 34 14 80 ➟ 01 46 34 51 79

M *Cluny, Saint-Michel* P ***68 rooms** (and 1 split-level suite)* ●● *extra* *selecthotel@wanadoo.fr*

The Select Hôtel has the unique advantage of being the only hotel on the medieval place de la Sorbonne. This is reinforced by the successful combination of contemporary decor with beams and stone walls, a fountain in the entrance hall and a unique view of the Sacré-Coeur ➥ 112, and the Tour Saint-Jacques from two rooms on the 6th floor.

Not forgetting

■ **Les Rives de Notre-Dame (50)** 15 quai Saint-Michel, 75005 ☎ 01 43 54 81 16 ➟ 01 43 26 27 09 ●●●●

■ **Hôtel Luxembourg (51)** 4 rue de Vaugirard, 75006 ☎ 01 43 25 35 90 ➟ 01 43 26 60 84 ●●

■ Where to eat ➥ 76
■ After dark ➥ 90 ■ What to see ➥ 120

49

46

Not far from the Jardin du Luxembourg, fountains murmur in the entrance halls and gardens of the hotels of the *Quartier latin.*

48

47

In the area
The Left Bank is famous for its literary and cultural circles. The universities and the Panthéon remain, but less studious visitors may prefer to visit the Jardin du Luxembourg ➥ 122. ■ After dark ➥ 98 ■ What to see ➥ 120 ➥ 122

Where to stay

Hôtel des Jardins du Luxembourg (52)
5 impasse Royer-Collard, 75005 ☎ 01 40 46 08 88 ➠ 01 40 46 02 28

M *Luxembourg* ***26 rooms*** ● *extra* *safe*

There is an atmosphere of studied elegance in this quiet hotel, designed by Haussmann in one of the city's old cul-de-sacs, only a stone's throw from the Jardin du Luxembourg ➥ 122. Its decor pays attention to detail – oak floor, kilims and mahogany furniture – in a sophisticated combination of the contemporary and the exotic. The small but elegant private rooms are extremely comfortable. Freud stayed here on his first visit to France.

Hôtel des Grands Hommes (53)
17 place du Panthéon, 75005 ☎ 01 46 34 19 60 ➠ 01 43 26 67 32

M *Luxembourg* ***30 rooms*** *(and 2 suites)* ●● *extra*

During the 1930s, this 18th-century hotel was popular with such Surrealist writers and artists as Breton and Soupault. Today, they are remembered in a contemplative and friendly atmosphere. All the rooms are decorated with different fabrics, and English furniture abounds. The attic rooms are particularly delightful and offer a magnificent panoramic view, from the Panthéon to the Sacré-Coeur ➥ 112.

Hôtel du Panthéon (54)
19 place du Panthéon, 75005 ☎ 01 43 54 32 95 ➠ 01 43 26 64 65

M *Luxembourg* ***34 rooms*** ●● *extra*

This 18th-century building offers a magnificent view of the city, especially room no. 64 which opens onto a terrace. The rooms are light and airy with Louis–XVI furniture and Louis-Philippe ceilings with exposed beams.

Hôtel des Grandes Écoles (55)
75 rue du Cardinal-Lemoine, 75005
☎ 01 43 26 79 23 ➠ 01 43 25 28 15

M *Cardinal-Lemoine, Monge* P ***51 rooms*** ●● *extra*

This truly exceptional Paris hotel stands at the end of a cul-de-sac. As you cross the threshold, you enter a miniature paradise of small rooms in a garden setting. Although in the heart of Paris, the peace and quiet of the slightly old-fashioned surroundings create the impression of being deep in the countryside. Breakfast outside to the chirping of the sparrows. In addition to its 'rural' setting, this is an eminently affordable hotel which offers warm and friendly service.

Not forgetting
■ **Le Clos Médicis (56)** 56 rue Monsieur-le-Prince, 75006
☎ 01 43 29 10 80 ➠ 01 43 54 26 90 ●●

53

52

Contemporary Provençal-style decor lies behind the 17th-century façade of the Clos Médicis.

Le Clos Médicis

54

56

52

55

In the area

Odéon is the most 'theatrical' of the left-bank districts. If you listen carefully, you may even hear strains of *Le Mariage de Figaro* from the Théâtre de l'Europe ➥ 90. Today, this busy district is the preserve of movie-goers, gourmets and shopaholics.

Where to stay

Prince de Conti (57)

8 rue Guénégaud, 75006 ☎ 01 44 07 30 40 ➠ 01 44 07 36 34

M *Odéon* ***26 rooms*** *(and 2 split-level suites)* ●●● *extra* *10.30am–10.45pm* *safe*

If you are looking for a cozy, English-style hotel, this is the one for you. The 18th-century building, refurbished in 1994, offers excellent facilities. Although its rooms are relatively small, they are always comfortable, and some have balconies that overlook the courtyard.

Relais Christine (58)

3 rue Christine, 75006 ☎ 01 40 51 60 80 ➠ 01 40 51 60 81

M *Odéon* ***34 rooms*** *(and 17 suites)* ●●●● *extra* *on request*

Behind a wrought-iron gate, one of the most delightful left-bank hotels occupies a former Augustinian convent and cloister (16th century). The interior decor is warm (rich colors and wood paneling) and in keeping with the traditional style of the building (Liberty prints, beams and roughcast flagstones). There is a charming central courtyard and several very pleasant split-level suites.

Left Bank Saint Germain Hôtel (59)

9 rue de l'Ancienne-Comédie, 75006
☎ 01 43 54 01 70 ➠ 01 43 26 17 14

M *Odéon* ***30 rooms*** *(and 1 suite)* ●● *included* *satellite* *safe*

This elegant and comfortable hotel is virtually next door to the Procope and opposite the Ancienne Comédie Française. Louis XIII furniture, damask wallpaper, Aubusson tapestry and walnut-paneled alcoves create a romantic atmosphere. The 17th-century building (renovated in 1989) is centered around three gardens and offers a splendid view of Notre-Dame from some of its rooms (on the fifth and sixth floors).

Relais Saint-Germain (60)

9 carrefour de l'Odéon, 75006 ☎ 01 44 27 07 97 ➠ 01 46 33 45 30

M *Odéon* ***21 rooms*** *(and 1 suite)* ●●●● *included* *6.30am–11pm* *safe* ***Le Comptoir du Relais*** *small meeting rooms*

Decorated with ancient prints and furniture, this delightful and luxuriously comfortable hotel has named its rooms after famous French authors. The room numbers ending in 4 – e.g. 'Ronsard' (no. 14) and 'Montesquieu' (no. 54) – overlook the street. ★ 'Balzac' (no. 56) is a small, split-level suite with African-style decor. It opens onto a sunny terrace that can, if required, communicate with 'Montesquieu' (no. 58).

Not forgetting

■ **Buci Latin (61)** 34 rue de Buci, 75006 ☎ 01 43 29 07 20 ➠ 01 43 29 67 44 ●●●

■ Where to eat ➥ 76

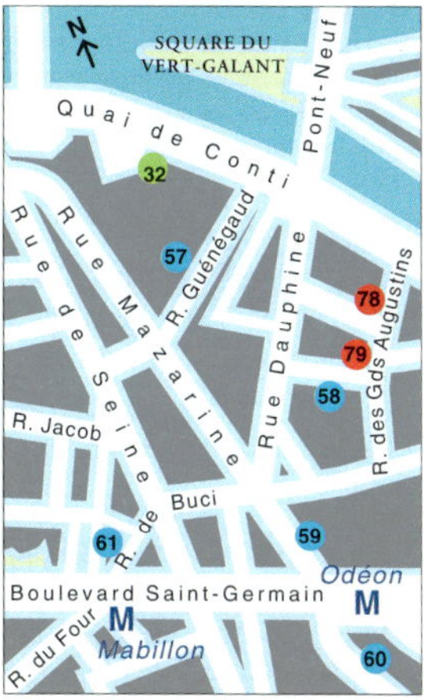

58

60

61

60

60

The doors of the rooms in the Buci Latin have all been decorated in different styles by young artists. One example of the originality of this delightful little hotel.

60

61

61

In the area
Saint-Germain is the literary heart of Paris, with most publishing houses established here. Its legendary cafés are still frequented by intellectuals. It is also becoming a luxury shopping district. ■ Where to eat ➥ 78
■ After dark ➥ 86 ➥ 88 ➥ 98 ■ What to see ➥ 116

Where to stay

Hôtel Montalembert (62)

3 rue Montalembert, 75007 ☎ 01 45 49 68 68 ➟ 01 45 49 69 49

M *Rue du Bac* P ***51 rooms** (and 5 suites)* ●●●●● *extra* safe *80 04 47 74 62*

This beautiful hotel, situated in the antiques district ➥ 160, is only a stone's throw from the Musée d'Orsay ➥ 116, and the church of Saint-Germain-des-Prés. Fronted by an elegant façade (1926), the Montalembert combines classic style with contemporary detail. Typically Rive Gauche.

Hôtel d'Angleterre (63)

44 rue Jacob, 75006 ☎ 01 42 60 34 72 ➟ 01 42 60 16 93

M *Saint-Germain-des-Prés **23 rooms** (and 4 suites)* ●● *extra* safe

Formerly the British embassy where the treaty of American Independence, signed on September 3, 1783, was prepared. Ernest Hemingway stayed here for some time in room no. 14. Quiet clientele and a historic (predominately Napoleon III-style) decor. Each of the spacious rooms is decorated in a different style and most overlook the central courtyard.

Villa Saint-Germain des Prés (64)

29 rue Jacob, 75006 ☎ 01 43 26 60 00 ➟ 01 46 34 63 63

M *Saint-Germain-des-Prés **29 rooms** (and 3 suites)* ●●● *extra* safe *La Villa*

An ideally situated 19th-century building that has achieved an extremely successful contemporary 'look'. It has the distinctive hallmark of Marie-Christine Dorner, who has used leather, nickel and sanded and marbled glass. It has a very good basement jazz club, La Villa ➥ 98. The hotel is regularly chosen by performers on tour.

Hôtel Guy-Louis Duboucheron (65)

13 rue des Beaux-Arts, 75006 ☎ 01 43 25 27 22 ➟ 01 43 25 64 81

M *Saint-Germain-des-Prés **25 rooms** (and 2 suites)* ●●●● *extra*

This is one of the most unusual hotels in Paris. Each room has its own story to tell and its own individual decor, often associated with its most famous occupant. For example, framed copies of bills still owing to the hotel hang in the room where Oscar Wilde died (uttering his last words, 'Either this wallpaper goes or I do.'), and the room once occupied by the French actress Mistinguett still contains the furniture she bequeathed to the hotel.

Not forgetting
■ **Hôtel d'Orsay (66)** 93 rue de Lille, 75007 ☎ 01 47 05 85 54 ➟ 01 45 55 51 16 ● ■ **Lenox (67)** 9 rue de l'Université, 75007 ☎ 01 42 96 10 95 ➟ 01 42 61 52 83 ●●

Where to shop ➥ 158

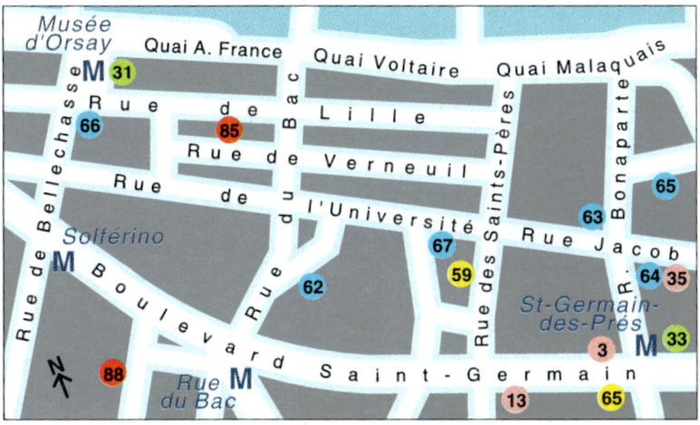

65

The rooms in the Hôtel Guy-Louis Duboucheron are centered around a beautifully lit gallery.

62

63

63

In the area

In striking contrast to the busy left-bank districts of Saint-Germain and Odéon, Sèvres offers a degree of respite and a calmer, more serene lifestyle. An ideal retreat after a day's sightseeing. ■ Where to eat ➡ 78 ➡ 82 ■ After dark ➡ 86 ➡ 88 ■ Where to shop ➡ 140 ➡ 156 ➡ 158

Where to stay

Duc de Saint-Simon (68)

14 rue Saint-Simon, 75007 ☎ 01 44 39 20 20 ➡ 01 45 48 68 25

M *Rue-du-Bac* ***29 rooms*** *(and 5 suites)* ●●● *extra* *7.30am–10.30pm*

This charming, small 18th-century house, off the rue de Grenelle, with its attractive courtyard, is much in demand from the fashion and art worlds. Although somewhat small, the rooms are comfortable and beautifully furnished, each in a different style. It is also worth mentioning the bathrooms, maginificently decorated with hand-made tiles from Salernes. Ask for a room overlooking the garden, or rooms 14, 24, 25 or 42, which have terraces. As for finding out if this hotel was the private residence of the Duke of Saint Simon, you will need to consult the very informative bi-lingual brochure made available by the hotel's managers.

Hôtel Lutétia (69)

45 boulevard Raspail, 75006 ☎ 01 49 54 46 46 ➡ 01 49 54 46 00

M *Sèvres-Babylone* P ***230 rooms*** *(and 20 suites)* ●●●●● *extra* *Le Lutèce* *Le Paris* ➡ *78; Brasserie Lutétia* *Salon Saint-Germain* *reception rooms* *Le Ernest Bar (cigar booth)*

The Hôtel Lutétia is one of the last luxury hotels on the Left Bank. The vast bulk of this huge art deco building reveals nothing of the very distinctive atmosphere of its many rooms and famous bar. Since it was built (1907–10) to accommodate the customers of the Bon Marché department store ➡ 140, famous guests have included General de Gaulle and his wife, who spent their wedding night here. Today, it has become the meeting place par excellence of the worlds of fashion, politics, art and literature. Its rooms have been redecorated in elegant 1930s style by Sybille de Margerie. The hotel also has a famous restaurant, Le Paris, and an exclusive bar, Le Lutèce, decorated in red and black by Sonia Rykiel.

Récamier (70)

3bis place Saint-Sulpice, 75006 ☎ 01 43 26 04 89 ➡ 01 46 33 27 73

M *Saint-Sulpice* ***29 rooms*** *(and 1 suite)* ● *included*

A quiet and attractive little hotel in the heart of Saint-Germain-des-Prés, only a minute's walk from the Jardin du Luxembourg ➡ 122. Its rooms have all the basic – if minimalist – comforts and occasionally surprising decor. ★ Choose the rooms overlooking the square and church. Although the least expensive may only have a W.C., they all enjoy a magnificent view. The hotel's delightful entrance, with its graceful canopy, is located in a quiet corner of the place Saint-Sulpice.

Not forgetting

■ **Hôtel des Saints-Pères (71)** 65 rue des Saints-Pères, 75006 ☎ 01 45 44 50 00 ➡ 01 45 44 90 83 ●●

■ **La Perle (72)** 14 rue des Canettes, 75006 ☎ 01 43 29 10 10 ➡ 01 46 34 51 04 ●●●

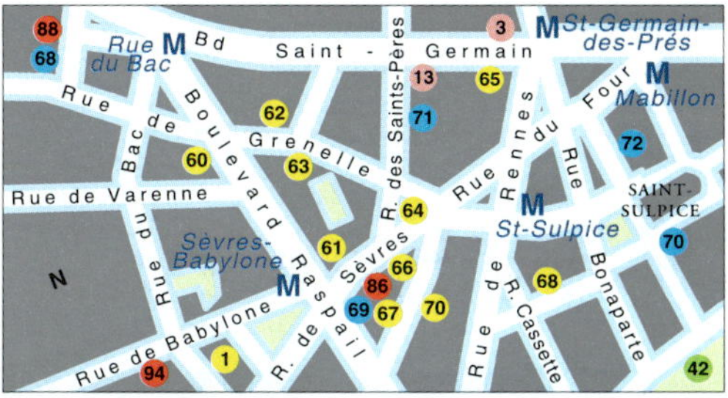

71

69

68

68

Spoilt for choice: romantic style in the Duc de Saint-Simon (room no. 41) or contemporary decor in the Lutétia (Suite Arman).

69

In the area

Once the haunt of writers and artists, the left-bank district of Montparnasse is now a busy cosmopolitan area boasting a main-line station, movie theaters, shops and myriad restaurants.

■ Where to eat ➡ 48 ➡ 66 ➡ 80 ■ After dark ➡ 86

Where to stay

Hôtel le Saint-Grégoire (73)

43 rue de l'Abbé-Grégoire, 75006 ☎ 01 45 48 23 23 ➡ 01 45 48 33 95

M *Saint-Placide* ***19 rooms*** *(and 1 suite)* ●● *extra* *hotel@saintgregoire.com*

This is more like a house than a hotel. The 18th-century building was decorated by David Hicks who has used kilims as well as his own fabrics, and set off pastel shades with Louis-Philippe sideboards, tables and wardrobes, and paintings tracked down in antique shops. The hotel's clientele (journalists and models) seems to be cast in the same mold and appreciates the charm of this distinctive building.

Le Sainte-Beuve (74)

9 rue Sainte-Beuve, 75006 ☎ 01 45 48 20 07 ➡ 01 45 48 67 52

M *Vavin* ***22 rooms*** *(and 1 apartment)* ●● *extra*

Close to the Jardin du Luxembourg ➡ 122, the Musée d'Orsay ➡ 116 and the Musée Rodin ➡ 108, the Sainte-Beuve occupies the perfect location. The David Hicks studio have created restful, English-style interiors in the public rooms, and the spacious private rooms reflect the same feeling of gentility and elegance.

L'Atelier Montparnasse (75)

49 rue Vavin, 75006 ☎ 01 46 33 60 00 ➡ 01 40 51 04 21

M *Vavin* ***16 rooms*** *(and 1 suite)* ●● *extra*

Not far from the famous La Coupole restaurant ➡ 66, L'Atelier Montparnasse is a small hotel with a very distinctive style. Each room is named after a painter and has a reproduction of a piece of that artist's work reproduced in *pâte-de-verre* mosaic in the bathroom. The reception area hosts temporary exhibitions.

Hôtel Raspail-Montparnasse (76)

203 boulevard Raspail, 75014 ☎ 01 43 20 62 86 ➡ 01 43 20 50 79

M *Vavin* ***36 rooms*** *(and 2 suites)* ●● *extra* *safe* *raspailm@aol.com*

In the 19th century, this hotel was known as the Hôtel de la Haute-Loire. The magnificent art nouveau canopy above the entrance – an exact copy of the original canopy that had disappeared – has restored the building to its former glory. The hotel overlooks the Carrefour Vavin and several rooms have a view of the Eiffel Tower. It was refurbished by Serge Pons in elegant art nouveau style, and each bedroom is dedicated to a particular artist and decorated with one of their works.

Not forgetting

■ **Villa des Artistes (77)** 9 rue de la Grande-Chaumière, 75006 ☎ 01 43 26 60 86 ➡ 01 43 54 73 70 ●

What to see ➥ 122
Where to shop ➥ 158

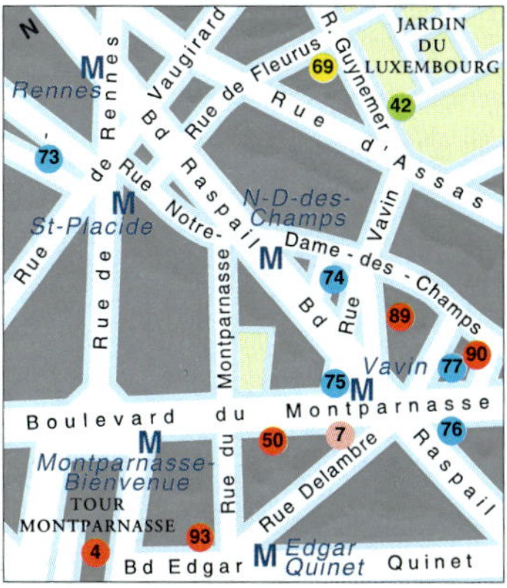

74

76

5

5

The wine waiter
The sommelier should advise customers on their choice of wine without influencing their decision.

Where to eat

Good value restaurants

Le Passage Brady(10e): the sounds, smells and colors of India in the center of Paris. The restaurants in the passage offer plain, unpretentious cooking at incredibly low prices.

La Butte aux Cailles (13e): far from the bustle of the main boulevards, this little village in the heart of the capital abounds in restaurants serving homely food. *Le Temps des Cerises* ☎ 01 45 89 69 48

Prices are inclusive of tax and a 15% service charge, although this doesn't mean you can't leave a tip. The categories below are based on menu prices or an à la carte three-course meal, without wine. But a word of warning, these may only apply to lunchtime menus.

99 Restaurants

THE INSIDER'S FAVORITES

INDEX BY CUISINE

AND PRICE RANGE
● less than F100
●● F100–F200
●●● F200–F300
●●●● F300–F400
●●●●● above F400

Basic facts

Some of the city's best restaurants offer splendid views of Paris. Eat during the day and you can pick out each area by the character of its buildings and parks; eat at night to see the city lights, with many of the major monuments spectacularly illuminated.

Where to eat

2

5

3

Maison Blanche (1)

15 avenue Montaigne, 75008 ☎ 01 47 23 55 99 ➡ 01 47 20 09 56

Alma-Marceau **Gourmet cuisine ●●●●** *à la carte F450* *Mon., Sat. 8-10.45pm; Tues.–Fri. noon–2.30pm, 8–10.45pm; closed in Aug.*

The decor of this restaurant, built on the roof of the Théâtre des Champs-Élysées ➡ 92, is austere, sophisticated and comfortable. The cuisine, by José Martinez, makes extensive use of seasonal produce and reflects an imaginative culinary flair. Elegant service. Steamed vegetables with passion fruit, pan-fried langoustines with vegetables and beetroot crisps, rhubarb crunch with acacia honey.

Les Célébrités (2)

61 quai de Grenelle, 75015 ☎ 01 40 58 21 29 ➡ 01 40 58 24 24

Bir-Hakeim **Gourmet cuisine ●●●** *à la carte F400* *daily noon–2.30pm, 7–10pm; closed in Aug.* *Le Benkay (same address)*

Master chef Joël Robuchon made his debut here. Today, one of his former sous-chefs, Jacques Sénéchal, continues the tradition of excellence with exquisite dishes such as his *marinière* of langoustines with morels. Excellent service.

Restaurants with a view

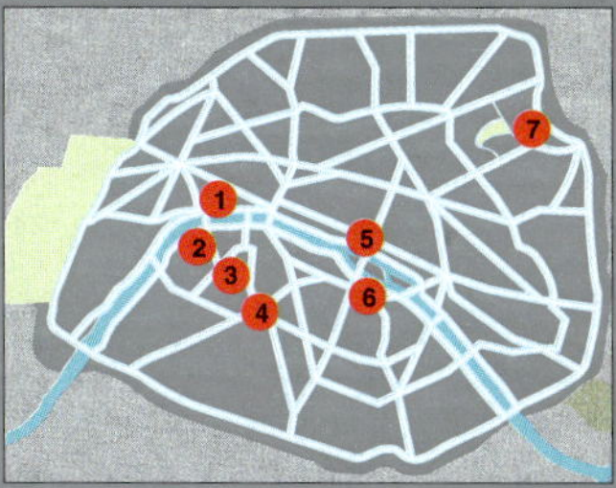

To gain a swift impression of the city, contemplate it from the Seine or discover one of the unusual quarters while enjoying a good meal.

1

6

4

Morot-Gaudry (3)

8 rue de la Cavalerie, 75015 ☎ 01 45 67 06 85 ➠ 01 45 67 55 72

M *La Motte-Picquet* P ***Gourmet cuisine*** ●● *à la carte F450*
Mon.–Fri. noon–2.30pm, 7.30–10.30pm

Jean-Pierre Morot-Gaudry's delightful restaurant on the 8th floor offers a truly remarkable view of the Eiffel Tower. An attractive menu offers traditional and modestly innovative cuisine, and ★ an excellent choice of more than a thousand French wines. An open-air terrace gives diners a front-row view of the fireworks on July 14!

Not forgetting

■ **Ciel de Paris (4)** Tour Montparnasse, 33 avenue du Maine, 75014 ☎ 01 40 64 77 64 ●●● *Great views and classic French cuisine on the 56th floor of the Montparnasse tower.* ■ **Toupary (5)** La Samaritaine, 2 quai du Louvre, 75001 ☎ 01 40 41 29 29 ● *Simple, affordable food at this Paris store.* ■ **La Tour d'Argent (6)** 17 quai de la Tournelle, 75005 ☎ 01 43 54 23 31 ●●●● *Renowned for its duck, its cellar, exceptional service and its view of the Seine and Notre-Dame.* ■ **Le Relais des buttes (7)** 86 rue Compans, 75019 ☎ 01 42 08 24 70 ●● *A small island of green in the heart of Paris. Marc Gautron and his wife delight a faithful neighborhood clientele, who also value this restaurant for its discretion and classicism. Reasonable prices.*

Basic facts

On Level 2 of the Eiffel Tower ➡ 106, the finest panoramic restaurant in Paris occupies a platform set between the pulleys and wheels that operate the lifts. The magnificent view takes in the Arc de Triomphe, Sacré-Coeur, Grand Palais, Notre-Dame…

Where to eat

Jules Verne (8)

Tour Eiffel, South (Level 2), Champs-de-Mars, 75007
☎ 01 45 55 61 44 ➡ 01 47 05 29 41

M *Bir-Hakeim, Champs-de-Mars* ***Gourmet cuisine*** ●●● *daily 12.15–2pm, 7.15-10pm*

The Jules Verne offers an exceptional dining experience – enjoy a magnificent view of Paris at sunset and savor the imaginative and meticulously prepared food of Alain Reix. Bread rolls souffléed with crab and served with creamed prawns or turbot cooked in lamb stock with two types of vermicelli. are just two of the inspired creations of this talented chef; the high price is justified. Piano bar and faultless service. Advance booking essential.

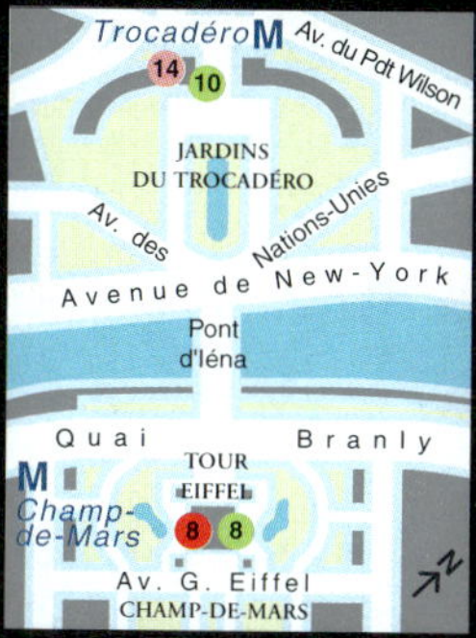

Some 400 feet above the ground, this restaurant opened in 1983 and was named after the French writer of science fiction and adventure, Jules Verne.

In the area

It will come as no surprise that the Place de l'Étoile is a district of prestigious restaurants, the sort that do not bow to short-lived, transitory fashions but remain loyal to established principles. Their relatively high prices are often justified. ■ Where to stay ➥ 18 ➥ 22 ■ After dark

Where to eat

Guy Savoy (9)

18 rue Troyon, 75017 ☎ 01 43 80 40 61 ➟ 01 46 22 43 09

M *Charles-de-Gaulle-Étoile* **Gourmet cuisine** ●●●●● *à la carte F800* ⊟ ⊙ *Mon.–Fri. 12.30–2.30pm, 7.30–10.30pm; Sat. 7.30–10.30pm* ◫ *Les Bookinistes* ●● *53 quai des Grands-Augustins, 75006 ☎ 01 43 25 45 94*

Sober but elegant modern decor and inventive cuisine using a limited range of basic flavors in a wide range of subtle variations. Guy Savoy is a chef at the height of his powers, a master of flavor: skate served with caviar and Breton vegetables, mussels and 'Homard-Carotte' with star anise, young spinach and scallop roe *court-bouillon*. The cellar represents most of the French wine-growing regions, with an especially wide choice of wines from the Rhône. A great restaurant.

Pierre Gagnaire (10)

6 rue Balzac, 75008 ☎ 01 44 35 18 25

M *GeorgesV* **Gourmet cuisine** ●●●●● *à la carte F800–1000* ⊟ ⊙ *Mon.–Fri. noon–2.30pm, 7.30–10pm; Sun. 7.30–10pm*

An inventive and improvisatory chef, who sets his imagination to work on seasonal products from all parts of the world. The one certainty is that you will enjoy a meal with diverse flavors and a very personal culinary esthetic. The wine list is still limited, but the restaurant's considerable success should allow it to expand.

Élysées Vernet (11)

25 rue Vernet, 75008 ☎ 01 44 31 98 98 ➟ 01 44 31 85 69

M *Charles de Gaulle-Étoile, Georges-V* **Provençal and gourmet cuisine** ●●●● ⊟ ⊙ *Mon.–Fri. noon–2.30pm, 7.30–9.30pm; closed in Aug. and on public holidays* Y

An Edwardian glass roof adorns one of the most elegant hotel restaurants in Paris. Alain Solivérès, a former sous-chef under Alain Ducasse, is famous for his game served with truffles, and such specialities as wheat risotto, chocolate puff turnover and ice cream flavored with roasted cocoa beans.

Taillevent (12)

15 rue Lamennais, 75008 ☎ 01 44 95 15 01 ➟ 01 42 25 95 18

M *Georges-V* **Gourmet cuisine** ●●●●● *à la carte* ⊟ ⊙ *Mon.–Fri. noon–2.30pm, 7.30–10.30pm; closed May 1, Dec. 25, Jan. 1, July 24–Aug. 25*

For 50 years, Taillevent has been the unrivaled guardian of tradition. Its classic dishes – traditional *boudin* of lobster cooked in a *court-bouillon* – reflect the credo of Jean-Claude Vrinat and his chef, Philippe Legendre. Luxurious decor, sophisticated service and an exceptional cellar.

Not forgetting

■ **Taïra (13)** 10 rue des Acacias, 75017 ☎ 01 47 66 74 14 ●● *French seafood cookery interpreted by Japanese chef Taïra Kurihara, trained in both traditions. Always a superb meeting of minds, and sometimes a love-match too.*
■ **Maison Prunier (14)** 16 avenue Victor-Hugo, 75016 ☎ 01 44 17 35 85 ●●●●● *Enjoy Gabriel Biscay's delicate seafood cuisine in a magnificent Art Deco setting. Cream of lobster soup with chorizo and haricot beans, Aquitaine caviar.*

➥ 86 ➥ 88
➥ 96
■ What to see ➥ 106

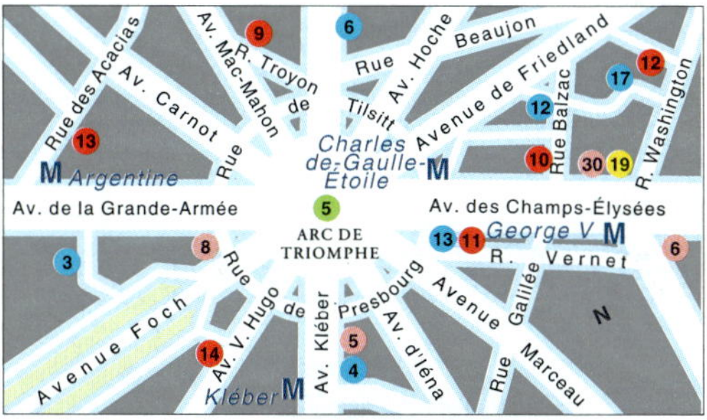

9

9

9

The clean lines of the decor chosen by Guy Savoy and the newly renovated interior of Taillevent.

10

12

In the area

The 17th *arrondissement* was originally renowned for its modest restaurants and *cuisine bourgeoise*. Over the last 20 years, the number of top-quality establishments has gradually increased and today the district offers a complete range of places to eat, from gourmet restaurants to modest bistros.

Where to eat

Michel Rostang (15)

20 rue Rennequin, 75017 ☎ 01 47 63 40 77 ➠ 01 47 63 82 75

Ternes ***Classic French cuisine*** ●●●● *à la carte F700* *Tue.–Fri. 12.30–2.30pm, 7.30–10.30pm; Mon., Sat. 7.30–10.30pm; closed Aug. 2–18* *Chez Raffatin et Honorine* ➡ 76

Michel Rostang was born and brought up in a region of lakes and Alpine meadows. He often uses freshwater fish and knows how to prepare it to the best advantage. He is one of the few chefs in Paris to offer char lakefish, perch and polar. A cuisine that uses seasonal vegetables (truffles, mushrooms) and traditional produce (Bresse) served in the friendly atmosphere maintained by Marie-Claude Rostang. An excellent choice of wines, ad hoc service.

Pétrissans (16)

30bis avenue Niel, 75017 ☎ 01 42 27 52 03 ➠ 01 40 54 87 56

Ternes ***Traditional cuisine*** ●● *à la carte F250* *Mon.–Fri. noon–2.30pm, 7.45–10.30pm; closed public holidays, Aug. 1–20*

An old wine cellar that has been converted into an atmospheric bistro. Simple cuisine: aubergine caviar, head-of-veal *ravigotte*, Salers sirloin and other bistro specialties. Friendly, efficient service. Local and vintage wines. Good range of cigars.

Amphyclès (17)

78 avenue des Ternes, 75017 ☎ 01 40 68 01 01 ➠ 01 40 68 91 88

Porte-Maillot ***Gourmet cuisine*** ●●● *à la carte F600, lunch menu F295* *Mon.–Fri. noon–2.30pm, 7–10.30pm; Sat. 7–10.30pm*

Philippe Groult, a fiery and creative chef, is a product of the Joël Robuchon school of excellence. His spider crab served in its shell alongside European crab and lobster or Dombes duckling with cherries in bitter orange sauce, achieve the blend of flavors, textures and aromas that is the quintessence of the very greatest French cuisine. Pleasant decor, courteous welcome and service.

Le Petit Colombier (18)

42 rue des Acacias, 75017 ☎ 01 43 80 28 54 ➠ 01 44 40 04 29

Ternes ***Classic French cuisine*** ●● *à la carte F350* *Mon.–Fri. 12.15–2.30pm, 7.15–10.30pm; Sat. 7.15–10.30pm; closed Aug. 1–20*

Old-fashioned decor, a muted atmosphere, a very friendly welcome and the masterly cuisine of Bernard Fournier, based on regional products: tenderloin of beef, lobster from Brittany and French game (when in season). A fine selection of 440 leading wines and a smoking area around an open fireplace.

Not forgetting

■ **Les Béatilles (19)** 11bis rue Villebois-Mareuil, 75017 ☎ 01 45 74 43 80 ●● *Classic French cuisine. Culinary expertise and good-quality ingredients.*

■ **La Marée (20)** 1 rue Daru, 75008 ☎ 01 43 80 20 00 ●●●●● *à la carte Seafood. Originality and tradition in a modestly luxurious setting. Excellent wines.*

■ After dark
➡ 100

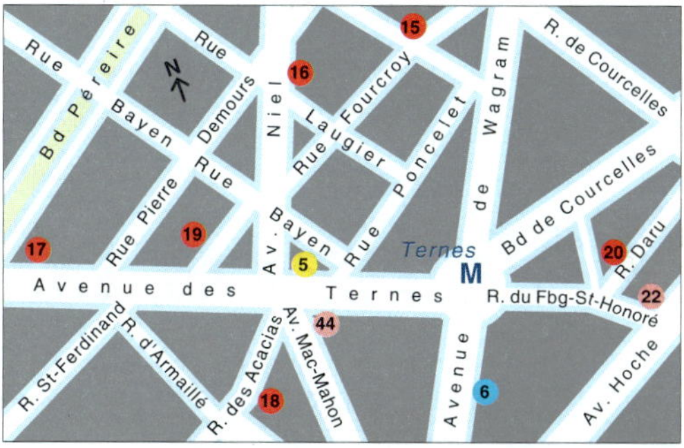

Michel Rostang continually extends his menu with dishes from his native Alps.

15

18

15

18

17

17

In the area
The *colline* (hill) of Chaillot, which witnessed the meteoric rise of Joël Robuchon, is today witnessing the success of Alain Ducasse. A district of beautiful tree-lined avenues. ■ Where to eat ➡ 74 ■ Where to stay ➡ 20 ■ What to see ➡ 106

Where to eat

Conti (21)

72 rue Lauriston, 75016 ☎ 01 47 27 74 67 ➡ 01 47 27 37 66

Boissière ***Italian gourmet cuisine*** ●● *à la carte F330 Mon.–Fri. noon–2pm, 7.30–10.30pm; closed for 3 weeks in Aug., Dec. 24–Jan. 2*

Michel Ranvier is passionately fond of Italy and takes his interpretation of its culinary repertoire very seriously. People love Italian opera, so why not Italian cuisine? Spaghetti with Mediterranean 'white caviar', poached scallops in *vin santo* and (in season) white truffles from Alba, are just a few of the specialties of the house. A fine list of Italian wines. Meticulous service. Good range of cigars.

Alain Ducasse (22)

59 avenue Raymond-Poincaré, 75116
☎ 01 47 27 12 27 ➡ 01 47 27 31 22

Trocadéro ***Gourmet cuisine*** ●●●●● *à la carte F1200 Mon.–Fri. noon–2pm, 7.45–10pm; closed July 13–Aug. 17, Dec. 23–Jan. 4*

Alain Ducasse, the first chef of the famous Louis XV restaurant in Monte Carlo, took over from Joël Robuchon on August 12, 1996. Robuchon's perfectionism was succeeded by Ducasse's brilliant contemporary vision of gourmet cuisine: high-precision preparation and an in-depth understanding of ingredients. Eclectic and luxurious decor. A richly stocked cellar lovingly tended by Gérard Margeon.

Jamin (23)

32 rue de Longchamp, 75116 ☎ 01 45 53 00 07 ➡ 01 45 53 00 15

Trocadéro, Boissière ***Gourmet cuisine*** ●●● *à la carte F600 Mon.–Fri. noon–2pm, 7.30–10pm*

The former restaurant of Joël Robuchon (closed since 1993) has been reopened by Benoît Guichard, who has particular style. Pan-fried scallops of foie gras, sweet-and-sour leeks and pig's cheek flavored with marjoram combine perfection and precision in a slightly lower key. Modestly priced wines.

Port Alma (24)

10 avenue de New York, 75116 ☎ 01 47 23 75 11

Alma-Marceau ***Seafood*** ●● *à la carte F400 Mon.–Sat. 12.30–2.30pm, 7.30–10.30pm; closed in Aug.*

Paul Canal is a Catalan who is passionate about fresh fish, which he prepares with simplicity and loving care. He seeks to highlight the natural qualities of bass, sole, scallops and abalone by means of simple but effective preparation. Bouillabaisse if ordered on the previous day.

Not forgetting

■ **Faugeron (25)** 52 rue de Longchamp, 75116 ☎ 01 47 04 24 53 ●●● *Modesty and dedication are Henri Faugeron's tribute to French cuisine.*

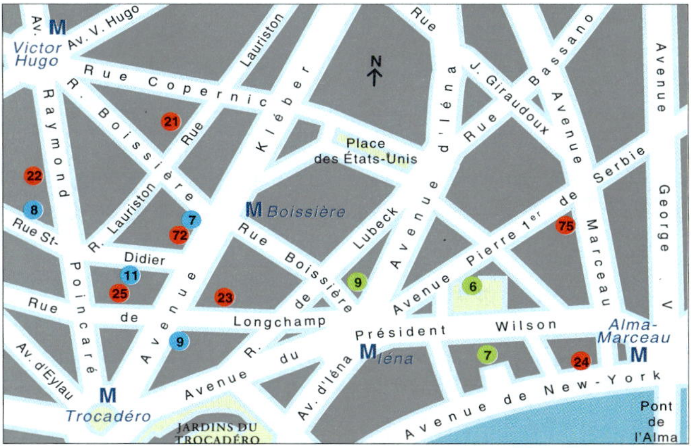

Alain Ducasse's restaurant in an early 20th-century mansion offers a conventional and intimate setting.

25

22

22

Basic facts

The River Seine divides Paris – creating two areas, each with a very different character. Parisians make the most of their river and its banks, not least as attractive places to dine.

Where to eat

Le Don Juan (26)

Yacht de Paris, port de Javel-Haut, 75015
☎ 01 44 37 10 20 ➟ 01 44 37 10 25

M *Javel* ***Gourmet cuisine*** ●●●●● *daily: boarding 8.15pm, departure 9pm, return 11.15pm* ***Acajou L'Acte III*** *same service*

A superb 1930s yacht that has been luxuriously renovated. Drinks are served on the upper deck, and dinner in the main saloon (14 places) and officers' wardroom (12 places), as you cruise beneath the bridges of Paris to the Grande Bibliothèque. Sophisticated cuisine devised by Gérard Besson, and prepared and served by his crew. A top-of-the-range *bateau mouche* with prices to match.

Pavillon Panama (27)

Port de Javel-Haut, 75015 ☎ 01 44 37 10 21 ➟ 01 44 37 11 25

M *Javel* ***Classic French cuisine*** ●● *daily noon–2.30pm, 8–11pm*

A pleasant riverside terrace, situated above the attractive new Parc André Citroën ➡ 123 in this rapidly developing district. The Pavillon has established a sound reputation among people who like something out of the ordinary. Eggplant mille-feuille with Provence herbs, chicken with cream of morilles... Trendy clientele. Very popular in fine weather.

La Plage Parisienne (28)

Port de Javel-Haut, 75015 ☎ 01 40 59 41 00

M *Javel* ***Classic French cuisine*** ●●● *à la carte* *daily noon–3pm, 8–11.30pm*

In fine weather, what could be more pleasant than to sit beneath the umbrellas of this delightful terrace on the banks of the Seine? Its 'healthy' cuisine of simple salads and vegetable dishes, correctly served, attracts a clientele from the world of fashion and advertising. Definitely out of the ordinary and an ideal place to enjoy a meal with friends, a pleasure enhanced (at lunchtime) by the presence of the sun.

Café Six-huit (29)

Quai Malaquais, 75006/quai Montebello, 75005 ☎ 01 46 34 53 05

M *Pont-Neuf* ***Classic French cuisine*** ● *à la carte* *Apr.–Sep.: daily noon–3pm, 7–11pm* *11pm–2am* ***Café-concert*** *Mon. 7pm–2am Wed. 9pm; Thu. 9.30pm; Fri., Sat. 10pm*

At the foot of the Passerelle des Arts, you can feast your eyes on the Palais du Louvre, the Pont Neuf and also – between April and September – on what is served on your plate (two affordable lunch and dinner menus). ★ For the rest of the year, the boat is a floating *café-concert* moored at the Quai Montebello. Relaxed, friendly atmosphere.

Not forgetting

■ **Bermuda Onion (30)** 16 rue Linois, 75015 ☎ 01 45 75 11 11 ●●
Flavorsome classic French cuisine and mixed clientele at this showcase restaurant where people come to see and be seen. Large terrace overlooking the Seine. Background music. Ideal for Sunday brunch.

28
26
29
28
26
26
27

In the area

In the 19th century, the Champs-Élysées replaced the Palais Royal and the *grands boulevards* as the fashionable place to be seen. Today, the recently renovated avenue is preparing for the new millennium. Its gardens and the neighboring avenues offer an ideal opportunity for an

Where to eat

L'Astor (31)

11 rue d'Astorg, 75008 ☎ 01 53 05 05 20 ➟ 01 53 05 05 30

Saint-Augustin ***Gourmet cuisine*** ●●● *à la carte F450* *Mon.–Fri. noon–2pm, 7.30–10pm*

Although Joël Robuchon is not actively involved in its preparation, he keeps a close eye on the cuisine of the Hôtel Astor ➡ 26. Those who have never tasted – or who cannot live without – caviar in aspic served with creamed cauliflower, prawn ravioli garnished with truffles and served with cabbage or the famous potato purée, should make their pilgrimage to this elegant restaurant with its glass roof, cabled columns and efficient service.

Yvan (32)

1 bis rue Jean-Mermoz, 75008 ☎ 01 43 59 18 40

Franklin-Roosevelt ***Gourmet cuisine*** ●● *à la carte F250* *Mon.–Fri. noon–2.30pm, 8–midnight; Sat. 8–midnight*

The atmosphere is of a happy night out with friends. Yvan has forgotten neither his training with the great Jacques Manière nor his Flemish origins — witness his dishes based on beer. Just as at the opera, the clientele is part of the show.

Laurent (33)

41 avenue Gabriel, 75008 ☎ 01 42 25 00 39 ➟ 01 45 62 45 21

Champs-Élysées-Clemenceau ***Gourmet cuisine*** ●●●● *à la carte F800* *Mon.–Fri. 12.30–2.30pm, 7.30–11pm; Sat 7.30–11pm; closed public holidays*

This exceptional restaurant in its garden setting is a monument to the Paris restaurant trade. Judging by the veal ravioli poached with purple artichokes, the large pan-fried langoustines and the macaroni with tomato and oregano, it is also a high-flying restaurant. It is managed by Philippe Braun, and Philippe Bourgignon keeps a very fine cellar.

Ledoyen (34)

1 avenue Dutuit, Carré des Champs-Élysées, 75008
☎ 01 53 05 10 01 ➟ 01 47 42 55 01

Champs-Elysées-Clemenceau, Concorde ***Gourmet cuisine*** ●●●● *à la carte F800* *Mon.–Fri. noon–2pm, 7.30–10pm; closed in Aug.* *Cercle Ledoyen (same address)* ***Classic French cuisine*** ●●● *☎ 01 53 05 10 02*

Christian Le Squer has taken charge of the restaurant. Offering a light and simple cuisine based on quality seasonal produce, he aims to bring out the full flavors, as with his king-sized crispy Breton langoustines, with citrus fruit purée and olive oil.

Not forgetting

■ **Lasserre (35)** 17 avenue Franklin D. Roosevelt, 75008 ☎ 01 43 59 53 43 ●●●●● *à la carte A historic restaurant with a celebrity clientele. Duck à l'orange a specialty.*

after-dinner stroll. ■ Where to stay ➥ 22 ➥ 26 ■ What to see ➥ 108 ■ Where to shop ➥ 142

35

34

In 1791, Antoine Nicolas Doyen rented a café on the Champs-Élysées and converted it into a restaurant.

5

34

33

In the area

Nearly every street in the Saint-Honoré district – which lies between La Madeleine, the Jardin des Tuileries and the Palais Royal, and not far from the Louvre – has a gourmet restaurant. ■ Where to eat ➡ 66 ➡ 74 ■ Where to stay ➡ 24 ➡ 28 ➡ 30 ■ What to see ➡ 104

Where to eat

Lucas Carton (36)

9 place de la Madeleine, 75008 ☎ 01 42 65 22 90 ➡ 01 42 65 06 23

M *Madeleine* ***Gourmet cuisine*** ●●●● *à la carte F1200* *Tue.–Fri. noon–2.30pm, 7.45–10.30pm; Mon., Sat. 7.45–10.30pm; closed Aug. 1–23*

Alain Senderens has become the guardian of this temple to innovative, as opposed to opportunist, cuisine. He is an impassioned perfectionist, achieving a precise balance of flavors and aromas and complementing his dishes with carefully chosen wines. Although his duck *Apicius* and hare *à la Royale* (simmered in red wine) are perennial masterpieces, each season brings a range of new dishes. A truly exceptional restaurant.

Les Ambassadeurs (37)

10 place de la Concorde, 75008 ☎ 01 44 71 16 16 ➡ 01 44 71 15 02

M *Concorde* ***Gourmet cuisine*** ●●●● *à la carte F700* *daily noon–2.30pm, 7–10.30pm*

★ Les Ambassadeurs forms part of the Hôtel de Crillon ➡ 24, and is famed as one of the city's most beautiful luxury-hotel restaurants. Its elegant and amiable service also make it one of the most convivial. Dominique Bouchet reinterprets classic dishes without flouting established principles. Marble and gilt decor.

Le Carré des Feuillants (38)

14 rue de Castiglione, 75001 ☎ 01 42 86 82 82 ➡ 01 42 86 07 71

M *Tuileries* ***Gourmet cuisine*** ●●●● *à la carte F550* *Tue.–Sat. noon–2.30pm, 7.30–10.30pm; Sat. 7.30–10.30pm; closed Aug. 1–20*

Alain Dutournier's cuisine may be inspired by the mountain streams of the Pyrenees and the River Adour, but it is far from being a mere repetition of the obvious regional dishes. A light touch, precise cooking and a carefully calculated use of chili peppers from the Basque village of Espelette give his roasted prawns a truly exquisite flavor. Fine cellar and meticulous service.

À la Grille Saint-Honoré (39)

15 place du Marché Saint-Honoré, 75001
☎ 01 42 61 00 93 ➡ 01 47 03 31 64

M *Tuileries* P ***Traditional cuisine*** ●● *à la carte F260* *Tue.–Sat. noon–2.30pm, 7–10.30pm; closed Aug. 1–20*

Generously cooked traditional ingredients, served in the old-fashioned comfort of a bistro whose chef, Jean Speyer, is keen to improve on classic recipes: game when it is in season, shellfish when they are affordable and frogs' legs. A study in professionalism and tranquility.

Not forgetting

■ **Goumard (40)** 9 rue Duphot, 75001 ☎ 01 42 60 36 07 ●●●● *An elaborate Art Nouveau setting and elegantly sophisticated seafood.*
■ **Le Manège (41)** Hôtel Meurice ➡ 24 ☎ 01 44 58 10 10 ●●●● *Louis XVI decor, gourmet cuisine by Marc Marchand. Excellent cellar.*

Where to shop ➥ 146 ➥ 148 ➥ 150

41

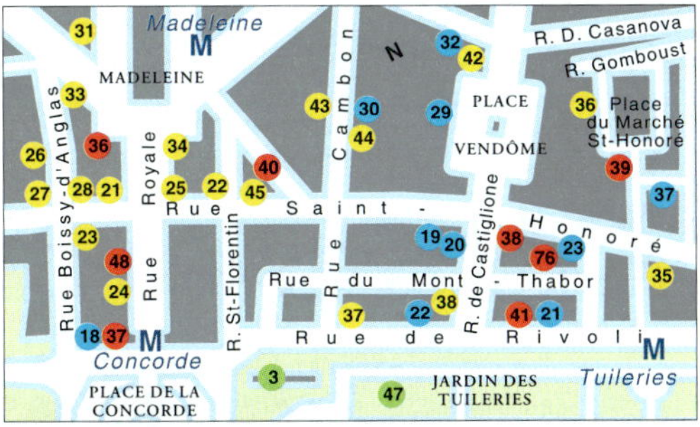

40

36

40

36

Almost 200 years separate Robert Lucas and Francis Carton, who gave their names to one of the finest restaurants in Paris.

38

41

In the area

The memory of the Second Empire is kept alive in several restaurants in the Opéra district, which played a major role in the life of Paris during the golden age of the *grand boulevard*. A number of brasseries and bistros maintain the culinary tradition. ■ Where to stay ➡ 28 ■ After dark

Where to eat

L'Œnothèque (42)

20 rue Saint-Lazare, 75009 ☎ 01 48 78 08 76 ➟ 01 40 16 10 27

M *Notre-Dame-de-Lorette* ***Traditional cuisine*** ●● *Mon.–Fri. noon–2.30pm, 7.30–11pm; closed Aug. 7–31*

This local restaurant occupies a former liquor store and has unusual decor: wall-to-wall bottles. The proprietor, Daniel Hallée, once a *sommelier* at Jamin ➡ 56, has entrusted the cooking to Jacques Marmonier. The cuisine – saddle of hare (in season), magnificent fish dishes and excellent beef – is complemented by excellent regional wines and Havana cigars.

Casa Olympe (43)

48 rue Saint-Georges, 75009 ☎ 01 42 85 26 01 ➟ 01 45 26 49 33

M *Notre-Dame-de-Lorette* ***Classic French cuisine*** ●● *Mon.–Fri. noon–2pm, 8–11pm; closed Aug., Dec. 24–Jan. 2, May 1–8*

Once the culinary queen of Montparnasse, Olympe, aka Dominique Versini, is returning to her roots with this modest bistro. The richly flavored dishes include guinea fowl ravioli, casserole of free-range pork and sage, and Sisteron lamb shoulder. Brisk service. Moderate prices.

Saint-Amour (44)

8 rue Port-Mahon, 75002 ☎ 01 47 42 63 82

M *Opéra* ***Classic French cuisine*** ●● *à la carte F220* *Mon.–Fri. noon–2.45pm, 7–11pm; Sat. 7–11pm; closed public hol., Aug. 15-31*

This modest two-story restaurant, which witnessed Édith Piaf's debut in Paris, reflects a discerning taste for the good things in life. It offers classic French dishes from Lyons and Burgundy washed down with a simple Beaujolais or another of its wide range of very reasonably priced wines. *Turbot au sel de Guérande* (salt turbot) and chocolate tart are two of the house favorites.

Drouant (45)

16–18 rue Gaillon, 75002 ☎ 01 42 65 15 16 ➟ 01 49 24 02 15

M *Opéra, Quatre-Septembre* ***Gourmet cuisine*** ●●● *à la carte F750* *daily noon–2.30pm, 7.15–10pm* ***Café Littéraire*** ●● *daily noon–2.30pm, 7pm–midnight*

This traditional restaurant is famous for its wrought-iron staircase by the interior designer, Jacques-Émile Ruhlmann, its 'marine' ceiling decorated with fish, shellfish and crustaceans, and its Salon Goncourt. Louis Grondard's cuisine deserves equal attention for its precise cooking, presentation and classic authenticity. Magnificent rooms on the upper floor where Jean Cocteau and Colette were regulars. Excellent wine list and impeccable service.

Not forgetting

■ **L'Entrecôte de Paris (46)** 101 rue Saint-Lazarre, 75009 ☎ 01 48 74 74 90 ● *Menus from F70 for lovers of red meat.*

➥ 88 ➥ 90 ➥ 92 ■ Where to shop ➥ 140 ➥ 150

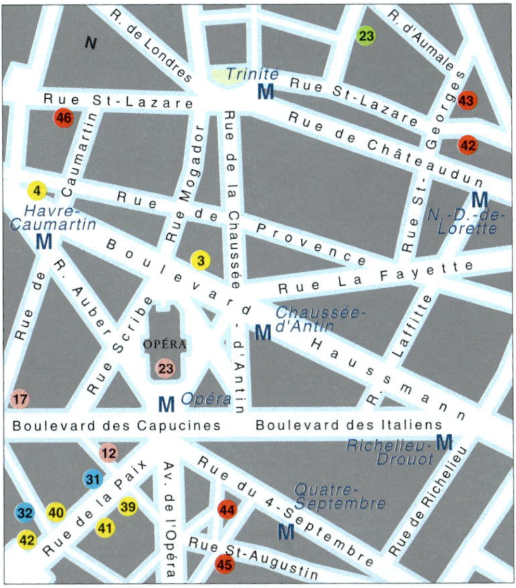

43

42

45

45

45

44

45

Basic facts

Some Parisian restaurants have become symbols of the city, recognized around the world. Many conjure up a particular era in the city's history, and boast wonderfully evocative interiors. Some have been connected with the literati of the city, and resonate with memories of a bygone era.

Where to eat

47

49

MAXIM'S

48

MAXIM'S

Le Pré Catelan (47)

Route de Suresnes, 75016 ☎ 01 44 14 41 14 ➡ 01 45 24 43 25

M *Porte Dauphine* ***Gourmet cuisine*** ●●● *à la carte F550*
Tue.–Sat. noon–2.30pm, 7–10.30pm; Sun. noon–2.30pm; closed for two weeks in Feb.

Frédéric Anton, who took over from Roland Durand in March 1997, keeps alive the gourmet tradition of this celebrated fin-de-siècle restaurant in the leafy Bois de Boulogne. Trained at the renowned Joël Robuchon school of excellence, he has established a cuisine that is a balanced blend of inspiration and expertise.

Maxim's (48)

3 rue Royale, 75008 ☎ 01 42 65 27 94 ➡ 01 40 17 02 91

M *Concorde* ***Classic French cuisine*** ●●●●● *à la carte*
Mon.–Sat. 12.30pm–2pm, 7.30–10pm; closed Sun.–Mon. during July and Aug.

From the Belle Epoque to World War Two, this was the place to celebrate. And Maxim's remains a name to conjure with. In the expert hands of chef Bruno Stril from 1998, Maxim's offers a menu that includes baked fillet of bass with red orach shoots and rabbit hash with sage.

50

51

53

Chartier (49)

7 rue du Faubourg-Montmartre, 75009
☎ 01 47 70 86 29 ➟ 01 48 24 14 68

M *Grands-Boulevards* **Home cooking** ● *à la carte F80* ▤ ◷ *daily 11.30am–3pm., 6–10pm*

A vestige of late-19th-century, working-class Paris when 'home cooking' was served in a luxurious setting, Chartier has lost none of its popularity and still serves good, plain dishes. An interesting and unusual place to eat.

53

Not forgetting

■ **La Coupole (50)** 102 boulevard du Montparnasse, 75014 ☎ 01 43 20 14 20 ➟ 01 43 35 46 14 ● *A 1920s Paris institution with huge dining room and wonderful decor. Controversially restored in 1988. Best for Sunday lunch or dinner.* ■ **La Grande Cascade (51)** Allée de Longchamp, bois de Boulogne, 75016 ☎ 01 45 27 33 51 ●●● *One of the 'meccas' of Parisian cuisine since the Second Empire, now under the watchful eye of Jean-Louis Nomicos, brought up in the school of Alain Ducasse.* ■ **La Fermette Marbœuf 1900 (52)** 5 rue Marbœuf, 75008 ☎ 01 53 23 08 00 ●● *Magnificent Art Nouveau settings, classic French cuisine.* ■ **Le Train Bleu (53)** Gare de Lyon, place Louis-Armand, 75012 ☎ 01 43 43 09 06 ●●● *Superb Edwardian railroad architecture. Unfortunately, meals are not always on time.*

In the area

Montmartre is busy with tourists throughout the year, and many of its restaurants are overpopulated and overpriced. However, if you avoid the main streets you can find some traditional gems. ■ After dark ➡ 92
■ What to see ➡ 112

Where to eat

Le Restaurant (54)

32 rue Véron, 75018 ☎ 01 42 23 06 22

M *Abbesses* ***Traditional cuisine*** ●● *à la carte F120* ▭ ⏲ *Mon., Sat. 8–11.30pm; Tue.–Fri. noon–2.30pm, 7.30–11.30pm*

Enjoy a pleasant interlude in this restaurant whose chef is a native of Pau and, not surprisingly, a devotee of gourmet cuisine. It is situated in the rue des Abbesses, an area of Montmartre that is late to bed and late to rise. A beautifully bright, peaceful restaurant in which to enjoy good, plain cuisine. Affordable prices.

A. Beauvilliers (55)

52 rue Lamarck, 75018 ☎ 01 42 54 54 42 ➡ 01 42 62 70 30

M *Lamarck-Caulaincourt* P ***Gourmet cuisine*** ●● *à la carte F600* ▭ ⏲ *Mon. 7.30–10.45pm; Tue.–Sat. noon–2pm, 7.30–10.45pm*

Everything in Édouard Carlier's restaurant contributes to the dining experience, from the delightful decor and slightly old-fashioned menu, to the efficient service and the delicious dishes from the past. A meal here is a true celebration, but one that can prove costly. Keep an eye on the *sommelier*!

Table d'Anvers (56)

2 place d'Anvers, 75009 ☎ 01 48 78 35 21 ➡ 01 45 26 66 65

M *Anvers* ***Modern gourmet cuisine*** ●●● *à la carte F500* ▭ ⏲ *Mon.–Fri. noon–2.30pm, 7–10pm; Sat. 7–11pm*

Innovative brothers Christian and Philippe Conticini combine forces in this welcoming restaurant. Christian concentrates on the savory dishes, experimenting with taste, texture and flavor, while Philippe focuses on wonderful desserts. Eclectic wine list.

L'Alsaco (57)

10 rue Condorcet, 75009 ☎ 01 45 26 44 31

M *Anvers* ***Alsatian cuisine*** ● *à la carte F150* ▭ ⏲ *Mon.–Fri. 9am–3.30pm, 7–11pm; Sat 7–11pm; closed in Aug.*

Typically simple cuisine and beer and a range of Alsatian wines at reasonable prices. Claude Steger, known as Klaus, has his cold meats sent from the Upper Rhine, and his magnificent sauerkraut from Masevaux. Often full, although the *patron*'s mood is as variable as the tab.

Not forgetting

■ **Le Moulin à Vins (58)** 6 rue Burq, 75018 ☎ 01 42 52 81 27 ●●
Open until 2am. The main attractions are Dany, the 'patronne' *and her Côtes du Rhône.*

■ **Aux Négociants (59)** 27 rue Lambert, 75018 ☎ 01 46 06 15 11 ●●
Wines from the Loire to accompany the rillons *(pork belly pieces cooked in lard until crisp),* boudin *(black pudding) and other specialties from the Loire valley.*

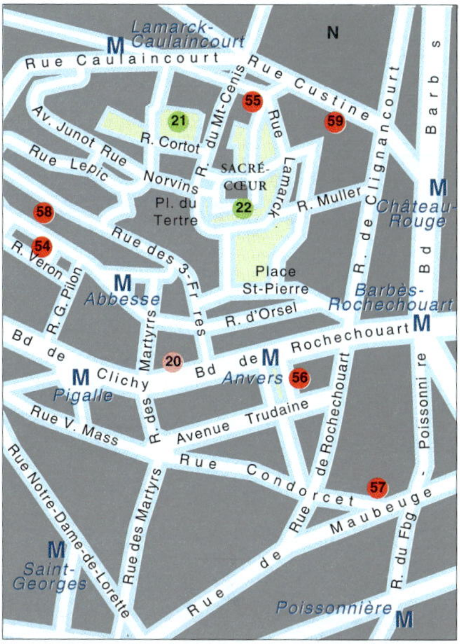

Dinner at Beauvilliers is an experience to remember.

In the area
Before the French Revolution, Paris had a mere 50 restaurants. The first establishment to offer *à la carte* was founded in 1782 in the rue de Richelieu. ■ Where to stay ➡ 30 ➡ 32 ■ After dark ➡ 90 ➡ 98 ➡ 102 ■ What to see ➡ 110 ■ Where to shop ➡ 152 ➡ 154 ➡ 160

Where to eat

Le Grand Véfour (60)

17 rue de Beaujolais, 75001 ☎ 01 42 96 56 27 ➡ 01 42 86 80 71

M *Palais-Royal* ***Gourmet cuisine ●●●●●*** *à la carte F400*
Mon.–Fri. 12.30–2.15pm, 7.30–10.15pm; closed in Aug.

Le Grand Véfour, beneath the arcades of the Palais-Royal, is one of the oldest and most famous of Paris restaurants. Today it is managed by Guy Martin, a native of Savoy, who maintains the restaurant's exceptionally high standard of cuisine. Le Véfour offers its well-to-do clientele a choice of simply prepared dishes, or creations based on what Escoffier called 'the great transformation'. Remarkable cellar and service.

Gérard Besson (61)

5 rue Coq-Héron, 75001 ☎ 01 42 33 14 74 ➡ 01 42 33 85 71

M *Louvre-Rivoli, Palais-Royal* ***Gourmet cuisine ●●●*** *à la carte F500*
Mon.–Fri. noon–2.30pm, 7.15–10.30pm; Sat. 7.15–10.30pm

The extensive culinary repertoire of Gérard Besson, a former student of Garin, is based on truffles and game. Scrambled eggs with truffles and noisettes of venison, complemented by a bottle of Burgundy, are among the culinary delights to be enjoyed in the modern decor of this former store in Les Halles. The chef insists on a respectful use of seasonal ingredients, and produces some wonderful new dishes.

Café Marly (62)

Palais du Louvre, 93 rue de Rivoli, 75001 ☎ 01 49 26 06 60

M *Louvre-Rivoli, Palais-Royal* ***Classic French cuisine ●*** *à la carte* *daily 8–2am*

One of the trendiest cafés in Paris, Café Marly is located inside the Louvre. Vast rooms with bay windows overlooking the glass pyramid, and a view over the museum rooms devoted to French sculpture. Go in the evening when the pyramid is lit up.

Ambassade d'Auvergne (63)

22 rue du Grenier-Saint-Lazare, 75003
☎ 01 42 72 31 22 ➡ 01 42 78 85 47

M *Rambuteau* ***Regional cuisine from the Auvergne and Aveyron ●●*** *à la carte F230* *daily noon–2pm, 7.30–11pm*

In spite of its rather eccentric and medieval appearance, the restaurant is popular with lovers of *tripoux* (highly seasoned variety meats tied up in small packs with gut casings) and other specialties from the Auvergne region. Regional wines.

Not forgetting
■ **Le Pied de Cochon (64)** 6 rue Coquillière, 75001 ☎ 01 40 13 77 00 ●● *According to a sign over the bar, 'All roads lead to Le Pied de Cochon'. Open round the clock.*
■ **Auberge Nicolas Flamel (65)** 51 rue de Montmorency, 75003 ☎ 01 42 71 77 78 ● *Simple cuisine served in the former house (1407) of the alchemist Nicolas Flamel.*

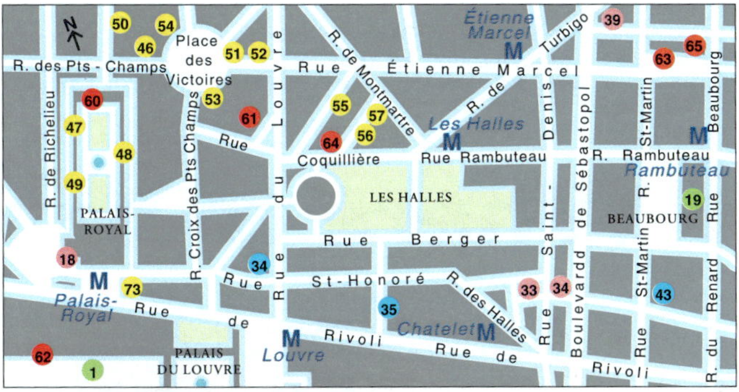

2

60

61

"If I hadn't got Louis [Vaudable] to take over the 'Véfour', the Americans would have bought the decor and taken it away". *Jean Cocteau*

In the area

The Marais, one of the most historic districts of Paris, is today a lively area and the center of the city's gay scene. ■ Where to stay ➥ 32 ■ After dark ➥ 92 ■ What to see ➥ 110 ■ Where to shop ➥ 160

Where to eat

Miravile (66)

72 quai de l'Hôtel-de-Ville, 75004
☎ 01 42 74 72 22 ➠ 01 42 74 67 55

M *Hôtel-de-Ville, Pont-Marie* ***Gourmet cuisine*** ●● *à la carte F350* *Tue.–Fri. noon–2.15pm, 7.30–10.30pm; Mon.,Sat. 7.30–10.30pm; closed for 3 weeks in Aug.*

In an attractive location on the banks of the Seine, next to Notre Dame, the Miravile offers the classic dishes of French cuisine in an imaginative partnership with the fragrances of Japan.

Le Monde des Chimères (67)

69 rue Saint-Louis-en-l'Île, 75004
☎ 01 43 54 45 27 ➠ 01 43 29 84 88

M *Pont-Marie* ***Traditional cuisine*** ● *à la carte F250* *Tue.–Sat. 12.15–2.30pm, 7.15–10.30pm*

Le Monde des Chimères became famous during the golden age of Nouvelle Cuisine. Today, Cécile Ibane uses her expertise to teach the younger generation that cuisine – like life – goes on. Splendid, slow-cooked dishes of Mediterranean inspiration.

L'Ambroisie (68)

9 place des Vosges, 75004 ☎ 01 42 78 51 45

M *Saint-Paul, Bastille* ***Gourmet cuisine*** ●●●●● *à la carte* *Tue.–Sat. noon–1.45pm, 8–9.45pm; closed for 2 weeks in Feb., 3 weeks in Aug.*

Bernard Pacard's style is based on the simple presentation of complex flavors using the very best ingredients. His cuisine – precise and faultless – encapsulates the best of gourmet cuisine, and on the place des Vosges to boot! The charlotte of foie gras from the Landes flavored with fennel and spiced caramel is an absolute must. Efficient, friendly service under the watchful eye of M. Pierre, a connoisseur of vintage wines and spirits.

Bofinger (69)

5–7 rue de la Bastille, 75004 ☎ 01 42 72 87 82 ➠ 01 42 72 97 68

M *Bastille* ***Alsatian cuisine*** ●● *à la carte F250* *Mon.–Fri. noon–3pm, 6.30pm–1am; Sat.–Sun; public holidays noon–1am*

Bofinger's clientele continues to enjoy the famous sauerkraut, seafood and essentially simple and soberly prepared cuisine beneath the restaurant's magnificent glass roof. Although the regulars of 30 years' standing had some reservations about the change of ownership, by and large the restaurant has remained as popular as in its heyday.

Not forgetting

■ **La Baracane (70)** 38 rue des Tournelles, 75004 ☎ 01 42 71 43 33
● *The 'confit de canard' washed down with a bottle of Cahors is said to guarantee long life. In any event, it's just what the doctor ordered!*

68

68

The decor (1919) of the Bofinger, by the architect Legay and the interior designer Mitdgen, is considered to be the archetypal brasserie.

69

69

7

69

67

66

Basic facts

Paris has many international restaurants where customers can enjoy dishes created from fresh ingredients flown in from all over the world. The city has several thousand Asian restaurants; Chinese cuisine is particularly popular, as is the more aromatic and lighter Vietnamese

Where to eat

75

73

73

Kim Anh (71)

15 rue de l'Église, 75015 ☎ 01 45 79 40 96 ➟ 01 40 59 49 78

M *Charles-Michel* ***Gourmet Vietnamese cuisine*** ●●● *à la carte F250* *daily 7.30–11.30pm*

Vietnamese cuisine and tradition bring the delights of southeast Asia to Paris. Kim Anh offers a delightful family welcome and an intimate atmosphere. Spring rolls, stuffed crab, prawns marinated in curry sauce, steamed stuffed snails, filleted cockerel and Tonkinese soup. Wines include Côtes du Jura, Saint-Julien and Graves.

Bertie's (72)

Hôtel Baltimore, 1 rue Léo-Delibes, 75016 ☎ 01 44 34 54 34

M *Boissières* ***English cuisine*** ●●● *à la carte F250* *Mon.–Fri. 12.30–2pm, 7.30–10pm; closed Aug. 1–15*

Located in the discreetly comfortable Hôtel Baltimore, this restaurant is named after Queen Victoria's husband, Prince Albert, known affectionately as 'Bertie'. Blond oak decor, large plaid-covered bench seats and pictures of the British royal family. Specialties: carved meats served from the trolley, roast Scottish lamb with mint sauce, roast duck with orange sauce, sherry trifle. Service quintessentially British.

cuisine. North African and European – especially Italian – culinary traditions are also well represented.

72

76

75

74

77

74

Tagine, couscous, mint tea, grissini sushi, *taboulé*, *khobz*… Unusual and evocative names that conjure up images of exotic lands and flavors.

Mansouria (73)

11 rue Faidherbe, 75011 ☎ 01 43 71 00 16 ➟ 01 40 24 21 97

M *Faidherbe-Chaligny* ***Moroccan cuisine*** ●● *à la carte F200* ▤ ◷ *Mon. 7.30–11.30pm; Tue.–Sat. noon–2.30pm, 7.30–11.30pm*

The famous Moroccan couscous offers a rich intensity of flavors: delicious meats accompany the grain, sauce and vegetables. The hostess, Fatima Hal, is also a sociologist and has written a book on this exceptional 'communal cuisine'. The house specialty is couscous made with lamb and conserve of onions.

Not forgetting

■ **Paolo Petrini (74)** 6 rue du Débarcadère, 75017 ☎ 01 45 74 25 95
●● *Paolo Petrini has introduced Parisians to sophisticated Italian cuisine, inspired by his native Tuscany. Even if the welcome is sometimes rather reserved, the restaurant is currently one of the best in Paris.*

■ **Pavillon Noura (75)** 21 avenue Marceau, 75116 ☎ 01 47 20 33 33
●● *This Lebanese restaurant offers a varied and constantly changing menu.*

■ **Kinugawa (76)** 9 rue du Mont-Thabor, 75001 ☎ 01 42 60 65 07
●● *One of the best Japanese restaurants in Paris where flavor takes precedence over ceremony. Minimalist decor, high prices.*

■ **Chen Soleil d'Est (77)** 15 rue Théâtre, 75015 ☎ 01 45 79 34 34
●●● *The best Chinese restaurant in Paris, situated in the Chinese quarter.*

In the area

After World War II, Saint-Germain-des-Prés became the center of the city's intellectual life and nightlife. In the 1980s the spotlight was turned on fashion, but the district retains its fine restaurants. ■ Where to stay ➡ 34 ➡ 38 ■ After dark ➡ 90 ➡ 96 ■ What to see ➡ 118 ➡ 120

Where to eat

Le Relais Louis XIII (78)

8 rue des Grands-Augustins, 75006 ☎ 01 43 26 75 96

Ⓜ *Saint-Michel* ***Classic French cuisine*** ●●● *à la carte F350* ⊟ ⏲ *Mon. 7.30–10.15pm; Tue.–Sat. noon–2.30pm, 7.30–10.45pm; closed for 1 week in Feb., Aug. 1–21*

The truly amazing medieval and Renaissance decor was designed by an art connoisseur who is also a flea-market enthusiast. The restaurant has been taken over by Manuel Martinez, former chef of La Tour d'Argent ➡ 48. One of a number of restaurants in the area serving diverse and unusual dishes. Good wine list.

Jacques Cagna (79)

14 rue des Grands-Augustins, 75006
☎ 01 43 26 49 39 ➡ 01 43 54 54 48

Ⓜ *Saint-Michel* ***Gourmet cuisine*** ●●● *à la carte F700* ⊟ ⏲ *Tue.–Fri. noon–2pm, 7.30–10.30pm; Mon., Sat. 7.30–10.30pm; closed Aug. 1–24, Dec 24–Jan 2*

The restaurant's classic cuisine is in keeping with the 'old Paris' setting in the style of an old inn. Updated classics include *petit-gris* snails or Houdan chicken. First-class cuisine always on the lookout for new ideas. Attentive service.

Campagne et Provence (80)

25 quai de la Tournelle, 75005 ☎ 01 43 54 05 17

Ⓜ *Maubert-Mutualité* ***Mediterranean cuisine*** ●● ⊟ ⏲ *Mon. 7.30–11pm; Tue.–Sat. noon–2.30pm, 7.30–11pm*

Sundrenched cooking with flavorful products — even the tablecloths are the color of pastis. This is a gastronomic mecca where the dishes are boldly flavored with aromatic herbs, especially suitable for a saddle or loin of lamb, or crab in a spicy mayonnaise sauce with purée of potatoes and almonds.

Chez Raffatin et Honorine (81)

16 boulevard Saint-Germain, 75005
☎ 01 43 54 59 10 ➡ 01 43 29 02 08

Ⓜ *Maubert-Mutualité, Jussieu* ***Regional cuisine from Lyon*** ●● ⊟ ⏲ *Mon.–Fri. noon–2.30pm, 7.30–11pm; Sat. 7.30–11pm* *Michel Rostang* ➡ *54*

The clientele can enjoy top quality food at very reasonable prices in a classic 50s interior, that of the old, but nonetheless famous, *Raffatin et Honorine*.

Not forgetting

■ **Allard (82)** 41 rue Saint-André-des-Arts, 75006 ☎ 01 43 26 48 23 ●●
The new proprietors have successfully maintained the bistro cuisine of Fernande Allard.

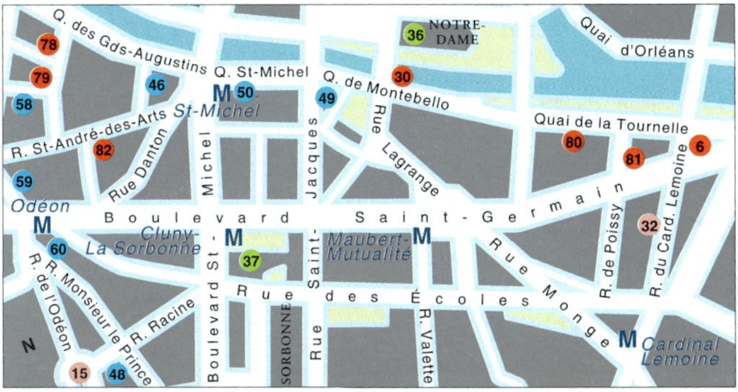

79

82

79

81

82

The secret of Jacques Cagna? High quality ingredients that he always treats with respect and simplicity.

In the area

This district's many eating places, which include some famous restaurants, attract workers from the government ministries and many publishing houses located here. ■ Where to eat ➡ 82 ■ Where to stay ➡ 40 ➡ 42 ■ After dark ➡ 94 ■ What to see ➡ 108 ➡ 116

Where to eat

Le Divellec (83)

107 rue de l'Université, 75007 ☎ 01 45 51 91 96 ➡ 01 45 51 31 75

Invalides **Seafood ●●●** *à la carte* *Mon.–Sat. 12.30–2.30pm, 8–10pm; closed Dec. 24, Jan. 1*

This veritable *conservatoire* of marine delicacies, where the catch is always fresh whatever the cost, attracts a clientele of celebrities and devotees of Jacques Le Divellec's famous seafood cuisine. His talent and force of circumstance have made Le Divellec a historic restaurant in its time, a 20th-century equivalent of the famous Rocher de Cancale.

Arpège (84)

84 rue de Varenne, 75007 ☎ 01 45 51 47 33 ➡ 01 44 18 98 39

Varenne **Modern gourmet cuisine ●●●●** *à la carte F800* *Mon.–Fri. noon-2.30pm, 7-11pm*

The asceticism of the surroundings here serves only to highlight the brilliance of the dishes prepared by Alain Passard. The genius of this chef lies in his culinary method, precise cooking and preparation techniques. Dedicated service in this top Paris restaurant – located in a quiet district not far from the Musée Rodin ➡ 108 – where cuisine is an art form.

Le Rouge Vif (85)

48 rue de Verneuil, 75007 ☎ 01 42 86 81 87

Rue-du-Bac **Traditional cuisine ●** *à la carte F180* *Mon.–Fri. 12–2.30pm, 8–11.15pm; Sat. 8–11.15pm*

The modest prices belie the quality of the cuisine in a restaurant that offers an unrivaled lunch menu. The warm atmosphere is as much due to a decor of natural stone and exposed beams as to the infectious enthusiasm of the proprietors. A clientele of regulars from the district's many publishing houses.

Paris (86)

43 boulevard Raspail, 75006 ☎ 01 49 54 46 90 ➡ 01 49 54 46 00

Sèvres-Babylone **Gourmet cuisine ●●●** *à la carte F500* *Mon.–Fri. noon–2pm, 7.30–10pm; closed in Aug., for 1 week in Feb. and Dec. 24–30*

The Paris is set in the 1930s decor of the only luxury hotel on the Left Bank – the Hôtel Lutétia ➡ 42. Philippe Renart's delightfully inventive cuisine is based on the availability of seasonal ingredients. Here, mushrooms, asparagus, truffles and baby vegetables are in the spotlight. Impressive chocolate dessert and a fine wine list.

Not forgetting

■ **Les Olivades (87)** 41 avenue de Ségur, 75007 ☎ 01 47 83 70 09 ●● *Authentic Provençale cuisine re-created with feeling. The chef was born in Avignon.*
■ **L'Œillade (88)** 10 rue Saint-Simon, 75007 ☎ 01 42 22 01 60 ●● *Simple cuisine, imaginatively prepared and full of flavor. Very reasonable prices.*

Where to shop ➥ 140 ➥ 156 ➥ 158

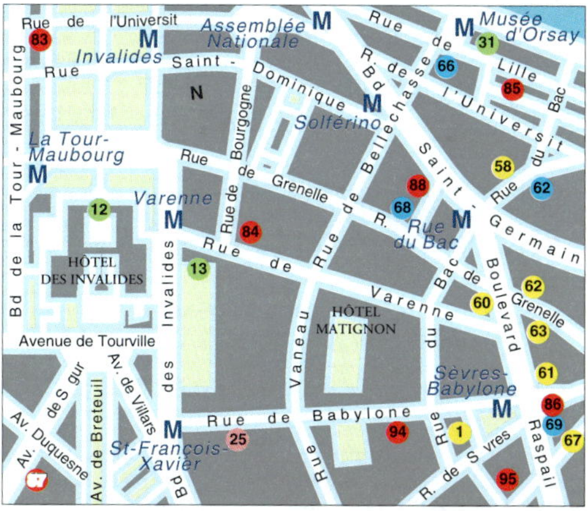

86

83

85

83

84

85

Arpège, situated between the National Assembly and the Hôtel Matignon, has an established clientele of political gourmets.

86

In the area

After World War I, Montparnasse became the preserve of artists and, later, of such writers as Ernest Hemingway, Jean-Paul Sartre and Simone de Beauvoir. Today, although the boulevard is monopolized by fast-food restaurants, the district still has a number of famous gourmet

Where to eat

Dominique (89)

19 rue Bréa, 75006 ☎ 01 43 27 08 80 ➟ 01 43 26 88 35

M *Vavin* ***Russian cuisine*** ●● *à la carte F250* ▭ ⏲ *Mon.–Sat. 7.30pm–1 am* 🍸 *Mon. 7.30pm–1 am; Tue.–Sat. noon–1 am*

Dominique is one of the last authentic restaurants of old Montparnasse, frequented by Russian princes and taxi drivers, which offers all the culinary splendors of Eastern Europe: *pirojki*, *chachliks*, eggplant caviar, beef Stroganoff and a wide range of vodkas. Managed by Françoise Dépée.

Le Caméléon (90)

6 rue de Chevreuse, 75006 ☎ 01 43 20 63 43

M *Vavin* ***Bistro cuisine*** ●● *à la carte F200* ▭ ⏲ *Mon.–Fri. noon–2pm, 8–10.30pm; Sat. 8–10.30pm; closed for 3 weeks in Aug.*

A real, old-fashioned Paris bistro where what is on your plate is more important than what is on the walls. For some time, the bar was one of the meccas of Montparnasse. The new proprietors are concentrating on the cuisine: lobster ravioli, home-made sausage and puréed potato, veal with fresh pasta. A good choice of light wines.

La Cagouille (91)

10 place Constantin-Brancusi, 75014
☎ 01 43 22 09 01 ➟ 01 45 38 57 29

(opposite 23 rue de l'Ouest) M *Gaîté* ***Seafood*** ●● *à la carte F260* ▭ ⏲ *daily noon–2.30pm, 7.30–10.30pm*

Gérard Almendou was one of the inventors of all-fish cuisine. When asked whether this is a culinary style or fashion, he counters that it is simply the produce of the sea and rivers prepared with care and simplicity. Whatever it is, it has proved a huge success. The renovated, modern setting – in a district that is still trying to establish its identity – and the famous dishes (including a superb mussels dish) represent a particular type of modern cuisine.

Vin et Marée (92)

108 avenue du Maine, 75014 ☎ 01 43 20 29 50 ➟ 01 43 27 84 11

M *Gaîté* ***Seafood*** ●● *à la carte* ▭ ⏲ *daily noon–2.30pm, 7.30pm–midnight* ♿

Vin et Marée, near the Gare Montparnasse, serves fish, shellfish and seafood amid 1930s decor. A promising new formula offered by an experienced team: good, simply prepared and inexpensive fish dishes served promptly and with a smile.

Not forgetting

■ **L'Opportun (93)** 62–64 boulevard Edgard-Quinet, 75014 ☎ 01 43 20 26 89 ●● *Simple dishes and modest regional wines in a bistro that is packed on market days.*

establishments. ■ Where to eat ➥ 48 ➥ 66 ■ Where to stay ➥ 44 ■ After dark ➥ 86

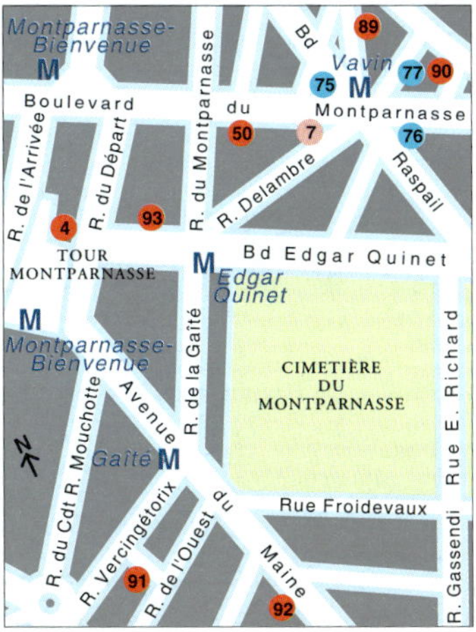

89

92

89

Seafood amid 1930s decor at the Vin et Marée (92), or the more contemporary La Cagouille (91).

91

89

Basic facts

Since the 1970s, there has been a trend among young talented chefs to take over bistros in the outlying – and less expensive – districts of Paris. Gourmets are attracted by the quality of their cuisine and their reasonable prices. The 'bistro formula' combines tables placed close

Where to eat

La Bamboche (94)

15 rue de Babylone, 75007 ☎ 01 45 49 14 40 ➟ 01 45 49 14 44

M *Sèvres-Babylone* ***Creative cuisine*** ●● *à la carte F250* *Mon.–Fri. noon–2.30pm, 7.30–11pm*

Amid polished decor that does not disguise the origins of this modest workshop, Claude Colliot creates an attractive culinary balance of seasonal products. This is first-class cuisine at bistro prices. You will have no cause for complaint, especially if you sample the sweetbreads, fried with pistachios grilled with truffles or Philippe Aléosse's cheeses.

L'Épi Dupin (95)

11 rue Dupin, 75006 ☎ 01 42 22 64 56 ➟ 01 42 22 30 42

M *Sèvres-Babylone* ***Classic French cuisine*** ● *Mon.–Fri. 12.30–2.30pm, 7.30–10.30pm*

Spontaneous and uncomplicated cuisine offering reasonable prices and high-quality ingredients. According to the season, the extremely popular *capilotade d'agneau* (tiny pieces of lamb) wrapped in eggplant skins, and the *pain perdu* with fruit capture the mood of this cuisine with its subtle Mediterranean undertones.

Le Restaurant d'Éric Frechon (96)

10 rue du General-Brunet, 75019 ☎ 01 40 40 03 30

M *Botzaris* ***Traditional cuisine*** ●● *à la carte F200* *Tue.–Sat. noon–2.15pm, 7–11pm*

Christian Constant's former second-in-command at the Hôtel de Crillon has caused great excitement at the foot of Buttes-Chaumont. People line up to try his subtle combinations of tastes from sea and farm. The lively staff wins over the clientele. Do go if you want to ensure a perfect evening with friends.

La Régalade (97)

49 avenue Jean-Moulin, 75014 ☎ 01 45 45 68 58 ➟ 01 45 40 96 74

M *Alésia* ***Bistro cuisine*** ●● *Tue.–Fri. noon–2.30pm, 7.30pm–midnight; Sat. 7.30pm–midnight; closed July 15–Aug. 15*

La Régalade is a dream come true – gourmet cuisine at affordable prices, courtesy of Yves Camdeborde, a native of the Béarn who trained in the top culinary schools. Although he decided on a bistro setting, his cuisine has other ideas. Even the all-pig platter – ear, snout and shoulder on a bed of braised cabbage – betrays the touch of a true chef. A warm and friendly welcome and an excellent choice of wines.

Not forgetting

■ **La Closerie des Lilas (98)** 171 boulevard du Montparnasse, 75006 ☎ 01 40 51 34 50 ●●● *Typical brasserie dishes or Mediterranean cuisine created by the new chef.*

■ **Le Terroir (99)** 11 boulevard Arago, 75013 ☎ 01 47 07 36 99 ●●● *Timeless classics of traditional cuisine augmented by judiciously chosen wines.*

together to create an atmosphere of conviviality, soberly elegant decor, and a cuisine that makes use of simple, seasonal produce.

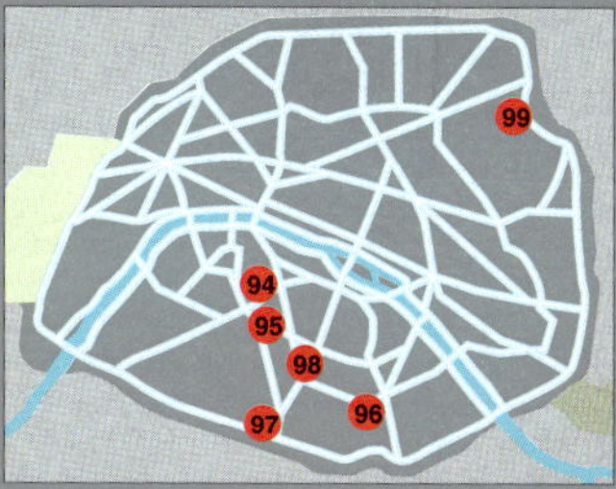

95

94

L'EPI DUPIN

97

98

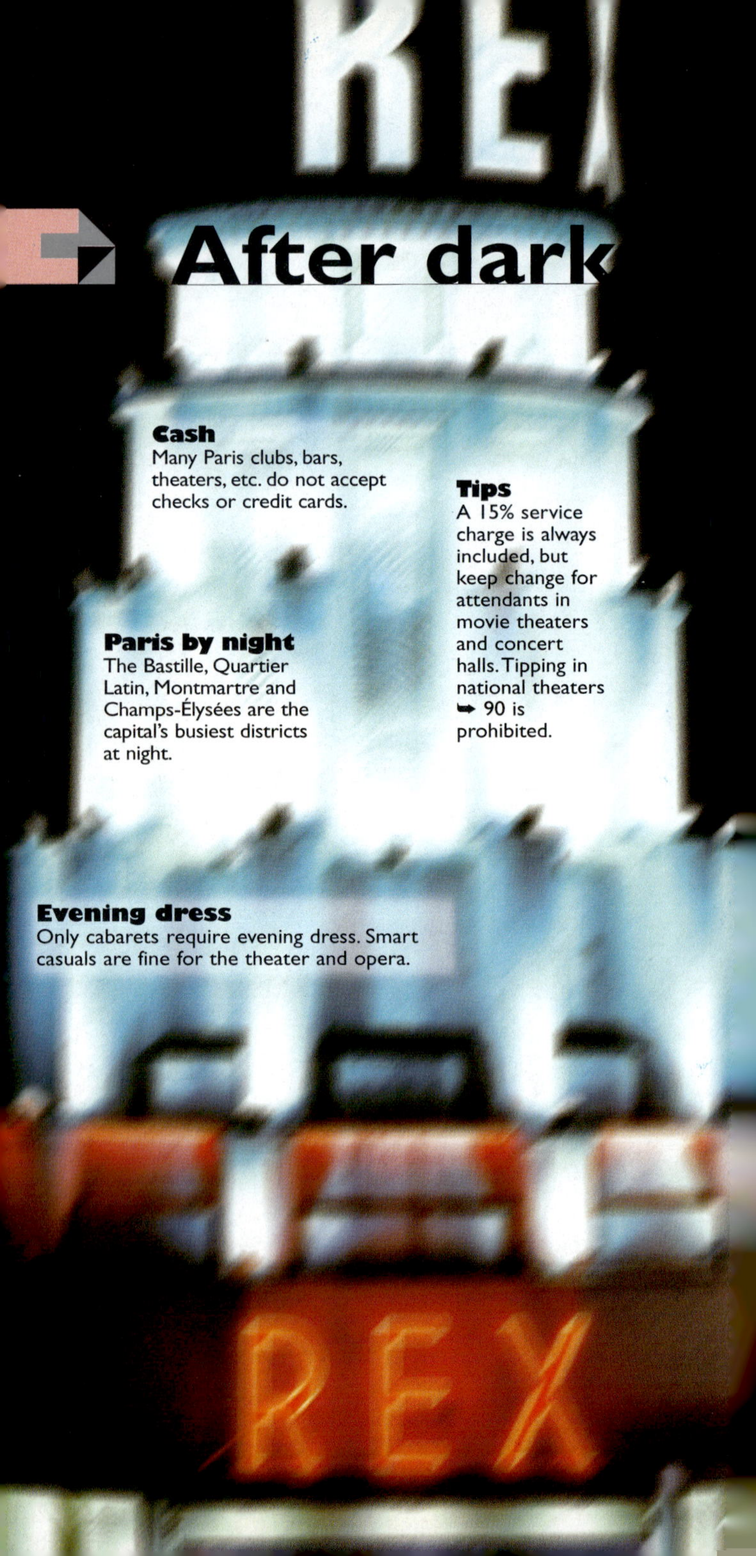

After dark

Cash
Many Paris clubs, bars, theaters, etc. do not accept checks or credit cards.

Tips
A 15% service charge is always included, but keep change for attendants in movie theaters and concert halls. Tipping in national theaters ➥ 90 is prohibited.

Paris by night
The Bastille, Quartier Latin, Montmartre and Champs-Élysées are the capital's busiest districts at night.

Evening dress
Only cabarets require evening dress. Smart casuals are fine for the theater and opera.

Entertainment on a budget

Theater tickets are half price if bought on the same day

Ticket Kiosks

Place de la Madeleine, 75008 or Paris de la gare Montparnasse, 75015

Tue.–Sat. 12.30–7.45pm; Sun. 12.30–3.45pm

Entertainment guides

Two weekly publications give dates and times of evening entertainments.

Le Pariscope • *F3* @ Pariscope.fr (includes a *Time Out* English section)

L'Officiel des Spectacles • *F2*

44 Nights out

THE INSIDER'S FAVORITES

Advance booking

Shows: it is best to book at least 24 hours in advance.

Virgin Megastore *52 Champs-Élysées, 75008*

☎ 0 803 023 024 Mon.–Sat. 10am–midnight; Sun. noon–midnight

FNAC *136 rue de Rennes, 75006*

☎ 0 803 808 803 Mon.–Sat 10am–7.30pm

Discos: telephone to avoid 'private party' evenings.

INDEX BY DISTRICT

Basic facts

Cafés – from the famous, trendy and exotic to the local neighborhood café – are an integral part of Parisian life. You can drop in for a *p'tit noir* (espresso), a *p'tit blanc* (glass of white wine), a *noisette* (espresso with a dash of milk), a *grand crème* (large white coffee) or a *demi* (half-pint of

After dark

Le Virgin Café (1)

52–60 avenue des Champs-Élysées, 75008
☎ 01 42 89 46 81 ➟ 01 49 53 50 40

Franklin-Roosevelt *daily 10am–11pm* ● *F24–F47* *daily 10am–11pm* *brunch noon–5pm*

The café is on the top floor of the beautiful 1930s building currently occupied by the Virgin Megastore, and is strategically located at the top of the impressive staircase overlooking the store's vast record departments. Customers can sip their drinks, perched on a high stool or sitting comfortably on a chair designed by Philip Starck, and watch the latest promo videos before making their purchases.

Le Café de la Musique (2)

213 avenue Jean-Jaurès, 75019 ☎ 01 48 03 15 91 ➟ 01 48 03 15 18

Porte-de-Pantin *daily 8–2am* ● *F26–F55* *11am–1am*
***Classical jazz** Wed. 10pm* ***World music** Fri. 10pm*

It comes as no surprise that this beautiful café is an extension of the Cité de la Musique. Sit on velvet-covered chairs in soft, restful colors and sip delicious classic cocktails served against a background of world music. An atmosphere of quiet luxury pervades, with all the discreet sophistication of Parisian design by Élizabeth de Portzamparc.

Le Flore (3)

172 boulevard Saint-Germain, 75006
☎ 01 45 48 55 26 ➟ 01 45 44 33 39

Saint-Germain-des-Près *daily 7–1.30am* ● *F24–F41* *26 rue Saint-Benoît: Mon. 2–8pm; Tue.–Sat. 11am–1pm, 2–8pm*

Since 1880 many well-known authors have frequented this discreetly charming and resolutely traditional café. It is still quite common to see literary prizewinners and celebrities savoring a perfect, if expensive, hot chocolate. Avoid weekends if you want to see it at its best.

Le Café de l'Industrie (4)

16 rue Saint-Sabin, 75011 ☎ 01 47 00 13 53 ➟ 01 47 00 92 33

Bastille *Sun.–Fri. 10–2am* ● *F10–F40* *12.30am*

This old neighborhood café has been ingeniously renovated by its owner to preserve its original 1940s charm. This dedicated antique-hunter and traveler has collected the pictures, photographs, period frames and crocodile skins that cover the walls. Every picture tells a story.

Not forgetting

■ **Le Bar de l'Hôtel Raphaël (5)** 17 av. Kléber, 75116 ☎ 01 44 28 00 28 *Enjoy an aperitif in the intimate wood-paneled bar.* ■ **Le Fouquet's (6)** 99 avenue des Champs-Élysées, 75008 ☎ 01 47 23 70 60 *A rendezvous for those who want to see and be seen!* ■ **Le Dôme (7)** 108 boulevard Montparnasse, 75014 ☎ 01 43 35 25 81 *Ideal for your first drink in a traditional Montparnasse café.*

beer) and drink it at the counter, at an inside table or on the terrace. Open from early morning through late at night – relax and watch the world go by.

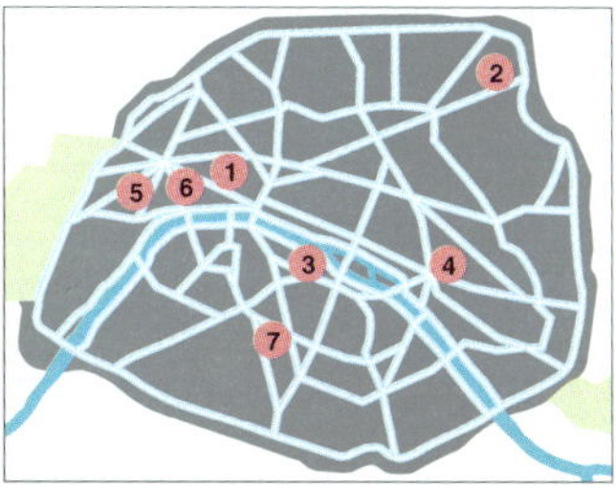

3

6

4

6

2

Basic facts

Many Paris bars stay open into the early hours and some don't close until morning. The favorite haunts of Paris nightbirds include the Champs-Élysées, Boulevard Saint-Germain, Boulevard Montparnasse, Pigalle, Les Halles and Bastille. Most late-night bars provide

After dark

Le Floridita (8)

19 rue de Presbourg, 75116 ☎ 01 45 00 84 84 ➟ 01 45 00 41 32

Charles-de-Gaulle-Étoile ***Cigar bar*** *Mon. 11am–4pm; Tue.–Sat. 11–2am 6pm–2am ● F15–F60 noon–3pm, 8pm–10pm*

Le Floridita, inspired by a bar of the same name in the Cuban capital of Havana, is devoted to cigar connoisseurs. Reddish-brown wood, wall hangings in dark green straw, soft lighting and wooden blinds create a restful and intimate atmosphere that has become the preserve of some very famous smokers. The cigars are reserved exclusively for customers and are stored in an unusual cellar: a bank strongroom!

Le Web Bar (9)

32 rue de Picardie, 75003 ☎ 01 42 72 66 55 ➟ 01 42 72 66 75

Temple, République ***Internet café*** *Mon.–Fri. 8.30–2am; Sat. 11.30–2am; Sun. 11.30–midnight ● Internet F40/h daily noon–3pm, 7–11pm*
@ webbar@webbar.fr

The classic entrance to this former goldsmith's workshop offers no hint of what lies beyond. A metal and glass roof illuminates two floors of galleries devoted entirely to the Internet, where surfers of all persuasions can browse the Net. The first story has a comfortable lounge area with club chairs and concrete tables. Jazz and world music help to block out the clicking and beeping of the computers. An atmosphere of trendy sophistication.

Le China Club (10)

50 rue de Charenton, 75012 ☎ 01 43 43 82 02 ➟ 01 43 43 79 85

Bastille, Ledru-Rollin ***Le Fumoir*** *Mon.–Thur. 7pm–2am; Fri.–Sat. 7pm–3am ● F60* ***Sing Song*** *Fri.–Sat. 10pm–3am ● F50 daily 7pm–12.30am*

A haven of peace and quiet which combines French sophistication and colonial energy, and where you are assured of being in good company. Le China Club has three different types of atmosphere to suit your mood. Le Fumoir, with its quiet English-club atmosphere and open fire, is an ideal place to enjoy a pure malt whisky and a game of chess against a background of classical music. Or you may prefer a cocktail in the American bar, ensconced in a Chesterfield sofa or perched on a stool at the monumental mahogany bar, listening to 1940s jazz. The teahouse decor of the Sing Song offers a touch of glamour with its weekend jazz and blues concerts.

Not forgetting

- **Le Moloko (11)** 26 rue Fontaine, 75009 ☎ 01 48 74 50 26
A modern bar with a friendly, lively atmosphere.
- **Harry's New York Bar (12)** 5 rue Daunou, 75002
☎ 01 42 61 71 14 *Take a trip down memory lane. Harry's was a favorite meeting place for performers and intellectuals of the post-war period. American-style comfort in a discreet atmosphere.*
- **La Casa del Habano (13)** 169 boulevard Saint-Germain, 75006
☎ 01 45 49 24 30 *A good menu with an opportunity to buy individual cigars.*

good-quality restaurant service throughout the night.

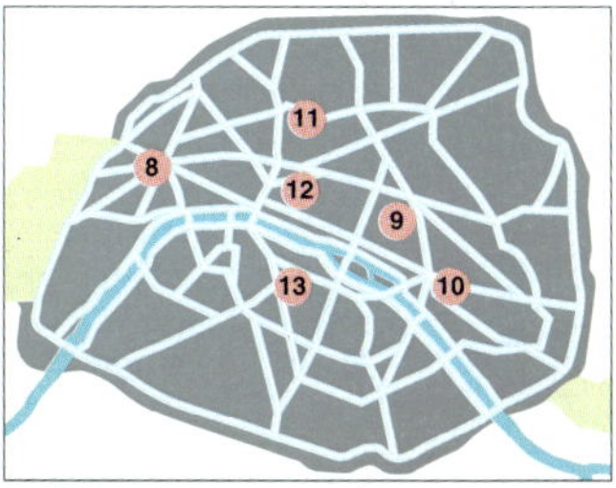

8

10

10

9

8

Basic facts

Paris has the largest number of theaters of any city in the world (276 in the city and suburbs) and performs the greatest number of plays (almost 1,000 per year). From the small private theaters (*théâtres de boulevard*) to the large, modern and heavily subsidized theaters, they

After dark

Théâtre national de Chaillot (14)

1 place du Trocadéro, 75116 ☎ 01 53 65 30 00

Trocadéro ***Reservations*** *by telephone 9am–7pm at theater 11am–7pm* ***Performances*** *Tue.–Sat. 8.30pm; Sun. 3pm ● F160; under-18s, over-60s F120* *Le Buffet* *@ culture.fr*

The Théâtre National Populaire (TNP), formed on November 11, 1920, moved into its permanent home in the Palais de Chaillot in 1938. Since then it has performed modern versions of classic works and helped to promote modern theater. Although renamed the Théâtre de Chaillot in 1972, it remains loyal to the image established by its unforgettable director, Jean Vilar. Its warm and friendly atmosphere goes with great artistic and professional expertise. The Grand Foyer (main entrance hall) offers an unrivaled view of the Trocadéro gardens and the Eiffel Tower.

Odéon-Théâtre de l'Europe (15)

Place de l'Odéon, 75006 ☎ 01 44 41 36 36 ➟ 01 44 41 36 01

Odéon ***Reservations*** *11am–7pm* ***Performances*** *Grande salle (main theater): Tue.–Sat. 8pm; Sun. 3pm ● F30–F170; Petit Odéon: Mon.–Sat. 6pm ● variable*

Built in 1782, this was the first Italian-style theater to provide seats in the stalls. Twice burned down and rebuilt, it has retained its sumptuous decor, resplendent with gilt and moldings, red-carpeted staircases, boxes with scarlet hangings and a ceiling by André Masson (1965). Since the 1960s, its repertoire has tended to focus on Europe, but Europe did not feature in the title until 1990. Performances are on a par with the magnificent surroundings and are enhanced by excellent acoustics. The Odéon offers a truly unique dramatic experience.

Théâtre national de la Colline (16)

15 rue Malte-Brun, 75020 ☎ 01 44 62 52 52 ➟ 01 44 62 52 90

Gambetta ***Reservations*** *Mon., Wed.–Sat. 11am–7pm; Tue. 11am–6pm (reserve 14 days before the performance)* ***Performances*** *variable ● F160; Tue. F110; under-30s, unemployed F80, over-60s F130*

The modern vocation of this theater (opened in 1988) was maintained brilliantly and with great enthusiasm by its former director, Jorge Lavelli. Its huge façade – several stories of glass and colored tubes – reflects its performances which are both daring and unusual, and use the full range of dramatic creativity. In addition, its two theaters are very comfortable and offer an almost panoramic view of the stage. ★ Before and after performances, the audience can enjoy a drink or dine in the Art-Deco bar which is also used by the actors.

Not forgetting

■ **Théâtre de l'Olympia (17)** 28 boulevard des Capucines, 75009 ☎ 01 47 42 25 49 *A former music hall which today presents a wide variety of artists and performers.* ■ **Théâtre national de la Comédie-Française (18)** 2 rue de Richelieu, 75001 ☎ 01 44 58 15 15 *Founded in 1680 by Louis XIV, the Comédie-Française is the most traditional of the French theaters. It presents a repertoire of some ten French classics in rotation.*

have an extremely varied repertoire in a wide variety of – often unusual – styles.

ODEON
THEATRE DE L'EUROPE

15

COMÉDIE FRANÇAISE
1680

COMÉDIE·FRANÇAISE

THÉÂTRE
DU VIEUX·
COLOMBIER

16

16

4

Basic facts
From classical music, ballet and opera to rock music and variety shows, the range of musical performances is as wide and varied as the theaters in which they are staged. The Parisian 'meccas' of music include two opera houses (the Garnier and the Bastille), the city's former cabaret

After dark

Théâtre des Champs-Élysées (19)

15 avenue Montaigne, 75008 ☎ 01 49 52 50 50 ➡ 01 49 52 07 41

M *Alma-Marceau* ***Concerts, opera, ballet*** ***Reservations** by telephone Mon.–Fri. 10am–noon, 2–6pm; at theater Mon.–Sat. 11am–7pm* ***Performances** times vary* ● *F50–F750* *Maison Blanche* ➡ *48*

This theater was founded in 1913 at the instigation of Gabriel Astruc in response to a real need. At the time, France had no large theater devoted to contemporary music. This modern building, combining German architectural techniques, English comfort and French art (frescos by Antoine Bourdelle ➡ 122 and Maurice Denis ➡ 130), was described by Proust as a 'Temple of Music, Art and Architecture'. Since it opened, it has played a leading role in the world of music, with such composers as Debussy, Saint-Saëns and Fauré directing their own works.

La Cigale (20)

120 boulevard Rochechouart, 75018
☎ 01 49 25 89 99 ➡ 01 42 23 67 04

M *Pigalle* ***Concerts, theater*** ***Reservations** Mon.–Sat. noon–7pm* ***Performances** times vary* ● *F80–F200*

Since 1887, this cabaret theater has presented an amazing combination of French singing stars (e.g. Arletty, Maurice Chevalier) and futuristic plays by such writers as Jean Cocteau. It was converted into a movie theater before once again becoming a theater in 1987 through the impetus of the French theater company Les Rita Mitsouko. Updated with a modifiable auditorium and redecorated by Philip Starck, the new Cigale is always on the lookout for anything and anyone of interest, from avant-garde performances (like the famous Stomp) to established stars.

Opéra Bastille (21)

120 rue de Lyon, 75012 ☎ 01 44 73 13 99 ➡ 01 40 01 25 40

M *Bastille* ***Opera, concerts*** ***Reservations** by telephone Mon.–Sat. 9am–7pm; at theater Mon.–Sat. 11am–6.30pm* ***Performances** times vary* ● *F60–F650* *01 40 01 19 70* @ *opera-de-paris.fr*

The Opéra Bastille was built, on this symbolic site, to commemorate the bicentenary of the French Revolution. The sweeping curves of the purpose-built structure are transformed at nightfall, when the light from inside the building shines out through the glass façade and shows off the architecture to its best advantage. The vast interior is light and spacious, with pear wood, black velvet and sculptures by Niki de Saint-Phalle and Yves Klein contributing to an impression of comfort, humor and elegance. A perfectly balanced light emanates from the ceiling of the Grande Salle (main auditorium), which has a seating capacity of 2,716.

Not forgetting

■ **Salle Pleyel (22)** 252 rue du Faubourg-Saint-Honoré, 75008 ☎ 01 45 61 53 00 *A modern theater with excellent acoustics.*
■ **Palais Garnier (23)** Place de l'Opéra, 75009 ☎ 01 44 73 13 99/ 01 40 21 25 47 *A magical, legendary theater and an absolute must… if you manage to reserve seats.*

theaters (which offer old-fashioned charm yet may be filled with the latest in modern sound), and the concert halls with their often eclectic programs.

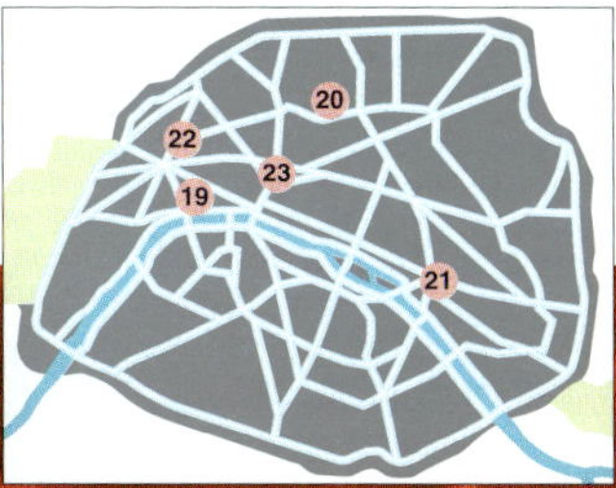

SALLE PLEYEL

OPERA NATIONAL DE PARIS

THEATRE DES champs élysées

19

Basic facts

Paris has no less than 112 movie theaters. Movie-goers can choose from the avant-garde and experimental movie theaters of the Latin Quarter, or the commercial movie theaters of Montparnasse, the Champs-Élysées, Les Halles and Odéon. Paris also prides itself on having two of

After dark

Le Grand Rex (24)

1 boulevard Poissonnière, 75002 ☎ 08 36 68 70 23

M *Bonne-Nouvelle* *varies daily* ● ***Grande Salle*** *Mon. F40; Tue.–Sun. F50* ***Petite salle*** *daily F45* *08 36 68 05 96* ***double ticket (film and visit)*** *Wed.–Sun., public holidays, school holidays 10am–7.00pm* ● *F70*

In 1932, the Paris smart set celebrated the opening of Europe's largest movie theater, with its art deco façade, a magnificent entrance hall decorated with palm trees, Spanish haciendas and Venetian palaces, a seating capacity of 3,300 and – at the time – the world's biggest screen. Although this splendidly kitsch movie theater was later converted into seven smaller studios, the Grande Salle (main studio) has retained all its original magic: a 'ceiling' consisting of a star-studded vault some 65 ft high, an even bigger screen (336 sq yds) inaugurated in 1988, and a special Christmas show consisting of *La Féerie des eaux* (a water extravaganza) followed by the latest Walt Disney film.

La Pagode (25)

57bis rue de Babylone, 75007 ☎ 01 45 55 48 48 ➟ 01 45 50 33 79

M *Saint-François-Xavier* *daily 1pm–midnight* ● *Thur.–Tue. F47, under-12s F32; Wed. F38* *Mon.–Sat. 4–9.45pm; Sun. 2–8pm*

La Pagode is not just a name – it is a genuine pagoda imported from Japan and rebuilt brick by brick. It was opened as a mainly avant-garde and experimental movie theater in 1927 and rapidly became the meeting place of such authors and film directors as Jean Renoir, Luis Buñuel and Jean Cocteau. Today its range may be wider but its atmosphere has remained unchanged: ★ somewhere between that of a local movie theater and a movie club. You can even go there for tea or to walk in its exotic garden.

Gaumont Grand Écran Italie (26)

30 place d'Italie, 75013 ☎ 01 45 80 86 78 ➟ 01 45 80 86 87

M *Place d'Italie* *Sun.–Fri. 12.30pm-12.30am; Sat. variable* ● *F46–F55; over-60s F39–F46; under-12s F33*

This ultra-modern aluminum and monochrome glass building by Kenzo Tange is the city's very latest movie theater. One of its three studios has a truly amazing screen (290 sq yds) and a seating capacity of 652. The audience has a unique audio-visual experience due to the double-system and digital-sound projection equipment. The films shown in this studio are, of course, of the more spectacular variety. Not recommended for lovers of literary films.

Not forgetting

■ **Max Linder (27)** 24 boulevard Poissonnière, 75009 ☎ 08 36 68 50 52 *This movie theater is its own movie star, of the 1930s vintage. Wonderful decor, comfort, luxury and, of course, a big screen!* ■ **Kinopanorama (28)** 60 avenue de la Motte-Picquet, 75015 ☎ 01 43 06 50 53 *The 'Kino', with its wide, curved screen (18 yds long) has been a cult movie theater for generations of movie-goers from Paris, the rest of France and other countries!*

the largest screens in Europe – one at the Gaumont Grand Écran Italie, and the other at Le Grand Rex.

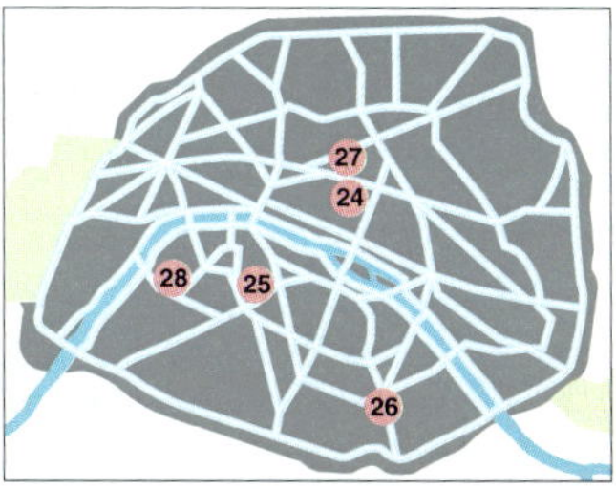

25

25

24

26

26

Built by Bluysen and Eberson, Le Grand Rex (1932) broke new ground with its dazzling façade and vast halls called 'atmospherics'.

24

Basic facts

Paris still has some of its legendary clichés: music halls, cabarets, the cancan and its famous revues. Although most date from the end of the 19th century, their names and music still fire the imagination. The districts of Montmartre, Pigalle, the Champs-Élysées and Montparnasse

After dark

Le Bal du Moulin Rouge (29)

82 boulevard de Clichy, 75018 ☎ 01 46 06 00 19 ➠ 01 42 23 02 00

M *Place-Blanche* **Performances** *daily 9pm, 11pm* ● *F550, F490* **Performance & dinner** *daily 7pm* ● *F770* ● *two drinks F360*

The English christened the high-kicking dance performed at the opening (1889) of the Bal du Moulin Rouge the 'French cancan'. Over one hundred years after La Goulue, the famous dancer immortalized by the posters of Toulouse-Lautrec, and after such great performers as Mistinguett, Josephine Baker, Édith Piaf, Maurice Chevalier and Yves Montand, the Moulin Rouge is still renowned for its atmosphere, variety shows, *joie de vivre*, ability to amaze and extremely talented performers.

Le Lido (30)

116bis avenue des Champs-Élysées, 75008
☎ 01 40 76 56 10 ➠ 01 45 61 19 41

M *George-V* **Performances** *daily 10pm, midnight* ● *F560 (daily 10pm; Fri., Sat. midnight); F460 (Sun.–Thu. midnight)* **Performance & dinner** *daily 7.30pm* ● *F815–F1015* ● *F385*

For its 50th anniversary, Le Lido 'touched up its make-up' and presented its 25th revue: *C'est Magique!* Of course, there were plenty of feathers and Bluebell girls. These 60 dancers, handpicked for their remarkable physique and classical dance training, perform a spectacular musical extravaganza worthy of the third millennium. With the help of laser projection, digital laser sound and other technological devices, the dancers take the audience through a series of four tableaux: a giant video game, an aerial ballet, a gambling inferno and a huge skating rink.

Crazy Horse (31)

12 avenue George-V, 75008 ☎ 01 47 23 32 32 ➠ 01 47 23 48 26

M *Alma-Marceau* **Performances** *Sun.–Fri. 8.30pm, 11pm; Sat. 8pm, 10.15pm, 12.15am* ● *F290–F560* **Performance & dinner** ● *F750, F850* @ *crazy-horse.fr*

Since 1951, Crazy Horse has been famous worldwide for its amazing nude performances. In an atmosphere of elegance and sophistication, dancers perform the sequences from their latest revue – *Teasing* – to the eternal delight of the audience!

Paradis Latin (32)

28 rue Cardinal-Lemoine, 75005 ☎ 01 43 25 28 28 ➠ 01 43 29 63 63

M *Cardinal-Lemoine* **Performances** *Wed.–Mon. 9.15pm* ● *F465* **Performance & dinner** *Wed.–Mon. 8pm* ● *F680* *Wed.–Mon. 9.15pm*

The framework of the Paradis Latin, built for the Paris Exhibition in 1889, was designed by Gustave Eiffel. As well as its spectacular revues in which a company of talented young dancers perform the wildly fantastical *Ville Lumière* (City of Light), it is also famous for its brigade of 25 waiters who are at your service to make this a truly memorable night out in Paris.

are traditionally associated with *Paris by night*!

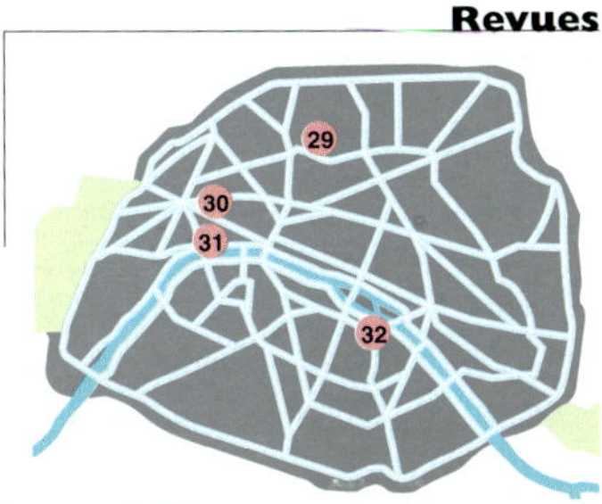

30

31

30

32

Feathers, diamanté, choreography and champagne in *Paris by night*.

29

Basic facts

The history of French jazz is closely linked to modern political history. Jazz was introduced into France by the Americans during World War II. Cellars, soundproof and naturally protected, proved to be ideal venues for jam sessions and concerts. The habit stuck and the city's cellars and

After dark

Baiser Salé (33)

58 rue des Lombards, 75001 ☎ 01 42 33 37 71 ➡ 01 42 36 24 40

M *Châtelet, Les Halles* **Latin, Afro, funk, blues, jazz** *Mon.–Fri. 7.30pm–6am; Sat.–Sun. 3pm–6am* ● *F28–F49* **Concerts** *10pm* ● *F50–F90; free Mon., Sun.*

Since it opened in 1983, this cellar club has presented every kind of jazz. This was world music ahead of its time! The club's eclectic approach is reflected in its comfortable setting and relaxed atmosphere. You feel immediately at ease among a clientele of all ages, styles and nationalities who share a common passion for jazz!

Duc des Lombards (34)

42 rue des Lombards, 75001 ☎ 01 42 33 22 88 ➡ 01 40 28 98 52

M *Châtelet* **Modern jazz** *Tue.–Sat. 7.30pm–3am. closed alternate Sun.* **Concerts** *times vary* ● *F100* @ *actua.com/Duc-Des-Lombards*

The Duc des Lombards has broken with the tradition of Saint-Germain-des-Prés in more ways than one. Not only is it on the Right Bank, it isn't in a cellar! Between velvet furnishings and wood paneling, poster-covered walls trace the history of jazz. The program is just as innovative, with the club always on the lookout for modern European jazz.

La Villa (35)

29 rue Jacob, 75006 ☎ 01 43 26 60 00 ➡ 01 46 34 63 63

M *Saint-Germain-des-Prés* **American jazz** *Mon.–Sat. 6pm–2am*
● *Mon.–Fri. F120; Sat.–Sun. F150*

La Villa has occupied the magnificent vaulted cellars of the modern Villa Saint-Germain hotel ➡ 40 since 1991. Its carefully designed and soberly elegant decor creates a muted atmosphere in which a sophisticated clientele listens to top-quality jazz played by American-led 'combos'.

Le Petit Journal (36)

71 boulevard Saint-Michel, 75005
☎ 01 43 26 28 59 ➡ 01 43 54 30 17

M *Luxembourg, Cluny* **New Orleans jazz** *Mon.–Sat. 11–2am, closed Aug.*
● *F100*

Le Petit Journal only opened in 1971, but its comfortable 1950s atmosphere gives the impression that it has been around much longer. Located in Saint-Germain-des-Prés, in the heart of the Latin Quarter, its exceptional program makes it one of the meccas of New Orleans jazz. Regulars include Claude Bolling, Marcel Zanini, Claude Luter and Benny Bailey.

Not forgetting

■ **Studio des Islettes (37)** 10 rue des Islettes, 75018 ☎ 01 42 58 63 33 *A varied program of jazz: Julie Monley Wed. evening; Laurent Bardainne Quintet Thur.; Trio Sphère Mon.; Slang Trio Tue.* ■ **New Morning (38)** 7–9 rue des Petites-Écuries, 75010 ☎ 01 45 23 51 41 *An absolute must for jazz lovers – memorable performances on stage and from the floor.*

basements still house most of its swing and jazz clubs.

35

34

.6

Basic facts

Paris nightbirds have a taste for themes and artistic directors are having to use their imagination and ingenuity to devise impressive theme evenings. For example, a 'snow' or 'tropical' evening involves covering the dance floor with 'snow' or hot sand. Admission is usually free for

After dark

Les Bains (39)

7 rue du Bourg-l'Abbé, 75003 ☎ 01 48 87 01 80 ➠ 01 48 87 13 70

M *Étienne-Marcel* 🕒 *daily 11.30pm–5am* ● *Sun.–Thu. F100; Fri.–Sat. F120* ▭ 🍸 🍴 *Mon.–Sat. 9pm–5am*

Walking through the attractive wrought-iron gate and up the steps of these converted, early 20th-century public baths, doesn't necessarily mean you will get in. This fashionable venue has a marked preference for celebrities from the movie, press and fashion world. ★ The easiest way to get in is to reserve a table in the restaurant: the cuisine – French – is sophisticated, and the original decor is often enhanced by an exhibition of photographs or paintings. From there, you can go straight on to the dance floor. Once you are there, it won't matter whether the pool is covered or open, empty or full, whether the atmosphere is tropical or freezing, or the music funk or techno. You'll simply be glad to be there!

Le Balajo (40)

9 rue de Lappe, 75011 ☎ 01 47 00 07 87 ➠ 01 47 00 09 69

M *Bastille* 🕒 *Wed. 9am–2am; Thu. 2.30–6.30pm, 10pm–5am; Fri., Sat. 11pm–5am; Sun. 3–7pm, 9pm–1am* ● *afternoon F50; Wed.–Sat. evening F100; Sun. evening F60* ▭ 🍸

In 1936, the 'Bal à Jo' opened with a performance by Mistinguett. It was an unmitigated success and the smart set flocked to dance to the sound of accordion music, the traditional accompaniment in the dance halls of Paris.

39

42

43

women, provided they are suitably dressed: après-ski or swimwear only!

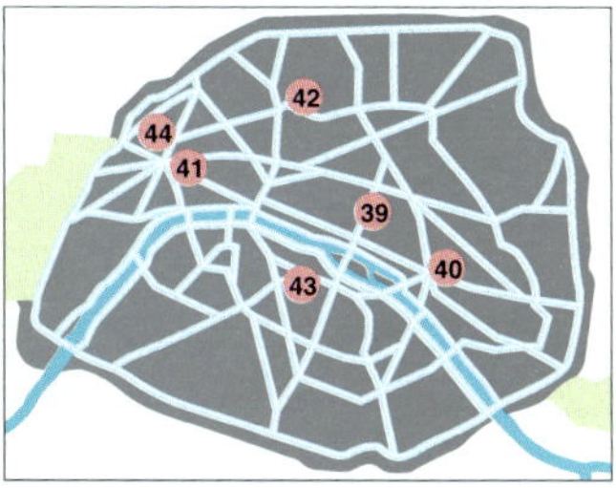

Although the music has changed – fresh-disco or house, depending on the night's theme – the atmosphere is still much the same. Le Balajo's clientele of committed and indefatigable young dancers can enjoy the atmosphere as they dance on a parquet floor amid period decor.

Le Queen (41)

102 avenue des Champs Elysées, 75008 ☎ 01 53 89 08 90

George-V *daily from midnight to dawn ● Mon. F50; Tue.–Thur., Sun. free; Fri.–Sat. F100* *● F50*

Here you are in the heart of Paris's gay nightlife. Since the beginning of the 90s, this club and its drag queens have become a real institution, a temple dedicated to underground dance and gay clubbing. You will hear plenty of house music played by famous DJs, and the stars that throng it guarantee a lively atmosphere. Unless accompanied by sexy young men, women find it difficult to get in from Thursday to Sunday. Fliers for specific evenings are circulated in the Marais bars.

Not forgetting

■ **La Locomotive (42)** 90 boulevard de Clichy, 75018 ☎ 01 53 41 88 88 *Each floor (including a 'machine room') in this club is in a different style.* ■ **Chez Castel (43)** 15 rue Princesse, 75006 ☎ 01 40 51 52 80 ➠ 01 40 51 72 74 *Recently taken over by a dynamic young team, this famous private club on the Left Bank seems to be up to speed again. There you will find babe-watchers, fashion gurus and intellectuals on the binge. Restaurant upstairs.* ■ **Niel's (44)** 27 avenue des Ternes, 75017 ☎ 01 47 66 45 00 *Popular with the show-business and fashion worlds.*

39

40

What to see

Special rates

30–50% reductions for children, students, senior citizens, groups and sometimes the 18–25s.
Free admission for minors in 65 Paris museums and monuments.
Carte Musée et Monuments (museums and monuments card) Offers a saving if you plan to visit several sights. • F80 (1 day); • F160 (3 days); • F240 (5 days). Available from museums, métro stations and tourist offices.

Underground Paris

Catacombs *Place Denfert-Rochereau, 75014* ☎ *01 43 22 47 63* Ⓜ *Denfert-Rochereau* 🕑 *Tue.–Fri. 2–4pm; Sat.–Sun. 9–11am, 2–4pm* • *F33*
Paris sewers *Quai d'Orsay 75007* ☎ *01 53 68 27 81* Ⓜ *Alma-Marceau* 🕑 *Sat.–Wed. 11am–4pm* • *F25*

Boat trips on the Seine
Bateaux parisiens Tour Eiffel ☎ *01 44 11 33 44* Ⓜ *Trocadéro*
Bateaux parisiens Notre-Dame ☎ *01 44 11 33 44* Ⓜ *Saint-Michel*
Vedettes du Pont-Neuf ☎ *01 46 33 98 38* Ⓜ *Pont-Neuf*
Bateaux Mouches ☎ *01 42 25 96 10* Ⓜ *Pont de l'Alma*

47 Sights

THE INSIDER'S FAVORITES

Information
Tourist Office *127 av. des Champs-Élysées, 75008* ☎ *08 36 68 31 12*
Museums Association *4 rue Brantôme, 75003* ☎ *01 44 61 96 60*
Paris Leisure Service ☎ *01 42 80 69 36*

INDEX BY TYPE

Basic facts

Built in the early 13th century as a fortress, the Louvre became a Renaissance palace during the reign of François I (1515–47). Merged with the 16th-century Palais des Tuileries in 1868, it was converted into a museum (1793), and extended and renovated between 1981 and 1993.

What to see

Musée du Louvre (1)

34–36 quai du Louvre, 75001 Paris ☎ 01 40 20 50 50

M *Palais-Royal, Louvre* ***Antiquities, paintings, sculpture, objets d'art, graphic art*** *Mon., Wed. 9am–9.45pm; Thur.–Sun. 9am–6pm; closed Tue. and some public holidays* ***Hall Napoléon*** *Mon., Wed.–Sat. 9am–10pm ● before 3pm F45; after 3pm; Sun. F26; under-18s, 1st Sun. of the month free*

The Musée du Louvre is divided into three main wings (named Denon, Sully and Richelieu) which can be reached from the Hall Napoléon on the ground floor of the famous glass pyramid (designed by I. M. Pei). The museum's extensive and magnificent collections, put together since the reign of François I, include the art of ancient civilizations, as well as western art from the Middle Ages to 1850. The Egyptian collection, recently reorganized, is arranged in a thematic order (Sully, ground floor) and a chronological order (Sully, first floor, closed Mon.). In such a huge museum it is best to concentrate on a particular period: French sculpture from the Early Middle Ages to the 19th century (Richelieu, *salles* 1–33); the Northern Schools 15th–17th century (Richelieu, *salles* 3–39); the French School 18th–19th century (Sully, *salles* 36–73). Three paintings in particular attract large numbers of visitors: Leonardo da Vinci's *Mona Lisa* (1503–06) (Denon, first floor, *salle* 6), Théodore Géricault's *Raft of the Medusa* (1819) (Denon, first floor, *salle* 77) and Jan Vermeer's *Lacemaker* (Richelieu, second floor, *salle* 38).

Musée de l'Orangerie (2)

Jardin des Tuileries, place de la Concorde, 75001 ☎ 01 42 97 48 16

M *Concorde* *Mon., Wed.–Sun. 9.45am–5pm; closed public holidays ● F30; 18–25s F20; under-18s free* .

Two Second-Empire buildings – the Musée de l'Orangerie and the Galerie du Jeu de Paume – flank the entrance to the Jardin des Tuileries, on the place de la Concorde. Since 1977, the former orangery of the Palais des Tuileries has housed the Walter-Guillaume collection, consisting of almost 150 paintings dating from 1870 to 1930. It includes masterpieces by Cézanne, Renoir, Picasso, Matisse, Utrillo, Soutine, Derain and Modigliani. Eight magnificent water lily compositions by Monet are displayed in two basement rooms.

Galerie du Jeu de Paume (3)

Place de la Concorde, 75001 ☎ 01 47 03 12 50

M *Concorde* *Tue. noon–9.30pm; Wed.–Fri. noon–7pm; Sat.–Sun. 10am–7pm ● F38; 13–18s, over-60s F28; under-13s free* *bookshop*

This former royal-tennis court, built during the reign of Napoleon III, was renovated in 1931. Since 1991, it has housed temporary exhibitions of modern art and seasons of movies.

Not forgetting

■ **Musée des Arts Décoratifs (4)** Palais du Louvre, 107 rue de Rivoli, 75001 ☎ 01 44 55 57 50 Tue.–Sun. noon–6pm; closed public holidays. *Paintings and decorative arts from the Middle Ages to the renaissance. Permanent collection partially closed due to renovation.*

b

a

Among the masterpieces contained in the Louvre Museum: Milo's *Venus* (a); *The Bolt* by Fragonard (b); Pei's Pyramid (c); Vermeer's *Lacemaker* (d); a Greek ceramic from the Campana gallery (e).

c

d

e

2

In the area
An impressive vista stretches from place de la Concorde to place Charles-de-Gaulle-Étoile and on to the Grande Arche of La Défense.
■ Where to stay ➡ 18 ➡ 20 ➡ 22 ■ Where to eat ➡ 50 ➡ 52 ➡ 56 ➡ 74 ■ After dark ➡ 86 ➡ 88 ➡ 90

What to see

Arc de Triomphe (5)
Place du Général-de-Gaulle, 75008 ☎ 01 55 37 73 77

Charles-de-Gaulle-Étoile *Apr.–Sep.: daily 9.30am–11pm / Oct–Mar.: daily 10am–10.30pm, closed Dec. 25, Jan. 1, May 1 ● F35; 12–25s, groups F23; under-12s free*

From its position in the center of place Charles-de-Gaulle-Étoile, the Arc de Triomphe offers a magnificent view of the Champs-Élysées. Built between 1806 and 1836, it is the symbol of the Napoleonic era. Beneath the archway, the tomb of the Unknown Soldier makes it a place of remembrance also. A small museum traces the history of the monument.

Musée de la Mode et du Costume (6)
Palais Galliéra, 10 av. Pierre-1er-de-Serbie, 75015 ☎ 01 47 20 85 23

Iéna *Tue.–Sun. 10am–6pm ● temporary exhibitions (vary)*

The Museum of Fashion and Costume is a pleasantly unusual museum. It traces the development of French society from 1735 through the history of fashion. And what better setting than the former palace of the Duchesse de Galliéra for its 30,000 costumes and 70,000 accessories?

Musée d'Art Moderne (7)
11 avenue du Président-Wilson, 75016 ☎ 01 53 67 40 00

Iéna *Tue.–Fri. 10am–5.30pm; Sat.–Sun. 10am–6.45pm; closed public holidays ● F30; concessions F20; variable: double ticket Museum-Exhibitions*

This temple of contemporary art was opened in 1961 in the Palais de Tokyo (1937). It features the Fauvist paintings of Matisse and Dufy, the Cubist works of Braque and Picasso, sculptures by Lipchitz and Zadkine, and the more recent works of Parisian and other European artists.

Tour Eiffel (8)
Champ-de-Mars, 75007 ☎ 01 44 11 23 45

Champ-de-Mars ***Elevator** Jun.12–Aug.30: daily 9am–midnight; Aug.31–Jun.11: daily 9.30am–11pm ● Level 1: F21; under 12s F12/ Level 2: F43; under 12s F22/ Level 3: F60; under 12s F31* ***Stairs** Jun.12–Aug.30: daily 9am–midnight; Aug.31–Jun.11: 9.30am–6.30pm ● Levels 1 and 2 F15* *Altitude 95 (Level 1); Le Jules Verne ➡ 50 (Level 2)* *Poste*

The Eiffel Tower, designed by Gustave Eiffel (1832–1923), was chosen from among 107 projects for the 1889 Paris Exhibition. The 984-foot tower – raised to 1052 feet in 1959 – is now the world-famous symbol of Paris. Magnificent views of the capital from Level 3.

Not forgetting
■ **Musée national des Arts asiatiques-Guimet (9)** 6 place d'Iéna, 75116 ☎ 01 45 05 00 98 Wed.–Mon. 9.45am–5.45pm; closed on public holidays. *Museum closed until Sep. 1999, but the Émile Guimet collections can be seen at the Hôtel Heidelbach (19 av. d'Iéna, 75116)* ■ **Musée de l'Homme (10)** Palais de Chaillot, 17 place du Trocadéro, 75116 ☎ 01 44 05 72 72 Wed.–Mon. 9.45am–5.15pm; closed public holidays.

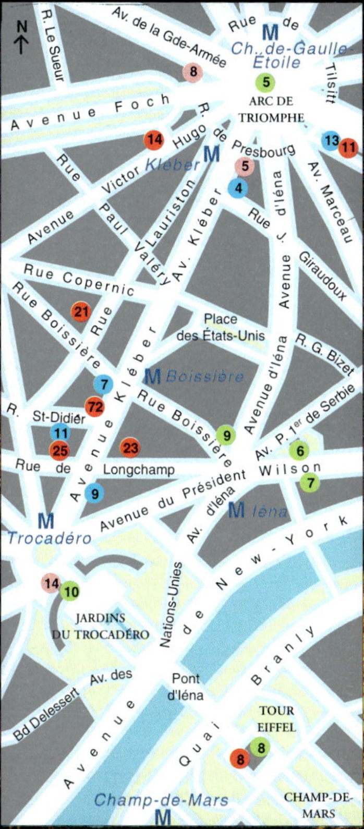
N
Av. de la Gde-Armée
Rue de Tilsitt
Ch.-de-Gaulle-Étoile
ARC DE TRIOMPHE
Avenue Foch
R. Le Sueur
R. Hugo
Rue Victor Hugo
Kléber
R. de Presbourg
Av. Marceau
Avenue Victor Hugo
Rue Paul Valéry
Rue Lauriston
Av. Kléber
Rue J. Giraudoux
Avenue d'Iéna
Rue Copernic
Rue Boissière
Place des États-Unis
R. G. Bizet
Boissière
Rue Boissière
Avenue Kléber
R. St-Didier
Avenue d'Iéna
Av. P. 1er de Serbie
Av. Wilson
Rue de Longchamp
Avenue du Président Wilson
Av. d'Iéna
Iéna
Trocadéro
Avenue de New-York
JARDINS DU TROCADÉRO
Av. des Nations-Unies
Bd Delessert
Pont d'Iéna
Quai Branly
TOUR EIFFEL
Avenue
Champ-de-Mars
CHAMP-DE-MARS

7

10

In the area

The sweeping avenues of the Invalides and Grand Palais districts are laid out with military precision. They are bordered by mansions, embassies, government ministries, and museums housed in historic residences or in buildings built for the 1900 Exhibition.

What to see

Galeries nationales du Grand Palais (11)

Avenue Winston-Churchill, 75008 ☎ 01 44 13 17 17

Champs-Élysées-Clemenceau ***Exhibitions*** *Thur.–Mon. 10am–8pm; Wed. 10am–10pm; closed public holidays ● F50; concessions F35* ***Films, Conferences*** *● free*

Some of the most famous French painters are displayed in a mixture of Art Nouveau and neo-Baroque. Built for the Universal Exhibition of 1900, the Grand Palais is Paris's main exhibition center. It hosts many prestigious artistic and cultural events such as the retrospectives on Renoir, Fragonard, Degas, Gauguin and Delacroix. Access to the auditorium is free; films and conferences accompany ongoing exhibitions.

Invalides (12)

Esplanade des Invalides, 75007 ☎ 01 44 42 37 72

Latour-Maubourg, Varenne ***Musée de l'Armée, Musée de l'Ordre de la Libération, Dôme des Invalides, Napoleon's tomb, Musée des Plans-Reliefs*** *Apr.–Sep.: daily 10am–6pm; Oct.–Mar.: daily 10am–5pm; closed public holidays ● F38; under-26s, F28 under-12s free*

An essential visit for anyone interested in French military history, the Hôtel des Invalides was built during the reign of Louis XIV (1670–1706) as a convalescent home for wounded soldiers. Today it houses the Military Museum, whose collections trace the military history of France from its origins to the present day, and the Museum of Relief Maps, with models of fortified towns illustrating the art of siege. The church of the Dôme contains the massive tomb of Emperor Napoleon I. The esplanade stretching between the Invalides and the Pont Alexandre III is one of the most beautiful in Paris.

Musée Rodin (13)

Hôtel Biron, 77 rue de Varenne, 75007 ☎ 01 44 18 61 10

Varenne *Tue.–Sun.: Apr.–Sep. 9.30am–5.15pm / Oct.–Mar. 9.30am–4.15pm; closed public holidays ● F28; Sun., concessions F18; under-18s free* *Tue.–Sun.: Apr.–Sep. 9.30am–6.45pm / Oct.–Mar. 9.30am–5pm ● F5* *in summer* ***Villa des Brillants*** *19 avenue Auguste-Rodin, 92190 Meudon ☎ 01 41 14 35 00*

When sculptor Auguste Rodin died in 1917, his 17th-century residence was converted into a museum dedicated to his life and works. Its rooms and gardens house such monumental sculptures as *The Burghers of Calais*, *The Thinker* and *Balzac*, as well as works by his former student and mistress Camille Claudel, and paintings by Monet, Renoir and Van Gogh.

Not forgetting

■ **Palais de la Découverte (14)** avenue Franklin-Roosevelt, 75008 ☎ 01 40 74 80 00 / Museum of science, in the west wing of the Grand Palais. Mysteries of science explained with simplified experiments. **Planetarium** ☎ 01 40 74 81 73 Tue.–Sat. 9.30am–6pm; Sun. 10am–7pm; closed public holidays

■ **Petit Palais (15)** avenue Winston-Churchill, 75008 ☎ 01 42 65 12 73 Tue.–Sun. 10am–5.40pm; closed public holidays *Paintings, Sculpture, Furniture and objets d'art from Antiquity to the 20th century.*

Where to eat ➥ 60 ➥ 78
Where to stay ➥ 22

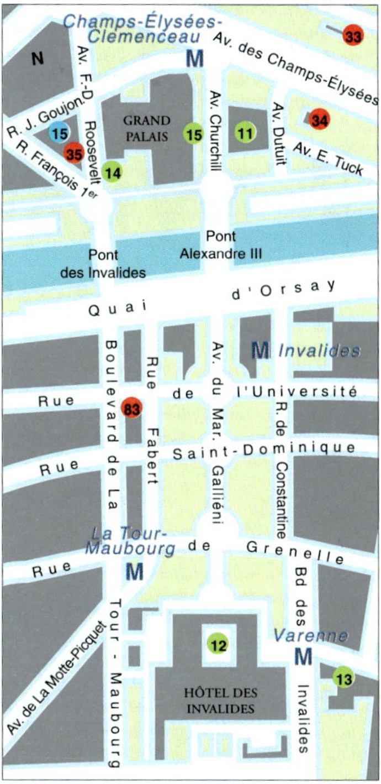

12

Many of the city's major buildings are decorated with gold, chosen by the monarchs of the Ancien Régime to symbolize faith, strength, durability and wealth.

11

13

12

3

11

In the area

The Marais, centered around place des Vosges, rue des Francs-Bourgeois and rue Saint-Antoine, is one of the few truly historic districts of Paris (16th–17th century). ■ Where to stay ➡ 32 ■ Where to eat ➡ 72 ■ After dark ➡ 86

What to see

Musée Picasso (16)

Hôtel Salé, 5 rue de Thorigny, 75003 ☎ 01 42 71 25 21

Chemin-Vert, Saint-Paul *Apr.–Sep.: Wed.–Mon. 9.30am–6pm / Oct.–Mar.: 9.30am–5.30pm; closed Dec. 25, Jan. 1 ● F30; 18–25s, Sun. F20; under-18s free* *01 42 71 70 84*

The 17th-century Hôtel Salé is one of the most beautiful buildings in Paris. Since 1985 it has housed the works of Pablo Picasso (1881–1973). The development of Picasso's work, from 1905 through 1973, is traced via over 250 paintings, including *Two women running on the beach* (1922), and *Self-Portrait* (1901), 158 sculptures, numerous reliefs, collages, ceramics and illustrated books, as well as 3000 drawings and engravings.

Hôtel de Soubise (17)

60 rue des Francs-Bourgeois, 75003 ☎ 01 40 27 60 96

Rambuteau, Hôtel-de-Ville ***Musée de l'Histoire de France** Wed.–Mon. noon–5.45pm; closed public holidays ● F20; concessions F15; under-18s free* ***National archives** Tue.–Fri. 9am–6pm; Sat. 1.45–5.45pm*

An ideal place to learn about the history of France. In 1808, Napoleon I chose the magnificent 18th-century Hôtel de Soubise to house the national archives. Since then, they have spread into the Hôtel de Rohan and four other neighboring mansions and currently occupy around 280 miles of shelving. The most original documents in the archives are on display in the Musée de l'Histoire de France.

Musée Carnavalet (18)

Hôtel Carnavalet, 23 rue de Sévigné, 75003 ☎ 01 42 72 21 13

Saint-Paul, Chemin-Vert *Tue.–Sun. 10am–5.40pm; closed Mon and public holidays ● F27 (except temporary exhibitions); 18–25s F14.50; under-18s free* *bookshop*

A truly magnificent museum consisting of two neighboring mansions linked by a passageway. The first is the beautiful Hôtel Carnavalet of Madame de Sévigné, which combines Renaissance and classical styles and provides the setting for the history of Paris from the Middle Ages to the 18th century. The second, the mansion of Le Pelletier de Saint-Fargeau, traces the history of the capital from the Revolution (1789) to the present day. The collections (paintings, engravings, models, sculptures, furniture and signs) are presented in rooms that re-create the atmosphere of Parisian mansions from different historical periods.

Not forgetting

■ **Centre Georges Pompidou ('Beaubourg') (19)** Piazza du Centre, 75004 ☎ 01 44 78 12 33 Mon., Wed., Fri.–Sun. 11am–9pm; Thu. 11am–10pm *Exhibitions and events in all spheres of modern art. Due to renovations (until Dec.31, 1999) temporary exhibitions are held in the Galerie Sud.* ■ **Hôtel de Béthune-Sully (20)** 62 rue Saint-Antoine, 75004 ☎ 01 44 61 20 00 Heritage bookshop: Tue.–Sun. 10am–7pm Guided visits only 3rd weekend in Sep. (reservations ☎ 01 44 61 21 69) *Magnificent 17th-century mansion, painstakingly restored.*

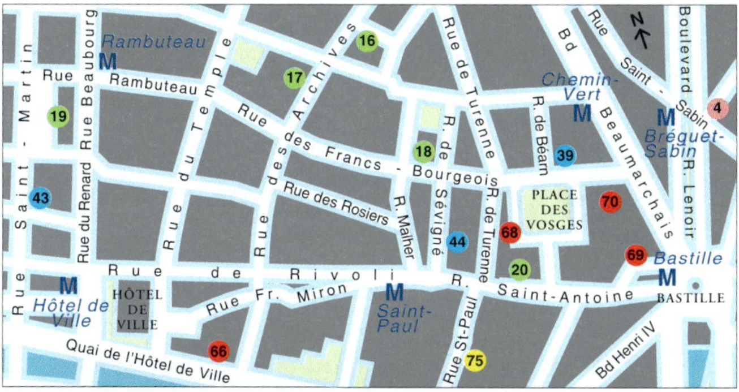

17

19

The Pompidou Center, a steel-and-glass modernist structure, attracts 8 million visitors every year.

17

18

17

17

In the area

Montmartre, a former wine-growers' village that became part of the capital in 1860, looks out across Paris from the top of its famous *butte* (hill). From the place du Tertre, a haunt of artists, a maze of steep streets and steps leads down to the *grands boulevards*. ■ Where to eat ➡ 64

What to see

Musée de Montmartre (21)
12 rue Cortot, 75018 ☎ 01 46 06 61 11

M *Abbesses, Anvers* ▭ ⌚ *Tue.–Sun 11am–6pm; closed public holidays* ● *F25; concessions F20; under-10s free*

The museum, housed in the *butte*'s oldest building (1650), was originally a private residence whose occupants have included artists (Dufy, Utrillo, Renoir) and poets (Reverdy). Its collections (posters, paintings and porcelain) reflect Montmartre's 'Bohemian period'. The Café de l'Abreuvoir and the studio of 19th-century composer Gustave Charpentier have been reconstructed.

Basilique du Sacré-Cœur (22)
33 rue du Chevalier-de-la-Barre, 75018 ☎ 01 53 41 89 00

M *Anvers* ⌚ ***Basilica** daily 6am–11pm* ● *free* ***Dome, crypt** daily: Apr.–Oct. 9am–7pm / Nov.–Mar. 9.30am–6pm* ● *F15*

The white dome of the Sacré-Coeur, dominating the Paris skyline from the *butte* of Montmartre, is one of the city's most famous landmarks. Built (1876–1910) in combined Romanesque and Byzantine styles, the basilica was originally intended for pilgrimages.

Musée Gustave Moreau (23)
14 rue de la Rochefoucauld, 75009 ☎ 01 48 74 38 50

M *Trinité* ▭ ⌚ *Mon., Wed. 11am–5.15pm; Thur.–Sun. 10am–12.45pm, 2–5.15pm* ● *F22; Sun., 18–25s F15; under-18s free*

The museum, devoted to the work of the French symbolist Gustave Moreau (1826–1898), was founded in the artist's studio in 1902. A collection of almost 1200 paintings (including *Jupiter and Semele*) and 5000 drawings presents a cohesive overview of Moreau's work. The Petit Musée in the artist's apartment offers a more personal view of his life.

Musée Grévin (24)
10 boulevard Montmartre, 75009 ☎ 01 47 70 85 05

M *Grands-Boulevards, Richelieu-Drouot* ▭ ⌚ *Apr.–Aug. daily 1–6pm; Sep.–Mar. daily 1–5.30pm; school holidays 10am–7pm* ● *F58; 6–14s F38; under-6s free*

This world-famous waxworks museum, opened in 1882, was the brainchild of journalist Arthur Meyer and cartoonist Alfred Grévin. A series of tableaux features several hundred waxwork models of famous historical figures and contemporary celebrities. The Palais des Mirages presents a *son et lumière*, while the Italian-style theater (which became a listed building in 1964) stages mime performances and magic shows.

Not forgetting

■ **Passage Jouffroy (25)** 10 boulevard Montmartre, 75002 *The city's first heated alleyway.* ■ **Passage des Panoramas (26)** 11 boulevard Montmartre, 75002 *The city's oldest alleyway, described by Émile Zola (1840–1902) in his novel* Nana.

➥ 68 ■ After dark ➥ 88 ➥ 92 ➥ 94 ➥ 96 ■ Where to shop ➥ 140

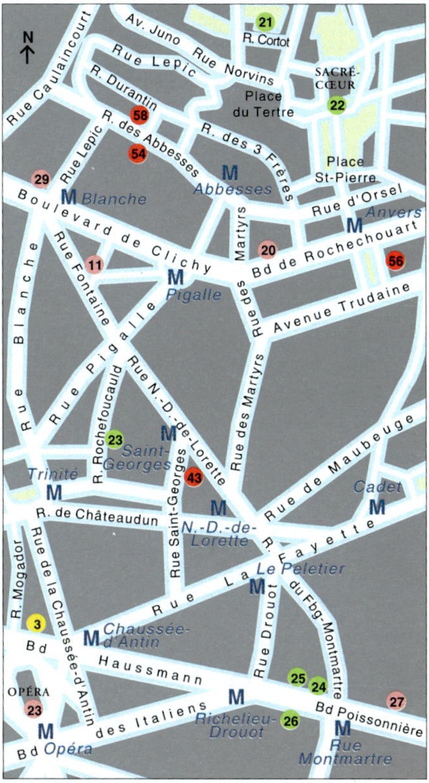

22

Built on a hill undermined by quarrying, Sacré-Coeur is supported by 83 underground pillars. According to locals, the basilica holds Montmartre together.

3

24

24

In the area

In the 19th century, working-class districts grew up around the former villages of La Villette and Belleville, and along the banks of the Ourcq and Saint-Martin canals. During the 1870s, the abattoirs of La Villette closed down and its population migrated into the suburbs, significantly altering

What to see

Cité des Sciences et de l'Industrie (27)

Parc de la Villette
30 avenue Corentin-Cariou, 75019 ☎ 01 40 05 70 00

Porte-de-La-Villette *Cité des Sciences, Planetarium* *Tue.–Sat. 10am–6pm; Sun. 10am–7pm ● F50; under-7s free* ***Cité des Enfants*** *Tue.–Sun. 10am–6pm ● F25* ***Techno cité*** *● F25* ***Cinaxe*** *Tue.–Sun. 11am–7pm ● F33;* ***Géode*** *Tue.–Sun. 10am–9pm ● F57;* *L'Aquarium*

The largest museum of modern science and technology in Europe offers additional attractions (planetarium, aquarium, introduction to technology, submarine visit). The Géode movie theater, a steel globe that houses the world's largest hemispherical screen, has become the symbol of the Cité. In the landscaped gardens are the Cité de la Musique and Grande Halle.

Parc des Buttes-Chaumont (28)

Place Armand-Carrel, 75019 ☎ 01 42 40 88 66

Botzaris, Buttes-Chaumont ***Park*** *daily 8.30am–10pm (7pm in winter)* ***Guignol (puppet show)*** *Apr.–Oct.: Wed., Sat., Sun. public holidays, school holidays 3pm, 4pm ● F12*

Created in 1867 by the civil engineer Jean-Charles Alphand, this was the archetype for the parks built during Georges Eugène Haussmann's period of office as prefect of Paris (1853–1870). It was laid out during the reign of Napoleon III to encourage working-class families to take Sunday walks rather than visit cabarets. It has a waterfall, two streams, a cave and a lake. The Temple de Sybille stands at the highest point on the island and offers a magnificent view of northern Paris.

Musée Édith Piaf (29)

5 rue Crespin-du-Gast, 75011 ☎ 01 43 55 52 72

Ménilmontant *Mon.–Thur. 1–6pm by appointment ● free*

The first museum to be dedicated to a French variety artist evokes the life and career of the popular singer Édith Piaf (1915–1963), née Édith Giovanna Gassion. Among the many memorabilia presented in this intimate museum is the famous 'little black dress' worn on stage by the singer affectionately known as 'the Little Sparrow'.

Père Lachaise Cemetery (30)

Boulevard de Ménilmontant, 75020 ☎ 01 43 70 70 33

Père-Lachaise, Philippe-Auguste *Mar. 16–Nov. 5: Mon.–Fri. 8am–6pm; Sat. 8.30am–6pm; Sun. 9am–6pm Nov. 6–Mar. 15: Mon.–Fri. 8am–5.30pm; Sat. 8.30am–5.30pm; Sun. 9am–5.30pm*

A maze of – often eccentric – tombs inscribed with such famous names as Molière, La Fontaine, Proust, Balzac, Colette, Jim Morrison… As well as the tombs, there is the *Mur des Fédérés*, the wall against which the last of the Communards (the supporters of the Paris Commune formed after the Franco-Prussian War in 1871) were executed in 1871, and memorials to the victims of the Nazi concentration camps.

the face of the Paris 'east-end', a process that continues.

■ Where to eat ➥ 48 ➥ 50
■ After dark ➥ 86 ➥ 90 ➥ 98

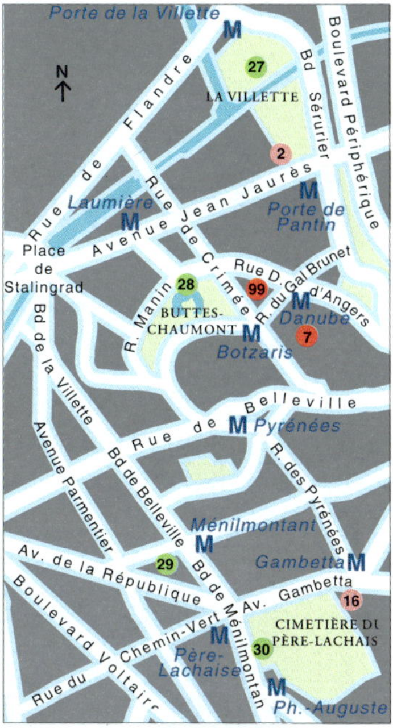

28

30

29

27

La Rotonde, a former toll-house used by tax collectors to administer the city toll. Built in 1784 by the architect Claude - Nicolas Ledoux (1736–1806).

27

In the area

Centered on the Musée d'Orsay, this district includes the Hôtel de la Monnaie (Mint), the Institut de France, the École des Beaux-Arts (School of Fine Arts) as well as art galleries and antique shops. ■ Where to stay ➥ 38 ➥ 40 ➥ 42 ■ Where to eat ➥ 78 ■ After dark ➥ 86

What to see

Musée d'Orsay (31)

62 rue de Lille, 75007 ☎ 01 40 49 48 14 (entrance: 1 rue de la Légion d'Honneur)

Solférino June 20–Sep. 20: Tue., Wed., Fri.–Sun. 9am–6pm; Thu. 9am–9.45pm / Sep. 21–June 19: Tue., Wed., Fri., Sat. 10am–6pm; Thu. 10am–9.45pm; Sun. 9am–6pm ● F40; concessions, under–18s free Le Café des Hauteurs Le Restaurant ☎ 01 45 49 11 11

The museum occupies the former Gare d'Orléans, built on the site of the Palais d'Orsay, which was burned to the ground during the Paris Commune in 1871. In 1900 the Orléans Railway Company built a new station, designed by the architect Victor Laloux (1850–1937). The station ceased operating in 1939 and remained empty for several decades. It was subsequently used as a sale room by Hôtel Drouot, the famous Paris auction house, and then as a theater by the Renaud-Barrault company before being saved from demolition in 1973 and converted into a museum in 1986. The luminous hall of the former station forms the central 'nave' of the museum, around which the collections are presented on terraces and mezzanines.

➡ 88 ➡ 98
■ Where to shop ➡ 156

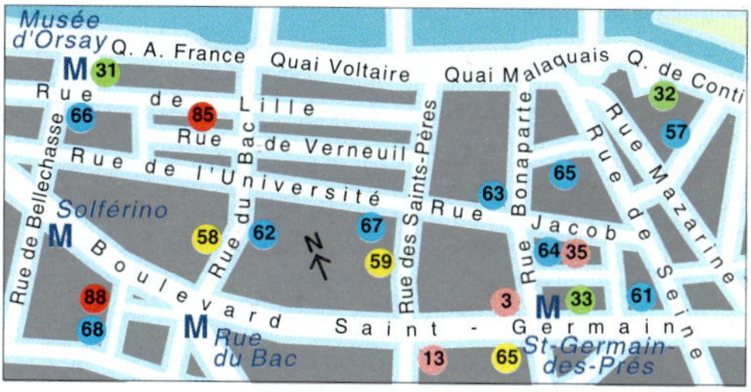

19th-century art

The collections of the Musée d'Orsay reflect western art from 1848 to 1914. They have been formed from national collections from three principal sources: the Louvre ➡ 104, the Jeu de Paume ➡ 105 and the Musée d'Art Moderne ➡ 106. The originality of the Musée d'Orsay lies in its presentation of a wide range of different art forms from a particularly fertile period. This gives a complete overview of painting, sculpture, decorative and graphic arts, as well as such visual arts as architecture and urban development, movies, photography, posters and book illustrations.

Paintings

The museum is organized chronologically on three levels, with rooms generally devoted to the work of one artist. Paintings are grouped according to theme and school. The museum possesses one of the finest collections of Impressionist paintings in the world (level 3), including Édouard Manet's *Olympia* (1863), Claude Monet's *La Cathédrale de Rouen: harmonie bleu et or, plein soleil* – one of the Rouen Cathedral 'series' – (1893), Renoir's *The Swing* (1876) and works by Pissarro and Sisley. However, it also gives an insight into modern art via the Naturalist (level 2) (Edgar Degas's *La Famille Bellelli*, 1860), Expressionist (Vincent Van Gogh's *La Nuit étoilée, Arles*, 1888), Pointillist (Paul Signac's *Femme à l'Ombrelle*, 1893), Nabi (level 3) (Pierre Bonnard's *La Loge*, 1908) and early Cubist (Paul Cézanne's *Le Pont de Maincy*, 1879) schools.

Not forgetting

■ **L'Hôtel des Monnaies (32)** 11 quai de Conti, 75006 ☎ 01 40 46 55 35 ⏲ Tue.–Fri. 11am–5.30pm *Engraving, medal manufacture and casting of objets d'art.* ■ **L'Église Saint-Germain-des-Prés (33)** 3 place Saint-Germain-des-Prés, 75006 ☎ 01 43 25 41 71 ⏲ Mon.–Sun. 7.30am–7.30pm

In the area
The Île de la Cité constitutes the historic and geographical center of Paris. Notre-Dame, the Sainte-Chapelle, Hôtel Dieu (rebuilt in the 19th century) and Conciergerie are all that remain of the former royal city. The Pont Neuf offers superb views of the island. ■ Where to eat ➡ 76

What to see

Conciergerie (34)
Palais de la Cité, 1 quai de l'Horloge, 75001 ☎ 01 53 73 78 50

Saint-Michel, Cité daily: Apr.–Sep. 9.30am–6.30pm / Oct.–Mar.: 10am–5pm; closed public holidays ● F35; 12–25s F23; under-12s free: **double ticket** *Conciergerie-Sainte-Chapelle F50 daily 11am, 3pm*

Originally the residence of the Capetians, built on the northern shore of the island in c.1300 by Philippe le Bel (1268–1314). In 1380, it became an annexe of the Grand Châtelet prison. The Salle des Gens d'Armes (hall of the men-at-arms) houses several pieces from this period. Many famous prisoners were detained here pending execution, especially in 1793 during the French Revolution. A visit to the Prisoners' Gallery, the dungeons and the cell of Queen Marie-Antoinette (converted into a chapel in 1816) gives some insight into these troubled times.

Sainte-Chapelle (35)
4 boulevard du Palais, 75001 ☎ 01 53 73 78 50

Saint-Michel, Cité daily: Apr.–Sep. 9.30am–6.30pm / Oct.–Mar. 10am–5pm; closed public holidays ● F35; 12–25s F23; under-12s free daily 11am, 3pm

Sainte-Chapelle, the work of Saint Louis and a real jewel of Gothic architecture which today stands within the walls of the Palais de Justice (Law Courts), used to stand in the main courtyard of the Palais de Saint-Louis. Built (1245–1248) as a royal shrine to house holy relics, it comprises two chapels, a lower chapel for the public and an upper chapel for the king. The absence of flying buttresses, which have been replaced by buttresses, made it possible to increase the size of the windows. Their fragile delicacy is accentuated by the relatively small dimension of the building and a very tall spire (250 feet). The windows illustrate the history of the Hebrew people, from the Creation to their arrival in Israel and the institution of a monarchy; they end with the story of Louis IX receiving the relics of the Passion.

Notre-Dame de Paris (36)
place du Parvis-de-Notre-Dame, 75004 ☎ 01 42 34 56 10

Cité ***Cathedral*** *daily 8am–6.45pm;* ***Towers*** *daily: summer 9.30am–6.15pm/ winter 10am–4.15pm ● F30; concessions F25* ***Treasure-house*** *Mon.–Sat. 9.30–11.30am, 1–5.30pm ● F15; concessions F10; under-12s F5* ***Crypt*** *daily: summer 9.30–6pm; winter 10am–4.30pm ● F32; 12–25s F21; under-12s free*

This magnificent Gothic cathedral (1163–1245) took more than 150 years to build. The sober harmony of its impressive bulk provides a striking contrast to its slender spire (295 feet) and the subtle balance of its flying buttresses. Among the interior details are the rose window in the north transept depicting scenes from the Old Testament, and the north and south walls (14th century) illustrating the *Life of Christ*. The towers (225 feet) offer a magnificent view of the city and such architectural details as the Galerie des Chimères with its gargoyles and monsters by Viollet-le-Duc (19th century). At the other end of the scale, the crypt, opened in 1980, enables visitors to see the cathedral's Gallo-Roman foundations.

Where to stay ➥ 34 ➥ 38 Where to shop ➥ 140

35

The bronze star in front of Notre-Dame represents not only the heart of Paris, but also the heart of France.

6

35

35

35

35

35

In the area

The universities, publishing houses and bookstores of the Latin Quarter have established its reputation as the intellectual center of Paris. It also offers a blend of monuments and medieval streets that are busy day and night. ■ Where to eat ➥ 48 ➥ 76 ■ Where to stay ➥ 34 ➥ 36

What to see

Thermes de Cluny (37)
Musée national du Moyen Âge
6 place Paul-Painlevé, 75005 ☎ 01 53 73 78 00

M *Cluny-La-Sorbonne* *Wed.–Mon. 9.15am–5.45pm ● F30; 18–25s F20; under-18s free* *Music and medieval poetry ☎ 01 53 73 78 22*

The Museum of the Middle Ages, founded in 1843, spans 15 centuries of history. The remains of its first- to third-century Gallo-Roman baths and the 16th-century mansion (*hôtel*) of the abbots of Cluny (a masterpiece of the Flamboyant style) make the museum the architectural embodiment of this period. The richness and diversity of medieval life is evidenced in the museum's sculptures, manuscripts, paintings and windows. The famous 16th-century tapestry, *Lady with the Unicorn*, is one of the museum's masterpieces.

Institut du Monde Arabe (38)
1 rue des Fossés-Saint-Bernard, 75236 Cedex ☎ 01 40 51 38 38

M *Jussieu, Cardinal-Lemoine* P *Tue.–Sun. 10am–6.05pm; closed May 1 ● F25; concessions F20; under-18s free* ***Library*** *Tue.–Sat. 1–8pm* ***Image and sound*** *Tue.–Sun. 10am–6pm* *panoramic restaurant*

Discover the Arab world via the Institut du Monde Arabe (IMA), founded in 1987. Its permanent collections are enhanced by regular exhibitions of large collections from the Institute's founder countries, while its print library (50,000 books) and multimedia reference library provide additional information on the civilizations and cultures of the Arab world.

Muséum National d'Histoire Naturelle (39)
57 rue Cuvier, 75005 ☎ 01 40 79 30 00

M *Jussieu* ***Grande Galerie de l'Évolution (Gallery of Evolution)*** *Wed.–Mon. 10am–6pm; Thur. 10am–10pm ● F40; concessions F30* ***Paleontology, anatomy and mineralogy*** *Nov.–Mar.: Wed.–Mon. 10am–6pm/ Apr.–Oct.: Wed.–Mon. 10am-5pm ● F30; concessions F20* ***Entomology*** *part of collection displayed in the Grande Galerie* ***Zoo*** *summer: daily 9am–6pm winter: daily 9.30am–6.30pm ● F30; concessions F20* ***Gardens*** *daily, sunrise to sunset*

Set in the Jardin des Plantes, this natural history museum was established in 1793. Its collections of natural history and ethnology are among the largest in the world today. Visit the late 19th-century *Grande Galerie de l'Évolution* with its huge glass roof, the gallery of paleontology with its reconstructed skeletons of prehistoric mammals, the botanical gardens and the menagerie.

Not forgetting

■ **Panthéon (40)** Place du Panthéon, 75005 ☎ 01 44 32 18 00 Apr.–Sep.: daily 9.30am–6.30pm; / Oct.–Mar.: daily 10am–6.15pm *"Aux Grands Hommes, la Patrie reconnaissante." (The mother land pays homage to its great men.)* ■ **Arènes de Lutèce (41)** 49 rue Monge, 75005 Sep.–mid-May: Mon.–Fri. 8am–9pm; Sat., Sun. 9am–9pm/mid-May–Aug.: Mon.–Fri. 8am–9.30pm; Sat., Sun. 9am–9.30pm *Beautiful Gallo-Roman amphitheater discovered in 1869.*

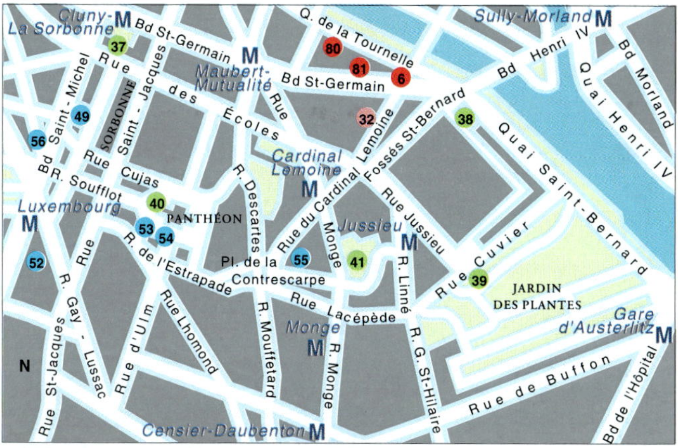

37

The Flamboyant ceilings of the Hôtel de Cluny chapel exemplify the final stylistic development of French Gothic architecture.

39

8

39

38

Basic facts
Green spaces have always been an important part of Paris life: the former private parks and formal gardens of the 17th-century royal and princely palaces, the public gardens of the 18th century, and the Bois de Boulogne and the Bois de Vincennes developed during the Second

What to see

Jardin du Luxembourg (42)
Boulevard Saint-Michel, 75006

Odéon *daily 9am–sunset* ● *free* *Puppet theater, hives*

The Jardin du Luxembourg was created at the same time as the palace built for Queen Maria de' Medici (17th century), today the seat of the French Senate. Together with the Jardin des Tuileries, it is one of the oldest gardens in Paris, designed by the first exponent of the French-style garden, Boyeau de la Bareaudière. Today children play around the garden's huge, ornamental pool and enjoy its puppet theater, and it is also a favorite rendezvous for students and residents of the Latin Quarter. The shady walkways offer glimpses of 19th-century sculptures (Cain, Bourdelle, Frémiet), including the fountain dedicated to Eugène Delacroix and decorated with a bronze sculpture by Jules Dado, and the famous Medici fountain.

Parc Monceau (43)
Boulevard de Courcelles, 75008 ☎ 01 42 27 08 64

Courcelles *daily Apr.–Oct.: 7am–10pm; / Nov.–Mar.: 7am–8pm* ● *free*

Created in 1778 by the Duc de Chartres, this park has the magical charm of an English-style garden. With ornamental pools, grottoes, mock Gothic ruins and ruined Greek temples, and statues of Musset (Antonin Mercié, 1906), Maupassant (Verlet, 1897) and Chopin (Froment-Meurice, 1906), the park is as popular with children as it is with adults. Near the north entrance, La Rotonde (built by Ledoux in 1784) is one of the oldest toll-houses used by tax collectors to administer the city toll. The park – a particular favorite of Marcel Proust – is surrounded by mansions, two of which house the Musée Cernuschi (Chinese art) and the Musée Nissim-de-Camondo (18th-century decorative arts).

45

42

Empire. The tradition continues, and today the capital has some 400 parks, private and public gardens and local squares.

Parc André-Citroën (44)

rues Balard, Leblanc, Montagne-de-la-Fage, 75015 ☎ 01 45 57 13 35

M *Balard* ⏲ *Mon.–Fri. 8.30am–sunset; Sat., / Sun. 8.30am–sunset* ● *free*

Parc André-Citroën was created by landscape designers Alain Provost and Gilles Clément, in the mid-1970s, on the site of the Citroën factories. It is probably the most sophisticated of the Paris parks and comprises the Jardin Blanc (white garden), used for games and walking, the Jardin Noir (black garden) with its dense, dark-colored plantings, and the large central park which descends toward the Seine. A series of six gardens, separated by waterfalls, completes the transformation of the site.

Not forgetting

■ **Jardin du Musée Bourdelle (45)** 18 rue Antoine-Bourdelle, 75015 ⏲ Tue.–Sun. 10am–5.40pm *Garden-museum of Bourdelle sculpture.* ■ **Parc Montsouris (46)** av. Reille, 75013 ⏲ daily, 8.30am–sunset *English-style garden.* ■ **Jardin des Tuileries (47)** Le Louvre ➡ *104* ⏲ daily, Apr.–Sep. 7am–9pm; / Oct.–Mar. 7.30am–7.30pm *A French-style garden created by Le Nôtre in 1666.* ■ **Parc des Buttes Chaumont (28)** *A picturesque garden.* ➡ *114.*

45

43

Cycle hire
Some railroad stations hire bicycles that can be returned to another station ● *F45 per day* **SNCF** ☎ *01 43 37 59 22*

Further afield

Rambles
Organized by the Paris ramblers' association: **Randonneurs d'Île-de-France** *67 rue du Moulin-Vert, 75014* ☎ *01 45 42 24 72*

Information

SNCF 24 hours ☎ *01 40 52 75 75 et* ***36 15*** *SNCF*
RATP 24 hours ☎ *08 36 78 77 14 et* ***36 15*** *RATP*
Prices ➡ 102; Tourist office ➡ 102; SNCF ➡ 10; RATP ➡ 12; Car rental ➡ 8

17 Days out

THE INSIDER'S FAVORITES

Festivals and events around Paris

Versailles ➡ 128 Concerts in Opéra Royal of the Château de Versailles *(Sep.–June)*; Grandes Fêtes de Nuit *(July, Aug. 28, Sep. 4–11)*; Grandes Eaux Musicales *(May–Aug.)*
Chantilly ➡ 132
Equestrian displays at the Musée Vivant du Cheval, Cheval & Gospel, Cheval & Fête *(1st Sun. every month)*; Nuits de Feu, international fireworks competition *(mid-June, alternate years)*
Saint-Denis ➡ 132
Religious dance and music *(June)*
Fontainebleau ➡ 134
Week of the Horse at the Grand Parquet hippodrome, week of breeding *(Aug.)*
Thoiry ➡ 136
Rhododendron and azalea festival *(May–June, Oct.)*; Rose and peony display *(2 weeks in June)*
Golf national ➡ 136
French Open *(end of June)*

INDEX BY TYPE

Basic facts

The forests around Paris were once royal hunting grounds. Today they are occupied by chateaux and museums for the culturally and historically minded, parks for visitors in search of fresh air, golf courses for sports enthusiasts and huge theme parks for the younger generation.

Further afield

Château de Versailles (1)

(45 mins) Autoroute A13 to Versailles exit.
RER *(30 mins) Line C to Versailles-Rive-Gauche.*
(30 mins) gare Saint-Lazare, to Versailles-Rive-Droite.
(20 mins) gare Montparnasse, to Versailles-Chantiers.

Musée National de la Céramique (4)

(45 mins) in the direction of porte de Saint-Cloud.
M *(35 mins) Line 9 to Pont de Sèvres.*

Château de Malmaison (5)

(45 mins) RN 13 dir. Saint-Germain-en-Laye.
M *(20 min) Line 1 to La Défense; bus no. 258, to Le Château station (5 min walk from the château).*

Château de Saint-Germain-en-Laye (6)

(45 mins) Autoroute A13 to Versailles-Ouest exit; RN 186 in the direction of Saint-Germain-en-Laye.
RER *(35 mins) Line A1 to Saint-Germain-en-Laye.*

Musée Maurice Denis (7)

(45 mins) Autoroute A13 to Versailles-Ouest exit; RN186 in the direction of Saint-Germain-en-Laye.
RER *(35 mins) Line A1 to Saint-Germain-en-Laye.*

Basilique Saint-Denis (8)

(20 mins) Autoroute A1 to Saint-Denis exit.
M *(25 mins) Line 13 to Saint-Denis-Basilique.*

Château d'Écouen (9)

(60 mins) Autoroute A1 to Pierrefitte-Beauvais exit; RN1 and RN 16 in the direction of Chantilly.
(25 mins) gare du Nord, to Écouen-Ezanville, bus no. 268 alighting at Mairie d'Écouen.

Château de Chantilly (10)

(75 mins) Autoroute A1 to Survilliers-Saint-Witz exit; RN16 in the direction of Chantilly.
RER *(45 mins) Line D to Chantilly-Gouvieux.*

Château de Vaux-le-Vicomte (11)

(60 mins) Autoroute A6 to Melun-Sénart exit.

Barbizon (12)

(50 min) Autoroute A6 to Fontainebleau exit in the direction of Barbizon.

Château de Fontainebleau (13)

(90 mins) Autoroute A6 to Fontainebleau exit.
(40 min) gare de Lyon to Fontainebleau-Avon, bus 'AB' to the chateau (15 min).

7

15

1

9

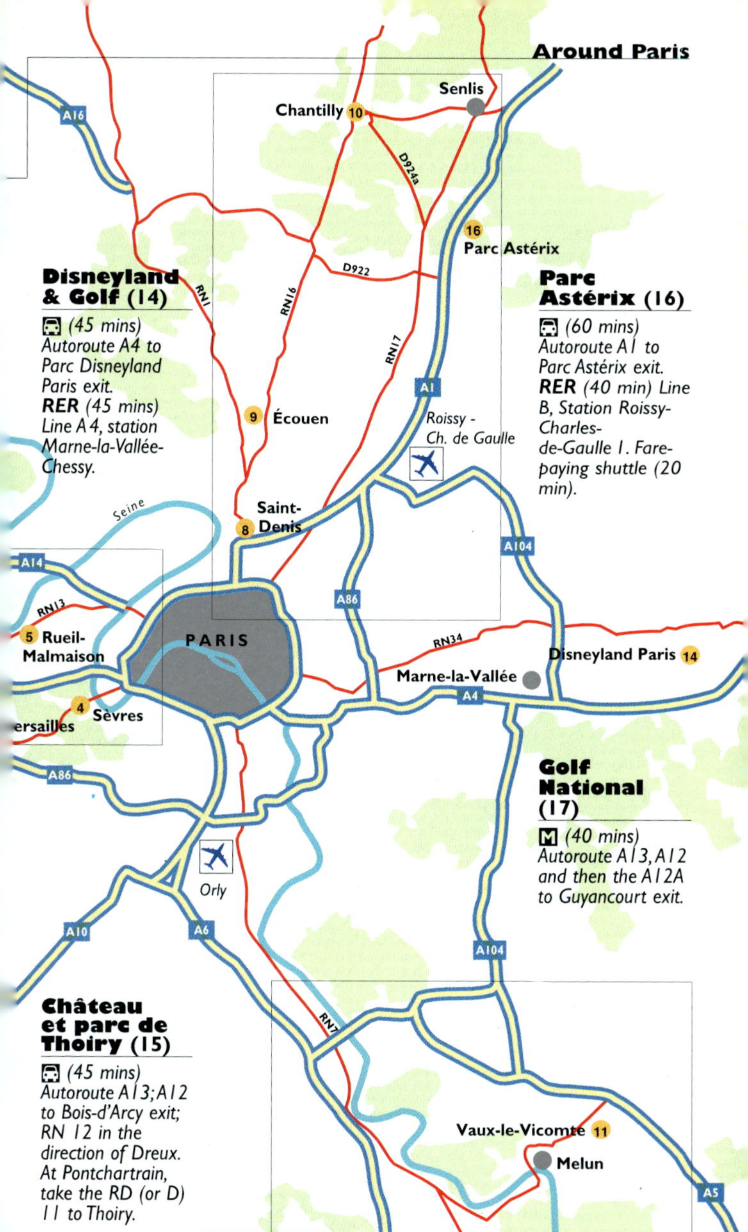

Disneyland & Golf (14)

(45 mins)
Autoroute A4 to Parc Disneyland Paris exit.
RER *(45 mins) Line A 4, station Marne-la-Vallée-Chessy.*

Parc Astérix (16)

(60 mins)
Autoroute A1 to Parc Astérix exit.
RER *(40 min) Line B, Station Roissy-Charles-de-Gaulle 1. Fare-paying shuttle (20 min).*

Golf National (17)

(40 mins)
Autoroute A13, A12 and then the A12A to Guyancourt exit.

Château et parc de Thoiry (15)

(45 mins)
Autoroute A13; A12 to Bois-d'Arcy exit; RN 12 in the direction of Dreux. At Pontchartrain, take the RD (or D) 11 to Thoiry.

16

13

Basic facts

It took 100 years and four royal reigns to build this impressive royal palace. Louis XIII's passion for hunting dictated the site, and the aspirations of Louis XIV, the Sun King, decided its vast size. Louis XV brought intimacy and elegance, and Marie-Antoinette added youthful

Further afield

Château de Versailles (1)

78000 Versailles ☎ 01 30 84 76 18

*Musée de l'Histoire de France May–Sep.: Tue.-Sun. 9am–6pm; Oct.–Apr.: Tue.–Sun. 9am–5pm ● F45; 18–25s F35; under-18s free; Museums and Monuments Card. Concerts in the **Opéra Royal** ☎ 01 39 02 30 00 La Flottille*

Built between 1661 and 1710 by Le Vau and decorated by Le Brun, Versailles is a fine example of classical architecture, with its buildings and wings arranged symmetrically around the main body of the chateau. In 1678, for reasons of politics and prestige, Louis XIV took up residence at Versailles along with the royal family, the royal Court and the French government. The chateau was extensively modified so that a strict hierarchy could be observed in the allocation of apartments. The North (1689) and South (1682) wings housed the princes and nobility. The royal apartments were located in the main chateau, with the queen's apartments to the south and the king's magnificent and lavishly ceremonial Grand Appartement to the north. The elegant sophistication of the Petits Appartements, commissioned by Louis XV, offer a striking contrast. Don't miss the Opéra, commissioned by Louis XVI and designed by Gabriel, or the famous Hall of Mirrors lined by 17 windows and 17 arcaded mirrors.

Gardens and Grand Canal (2)

*daily 7am–sunset ● admission free (except during Grandes Eaux) **Grandes Eaux Musicales** Apr.–Oct. ● F25 **Grandes Fêtes de Nuit** June–Sep. ☎ 01 30 83 78 78*

Designed by Le Nôtre and embellished by Mansart, the park of Versailles provided the setting for some lavish celebrations and entertainments. At the foot of the chateau are the 'open' gardens whose broad, sweeping vistas are punctuated by terraces and ornamental pools. Beyond these lie the groves, garden rooms furnished with almost 300 ornamental basins and statues. The majestic Grand Canal draws the eye into the distance, where the park merges with the vast forest of Versailles.

frivolity. King Louis-Philippe gave it to the nation as a museum.

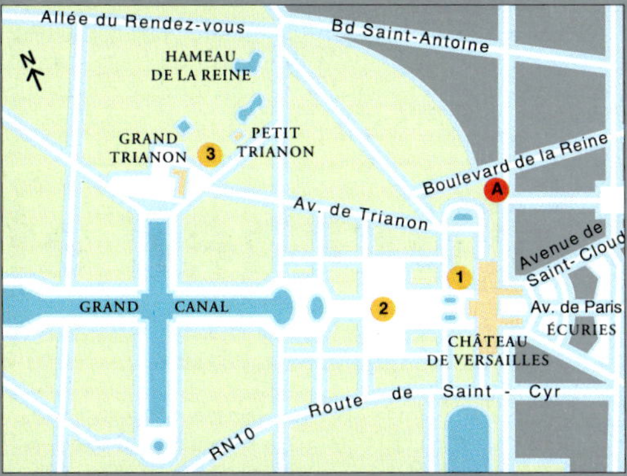

Under Louis XIV, the Grand Canal provided the setting for lavish entertainments.

Le Grand et le Petit Trianon (3)

May–Sep.: Tue.–Sun. 10am–6pm; Oct.–Apr.: Tue.–Sun. 9am–6.30pm, ● ***Grand Trianon*** *F25; 18–25s, Sun. F15; under-18s free Musée et Monuments card* ● ***Petit Trianon*** *F15; 18–25s, Sun. F10; under-18s free; double ticket Grand-Petit Trianon F30; 18–25s F20; under-18s free*

The long Italianate building of the Grand Trianon (1887) and the neoclassical residence known as the Petit Trianon (1762) were Louis XIV's and Louis XV's favorite parts of the chateau. Marie-Antoinette made Trianon her own domain and added the Hameau de la Reine (queen's hamlet). This reconstruction of a farm enabled her to enjoy the pleasures of 'rural' life, as advocated by writer Jean-Jacques Rousseau (1712–78). Centuries later, these 'miniature' palaces continue to delight visitors.

Not forgetting

Les Trois Marches (A) 1 boulevard de la Reine, 78000 Versailles
☎ 01 39 50 13 21 *Gastronomic restaurant.* ●●●●●

Basic facts

The Bourbon kings' passion for hunting meant that the court was constantly traveling between the Palais du Louvre and Saint-Germain-en-Laye, Vincennes and Saint-Cloud. This 'nomadic existence' came to an end when Louis XIV took up residence at Versailles. Today, the former

Further afield

Musée national de la Céramique (4)

Place de la Manufacture, 92310 Sèvres ☎ 01 41 14 04 20

Wed.–Mon. 10am–5pm; closed public holidays ● F22; concessions F15; under-18s free; Musées et Monuments card ☎ 01 41 14 04 23

It was the Manufacture Nationale de Porcelaine, on the edge of the park of Saint-Cloud, that established the reputation of Sèvres porcelain in the 18th century. The museum, founded in 1824, has a collection of over 12,000 pieces, dating from the Renaissance to the present day. It includes Italian majolica pottery, faience from Chantilly and Mennecy, porcelain from Saxony and Sèvres, and contemporary pieces made in the factory.

Musée national du Château de Malmaison (5)

Avenue du Château, 92500 Rueil-Malmaison ☎ 01 41 29 05 55

Malmaison *Apr., Aug.–Sep.: Mon., Wed.–Fri. 10am–noon, 1.30–5pm; Sat., Sun. 10am–5.30pm / May–July: Mon., Wed.–Fri. 10am–5pm; Sat., Sun. 10am–5.30pm / Oct.–Mar.: Mon., Wed.–Fri. 10am–noon, 1.30–4.30pm; Sat., Sun. 10am–5pm / closed Dec. 25, Jan. 1 ● F30; 18–25 F20; under-18s free*

This 18th-century chateau stands in a magnificent English-style park dotted with pavilions. It enshrines the memory of Napoleon Bonaparte and Joséphine de Beauharnais, for whom it was built. It became a national museum in 1906. Don't miss the library, still in its original form.

Château de Saint-Germain-en-Laye (6)

Musée des Antiquités nationales
Château BP 3030, 78103 Saint-Germain-en-Laye ☎ 01 39 10 13 00

Wed.–Mon. 9am–5.15pm ● F25; 18–25s F17; under-18s free; Musées et Monuments card

From royal fortress (12th century) to Renaissance palace (16th century), the chateau refurbished by Louis XIV became a museum in 1862. It is the richest prehistoric museum in the world, with collections that span a million years. One of its finest exhibits is the reconstruction of the Grotte de Lascaux (Dordogne).

Musée Maurice-Denis "Le Prieuré" (7)

2bis rue M. Denis BP 5251, 78175 Saint-Germain-en Laye Cedex ☎ 01 39 73 77 87

Wed.–Fri. 10am–5.30pm; Sat., Sun., public holidays 10am–6.30pm; closed Dec. 25, Jan. 1, May 1 ● F25; concessions F15; under-12s free; Musées et Monuments card

In 1914, this former royal general hospital (1680) was bought by Maurice Denis (1870–1943), a leading artist in the symbolist Nabi group. In 1980, 'Le Prieuré' became a museum devoted to the works of Denis and other 19th- and 20th-century artists.

Not forgetting

■ **Cazaudehore (B)** 1 avenue du Président-Kennedy, 78100 Saint-Germain-en-Laye ☎ 01 34 51 93 80 *Gastronomic cuisine.* ●●

hunting-grounds exist as parks, offering spectacular views of the city, as well as unusual museums. Well worth a visit.

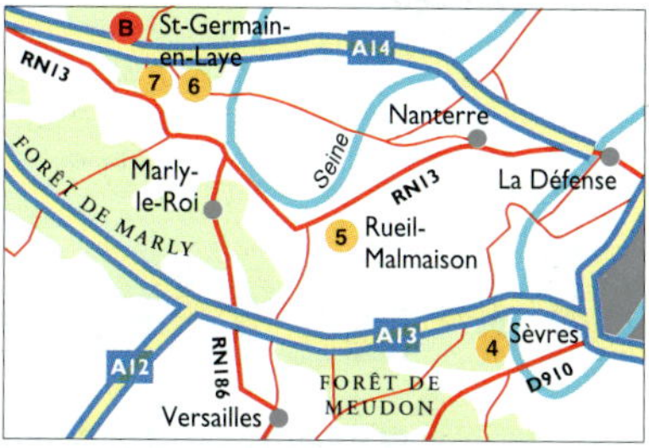

7

7

7

The *Dame de Brassempouy* (20,000 BC), discovered in south-west France, is exhibited in the Musée des Antiquités (6).

5

6

Basic facts

Three splendid buildings lie within easy reach of Paris to the north – the Basilique de Saint-Denis (the first major Gothic structure, and the mausoleum of the kings of France), Château d'Ecouen (a 16th-century chateau, now the setting for the Musée National de la Renaissance) and

Further afield

Basilique de Saint-Denis (8)

1 rue de la Légion-d'Honneur, 93200 Saint-Denis ☎ 01 48 09 83 54

Tombs-Crypt *Apr.–Sep.: Mon.–Sat. 10am–6.30pm; Sun. and public holidays noon–6.30pm / Oct.–Mar.: Mon.–Sat. 10am–4.30pm; Sun. and religious festivals noon–4.30pm; cemetery closed to public on public holidays and 30mins. before religious services ● F32; 12–25s F21; under-12s free;* ***Festival of religious music and dance*** *in June*

The Basilique de Saint-Denis (1122), built on the site of a 4th-century shrine of Saint Denis, became the prototype for later French cathedrals. Consecrated as the royal mausoleum by Louis VI, it houses the tombs of the kings of France, from Hugues Capet (d. 639) to Louis XVIII (d. 1824). The royal sepulchers and recumbent statues trace the history of the nation's royal dynasties. The only museum of funereal art of its kind in the world.

Château d'Écouen (9)

Musée national de la Renaissance, 95440 Écouen ☎ 01 34 38 38 50

Museum *Wed.–Mon. 9.45am–12.30pm, 2–5.15pm; closed Dec. 25, Jan. 1, May 1* ***Park*** *daily: Oct.–Mar. 8am–6pm; Apr.–Sep. 7.30am–7pm ● F25; 18–25s F17; under-18s free; Sun. F17 Sat.-Sun.*

This magnificent building, built for Anne de Montmorency (1493–1567), was converted into a museum (1969) at the instigation of the French writer and minister for Cultural Affairs, André Malraux. Its architectural wealth and remarkable collections are dominated by magnificent Renaissance tapestries depicting the story of David and Bathsheba. The park was designed by Jules Hardouin-Mansart.

Château de Chantilly (10)

60631 Chantilly ☎ 03 44 62 62 62

Musée Condé *Mar.–Oct.: Wed.–Mon. 10am–6pm / Nov.–Feb.: Wed.–Mon. 10.30am–12.45pm, 2–5pm ● F39; 12–18s F34; 3–11s F12; La Capitainerie* ***Musée Vivant du Cheval*** *Apr., July–Oct.: Wed.–Mon. 10.30am–6.30pm / May–June daily 10.30am–6.30pm / Nov.–Mar.: Mon., Wed.–Fri. 2.–6pm; Sat.–Sun., public holidays 10.30am–6.30pm ● concessions F45; 4–16s F35; Le Carrousel Gourmand*

At the center of a vast estate, this chateau was converted into a museum in 1886. The Petit Château (1560) houses the apartments of the princes de Condé, while the Grand Château (1875–85) holds collections of paintings and a magnificent library. The park, designed by Le Nôtre, includes the Grand Canal, formal flowerbeds, an Anglo-Chinese garden and the Grandes Écuries (1719), considered the most beautiful stables in the world. They were converted into the Musée Vivant du Cheval (living museum of the horse) in 1982. A trip in a hot-air balloon enables visitors to appreciate this remarkable estate from above.

Not forgetting

■ **Mets du Roy (C)** 4 rue de la Boulangerie, 93200 Saint-Denis ☎ 01 48 20 89 74 *Classic French cuisine* ●●● ■ **Les Goûters Champêtres (D)** Terroir et châteaux BP 80411, 60635 Chantilly cedex ☎ 03 44 57 46 21 *Country cuisine* ●

Château de Chantilly (an imposing building, set in an extensive park, and which houses the art collection of the Musée Condé).

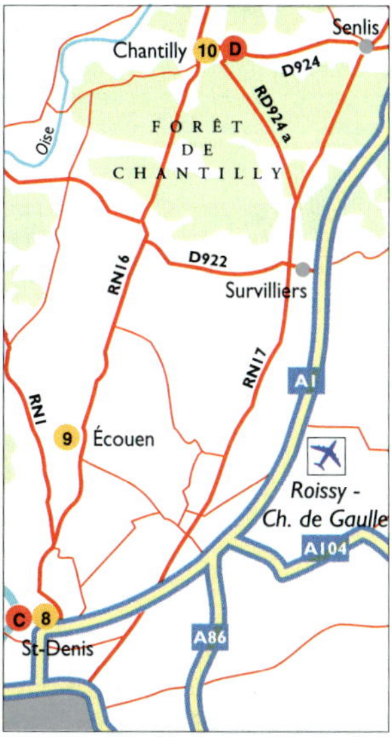

9

The equestrian displays at the Musée Vivant du Cheval are very popular.

9

10

Basic facts

The passion for hunting shared by most French monarchs led to the construction of hunting lodges on the edge of the vast game-filled forests of the Île-de-France region. This was how such royal residences as the Château de Fontainebleau were first established, while other

Further afield

Château de Vaux-le-Vicomte (11)

77950 Maincy ☎ 01 64 14 41 90

Gardens, museum, château *Mar. 11– Nov. 11: daily 10am–6pm* ***Candlelit visits*** *May 4–Sep. 30: Thu., Sat., public holidays, May 7, June 11, Aug. 15 8pm–midnight* ***Jeux d'eaux*** *Apr. 1–Oct. 31: 2nd and last Sat. in the month 3–6pm* ● ***Gardens-museum*** *F30, concessions F27, under-6s free* ***Gardens, museum, château*** *F62, concessions F49, under-6s free* ***Dome*** *F10 supplement Candlelit visits F80, concessions F70, under-6s free*

This great 17th-century palace – commissioned by Fouquet, minister of finance to Louis XIV – was the work of architect Le Vau, interior designer Le Brun, and landscape designer Le Nôtre, all of whom were later to work for Louis XIV and XV. The sumptuous apartments painted by Le Brun are furnished with 17th-century furniture, and the tapestries are amongst the most beautiful in France. Glorious gardens by Le Nôtre, immaculately restored. Summer candlelit tours are well worth the effort. The stables house an équipage museum.

Musée de l'École de Barbizon (12)

Auberge Ganne, 92 Grande-Rue, 77630 Barbizon ☎ 01 60 66 22 27

Nov.–Mar.: Mon., Wed.–Fri. 10am–12.30pm, 2–5pm / Apr.–Oct.: Mon., Wed.–Sun. 10am–12.30pm, 2–6pm ● *F25*

Between 1830 and 1870, this former woodcutters' village in the forest of Fontainebleau became the favorite haunt of the landscape painters of the Barbizon School (Millet, Rousseau, Daubigny, Corot, Courbet). They stayed in the Auberge Ganne, which was converted into a municipal museum in 1995 and today holds temporary exhibitions. Its doors, walls and sideboards are still covered in paintings by anonymous artists. The house and studio of Théodore Rousseau (55 Grande-Rue) is open to the public.

Musée national du château de Fontainebleau (13)

Château de Fontainebleau, 77300 Fontainebleau ☎ 01 60 71 50 70

May–June, Sep.–Oct.: Wed.–Mon. 9.30am–5pm; / July–Aug.: Wed.–Mon. 9.30am–6pm / Nov.–Apr.: Wed.–Mon. 9.30am–12.30pm, 2–5pm; closed public holidays ● ***Parc*** *free* ***Grands Appartements, Musée chinois*** *F35; 18–25s F23; under-18s free* ***Musée Napoléon Ier, Petits Appartements*** *F16 each; 18–25s F12 each; under-18s free*

A royal residence since the Middle Ages, the chateau became a Renaissance palace (1527) during the reign of François I. It was Napoleon I's favorite residence and it was here that he took leave of his army in 1814. The palace, now a national museum, has retained both influences: Renaissance (Galerie François Ier), and the Empire. The gardens were designed by Le Nôtre. A glorious day out.

Not forgetting

■ **Le Grand Veneur (E)** 77630 Barbizon ☎ 01 60 66 40 44 *Gastronomic cuisine* ●●● ■ **Croquembouche (F)** 43 rue France, 77300 Fontainebleau ☎ 01 64 22 01 57 *Classic French cuisine* ●●
■ **Auberge de Crisenoy (G)** 23 Grande-Rue, 77390 Crisenoy ☎ 01 64 38 83 06 *Classic French cuisine* ●●

chateaux represented the aspirations of high-ranking officials (such as Vaux-le-Vicomte built by Louis XIV's finance minister).

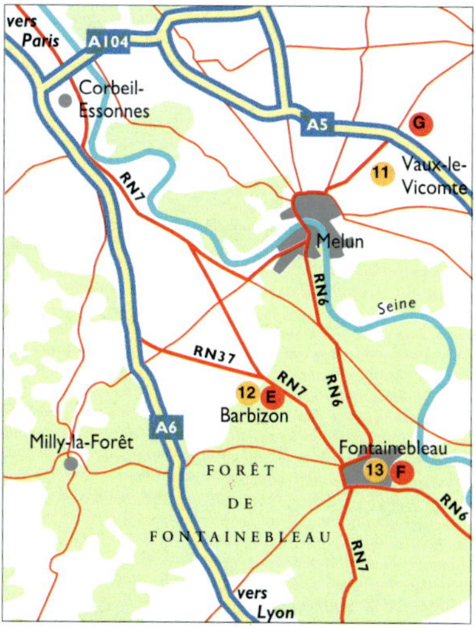

13

11

12

The doors and walls of the Auberge Ganne are decorated with frescoes, paintings and *trompe-l'oeil* effects.

2

Basic facts

Since the 1970s vast leisure areas and theme parks have been developed in the Paris region. Today, people come from all over the world to visit its three theme parks (among the largest in Europe) and 50 golf courses (10% of the golf courses in France).

Further afield

15

Disneyland Paris (14)

77777 Marne-la-Vallée ☎ 01 60 30 60 30

Mon.–Fri. 10am–6pm; Sat.–Sun., public holidays 9am–8pm; ● *Nov.–Mar. F160, 3–11s F130, under 3s free/ Apr.–Oct. F200, 3–11s F155, under 3s free* *hotels, golf courses*

Disneyland Paris re-creates the magical world of Walt Disney, in five fantasy landscapes. A golden opportunity to meet heroes from children's books, legendary figures from the American Wild West and favorite Walt Disney characters. Attractions – and distractions – for all ages include Space Mountain (intergalactical voyage), The Castle of Sleeping Beauty and Big Thunder Mountain.

Château de Thoiry and park (15)

78770 Thoiry-en-Yvelines ☎ 01 34 87 52 25

African game reserve *Apr.–Sep.: Mon.–Sat. 10am–6pm; Sun., public holidays 10am–6.30pm / Oct.–Mar.: Mon.–Sat. 10am–5pm; Sun., public holidays 10am–6.30pm* ● *F100; 3–12s F79*
Château *Mon.–Fri. 2–5pm; Sat.–Sun. 2–6pm* ● *F28; 3–12s F22*

The chateau (1564) was built by Philibert de l'Orme according to the 'golden section' principle. It creates a bridge of light through which the sun rises and sets on the days of the summer and winter solstices – a truly unique spectacle. The park is divided into French and English gardens, and a wildlife park that is home to some 800 animals. ★ Visitors can drive through the 'African game reserve' and see the animals at close quarters, with the added protection of a double security fence for the lions and tigers. Don't miss the breathtaking aerial acrobatics of the birds of prey.

16

17

14

Parc Astérix (16)

BP 8 60128 Plailly ☎ 03 44 62 31 31

Apr.–July 15: Mon.–Fri. 10am–7pm; Sat.-Sun. 9.30am–8pm / July 15–August: daily 9.30am–8pm; Sep.–Oct. 15: Wed. 10am–7pm, Sat.–Sun. 9.30am–8pm ● F170, 3–11s F120, under-3s free, season tickets F350, 3–12s F250

The park is based around Asterix the Gaul, the 'invincible' cartoon character created by Uderzo and Goscinny. Meet Asterix and his friends in their village. The park's other attractions include *rue de Paris* (Paris street), which traces the city's history, the Descente du Styx – a trip in a rubber dinghy on the underworld river of Greek mythology – and the Dolphinarium, with regular dolphin displays.

Golf national (17)

2 av. du Golf, 78280 Guyancourt ☎ 01 30 43 36 00

***Albatros** PAR **72**, **Aigle** PAR **71**, **Oiselet** PAR **32** Mon.–Fri. 8am–7.30pm; Sat., Sun. 7am–8.30pm ● Mon.–Fri. F100–F260; Sat.-Sun. F100–F390 Côté Jardin ●● Le Fairplay Pro-shop*

14

This showcase of the French Golf Federation has three courses: the 9-hole Oiselet (Birdie), the Aigle (Eagle), an 18-hole links-style course, and the Albatros (Albatross), ranked fourth in Europe, and the venue for the French Open, held every June. Stepping onto the Albatros is like stepping into another world, with a definite feel of Ireland about it. It is certainly an ideal course for improving your score! The friendly and professional welcome is 'on a par' with the quality of the courses.

Calling all bargain hunters

Designer seconds, ends of lines, factory stocks and second-hand items:

Le Mouton à cinq pattes *19 rue Grégoire-de-Tours, 75006* ☎ *01 43 29 73 56*
Réciproque *89, 92, 97, 101, 123 rue de la Pompe, 75016* ☎ *01 47 04 82 24*
Les Stocks de la rue d'Alésia *64–122 rue d'Alésia, 75016*

Where to shop

Tax refund

If you spend F2000 in one of the major department stores or in a store displaying the ***Tax-Free Shopping*** or ***Cashback*** logo, you can claim a VAT refund of around 14%. Make sure you take your passport.

Sales

The main sales periods are early January and July–August.

Salerooms

The largest auction house in Paris (buy a catalog at newspaper kiosks) is the **Hôtel Richelieu - Drouot** *9 rue Drouot, 75009* ☎ *01 48 00 20 20*

On rainy days

Carrousel du Louvre *rue de Rivoli, 75001* A gallery of shops beneath the glass pyramid of the Louvre: Boutique des Musées de Paris, Virgin Megastore.
Galerie Véro-Dodat *19 rue Jean-Jacques-Rousseau, 75001* Includes, among others, Capia: a wonderful shop that sells old-fashioned dolls.
Galerie Vivienne *4 rue des Petits-Champs / 6 rue Vivienne, 75002* Original workshops and *salons de thé* in a period (1823) setting.

78 Shops

THE INSIDER'S FAVORITES

INDEX BY TYPE

Basic facts

As well as being an integral part of everyday life in Paris, the city's huge, 19th-century department stores are also part of its cultural heritage. Life just wouldn't be the same without their back-to-school promotions, their wonderful Christmas window displays, their spring weddings lists or their

Where to shop

Le Bon Marché Rive Gauche (1)

22 rue de Sèvres, 75007 ☎ 01 44 39 80 00 ➠ 01 44 39 80 50

Sèvres-Babylone *Mon.–Sat. 9.30am–7pm* ***La Grande Épicerie*** *Mon.–Sat. 8.30am–9pm* *Duty free for export, Reception desk*

Le Bon Marché offers its customers an international food hall, an antiques gallery and a reading area with easy chairs. The atmosphere is intimate and the emphasis is on old-fashioned personal service: on the ground floor, devoted to menswear and accessories, you will find expert advice, a free alteration service and a rest area with fax and telephone.

La Samaritaine (2)

19 rue de la Monnaie, 75001 ☎ 01 40 41 20 20 ➠ 01 40 41 28 28

Pont-Neuf *Mon.–Wed., Fri.–Sat. 9.30am–7pm; Thur. 9.30am–10pm* *Le Toupary* ➡ *48*

A store with a popular appeal and a long-standing reputation for its particularly good DIY department. In 1996, it opted for a more stylish image when it opened its Grande Parfumerie, offering 40,000 leading beauty products, including perfumes and cosmetics, and giving over space to in-house beauty parlors by some of the top names. La Samaritaine's restaurant, Le Toupary, has a superb panoramic view of the city.

Les Galeries Lafayette (3)

40 boulevard Haussmann, 75009 ☎ 01 42 82 34 56

Havre-Caumartin, Opéra *Mon.–Wed., Fri.–Sat. 9.30am–7pm; Thur. 9.30am–9pm* *Duty-free for export, Customer service desk*

Les Galeries Lafayette offer a truly amazing range of services: easy shopping, while-you-wait heel bar, made-to-measure suits, hairdressing salons, travel agencies, booking agencies, as well as seven restaurants and a sushi bar. There are also regular in-store events such as fashion shows and concerts. On the home front: an entire floor is given over to home decoration, with an area specially reserved for exclusive ideas by leading interior designers.

Le Printemps (4)

64 boulevard Haussmann, 75009 ☎ 01 42 82 50 00 ➠ 01 42 82 45 62

Chaussée-d'Antin, Opéra *Mon.–Wed., Fri.–Sat. 9.35am–7pm; Thur. 9.35am–10pm* *Duty-free for export, Priority desk* *Brasserie Flo*

This 19th-century listed building is worth a visit in its own right. 9500 sq. yards are devoted to women's fashion and another 18,000 sq. yards to accessories. Simplified decor enables customers to identify with themes and lifestyles without being distracted by the surroundings. In the basement a new space of 3000 sq. yards, *L'esprit libre*, is devoted to leisure.

Not forgetting

■ FNAC (Fédération nationale d'achat des cadres) (5)
26 avenue des Ternes, 75017 ☎ 01 44 09 18 00 *Active since 1954. This popular store sells books and records, as well as photographic, hi-fi and computer equipment, in permanent defiance of its rivals.*

big summer sales. Five major stores compete to offer the very best in brand names and labels, special presentations and events, and customer services.

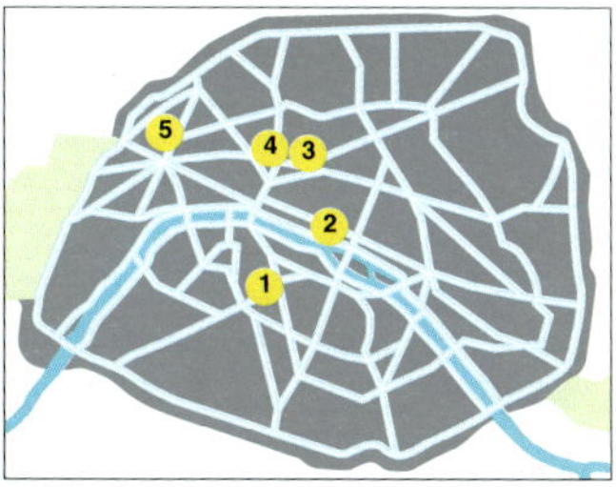

2

I

4

I

2

In the area

Elegant and expensive, the avenue Montaigne is the showcase for every kind of luxury and every kind of extravagance by the city's grand couturiers. All the top names are there. ■ Where to stay ➡ 22 ■ Where to eat ➡ 48 ■ After dark ➡ 92 ➡ 96

Where to shop

Inès de la Fressange (6)

14 avenue Montaigne, 75008 ☎ 01 47 23 08 94 ➡ 01 47 23 05 54

Ⓜ *Alma-Marceau, Franklin-Roosevelt* ***Women's off-the-peg fashion, home decor*** 🕒 *Mon.–Sat. 10am–7pm* ▭ *Duty-free for export, purchases mailed abroad*

A delightful designer boutique belonging to ex-Chanel supermodel Inès de la Fressange. Choose from a range of attractive personal items and decorative objects for the home in natural materials and 'healthy' colors. Take time out to try something on in the padded, boudoir-size cubicles.

Christian Lacroix (7)

26 avenue Montaigne, 75008 ☎ 01 47 20 68 95 ➡ 01 42 20 09 31

Ⓜ *Alma-Marceau, Franklin-Roosevelt* ***Haute couture, women's off-the-peg fashion*** 🕒 *Mon.–Sat. 10am–7pm* ▭ *Duty-free for export, purchases mailed abroad*

While Lacroix's haute couture is the embodiment of beauty and elegance, the boutique's off-the-peg ranges are inspired by the warmth, color and baroque sentimentality of the designer's Provençal origins.

Christian Dior (8)

30 avenue Montaigne, 75008 ☎ 01 40 73 54 44 ➡ 01 40 73 57 95

Ⓜ *Alma-Marceau, Franklin-Roosevelt* ***Haute couture, men's, women's and children's off-the-peg fashion, leather goods, perfume, home decor*** 🕒 *Mon.–Sat. 10am–7pm* ▭ *Duty-free for export*

In this building Christian Dior launched the historic 'new look'. Dior's latest innovation is *Lady Dior*, a shopping bag whose topstitched canework motif is reminiscent of the Louis XV chairs on which customers used to sit when viewing collections. Such is its success that it is available in three sizes, eight different materials and twelve colors.

Céline (9)

36–38 avenue Montaigne, 75008 ☎ 01 49 52 12 02 ➡ 01 49 52 12 21

Ⓜ *Franklin-Roosevelt, Alma-Marceau* ***Off the peg fashion, accessories, shoes*** 🕒 *Mon.–Sat. 10am–7pm* ▭ *Duty-free for export* ◫ *3, ave Victor Hugo 75016 ☎ 01 45 01 80 01; 58 rue de Rennes 75006 ☎ 01 45 48 58 55*

Its unique ambience is immediately apparent in the lobby with its fine leather goods, the perfume and jewelry department and the fashion hall. Each area has been created by designers Ory and Gomez as a dramatic space where fine materials sparkle in the light, creating a contemporary yet serene and seductive shopping environment.

Not forgetting

■ **Joseph (10)** 14 av. Montaigne, 75008 ☎ 01 47 20 39 55 *Women's off-the-peg fashion.*
■ **Vuitton (11)** 54 av. Montaigne, 75008 ☎ 01 45 62 47 00 *Accessories.*
■ **Caron (12)** 34 av. Montaigne, 75008 ☎ 01 47 23 40 82 *Perfume.*
■ **Mugler (13)** 49 av. Montaigne, 75008 ☎ 01 47 23 37 62 *Off-the-peg fashion.*

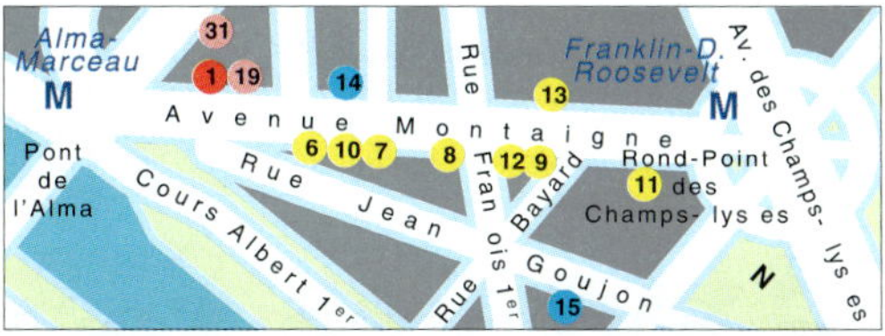
Alma-Marceau
M
Pont de l'Alma
Avenue Montaigne
Rue Jean Goujon
Cours Albert 1er
Rue Fran ois 1er
Rue Bayard
Franklin-D. Roosevelt
M
Rond-Point des Champs- lys es
Av. des Champs- lys es
N
31
1
19
14
13
6
10
7
8
12
9
11
15

CHRISTIAN LACROIX

7

9

13

10

8

11

6

In the area

This is a district of luxury hotels, radio stations, restaurants, theaters and movie theaters. In spite of the presence of the prestigious houses of Courrèges, Balmain and Rochas, the so-called 'golden triangle' is a predominately male preserve. The air is thick with tweed and resounds

Where to shop

Maison de la Vigne et du Vin (14)

21 rue François-Ier, 75008 ☎ 01 47 20 20 76

M *Franklin-Roosevelt* ***Wines and related items*** *Mon.–Thur. 10am–12.30pm, 1.30–6.30pm; Fri. 10am–12.30pm, 1.30–5.30pm*

Everything you always wanted to know about wine. When it opened in 1982, this shop was only an information bureau, but since 1992 it has become a center for the promotion of wines with a sales area attached. All the wine-making regions of France are represented, with of course tasting sessions.

Guerlain (15)

68 avenue des Champs-Élysées, 75008
☎ 01 45 62 52 57 ➠ 01 40 74 09 91

M *Franklin-Roosevelt* ***Perfume*** *Mon.–Sat. 9.45am–7pm; Sun. 3–7pm*
Duty-free for export

In a decor that reflects the early 20th-century luxury of the most beautiful avenue in the world, Guerlain displays its magnificent perfumes (*Shalimar, Habit Rouge, Samsara* and *Héritage*) and eaux de toilette (*Impériale, Eau du coq*) like national treasures. They represent 150 years of perfumed seduction in all its forms: oils, essences, talcs, soaps, pot-pourri and candles.

La Maison du Chocolat (16)

52 rue Francois Ier, 75008 ☎ 01 47 23 38 25 ➠ 01 40 70 01 63

M *Franklin-Roosevelt* ***Confectionery*** *Mon.–Sat. 9.30am–7pm*

A vice becomes a virtue in the 'house of chocolate', where addicts can unashamedly enjoy the delights of creamy hot chocolate made with bitter chocolate, and laced with rum or flavored with spices. The confectionery range includes 30 varieties of dark-chocolate ganache (flavored with jasmine, basil, rosemary, bush peach, cherry plums) and champagne truffles.

Faguais (17)

30 rue de la Trémoille, 75008 ☎ 01 47 20 80 91

M *Alma-Marceau, F-Roosevelt* ***Delicatessen*** *Mon.–Sat. 9.30am–7pm*

French regional specialties feature prominently among the distinctive flavors of this traditional delicatessen. Its range of some 2000 traditionally made products conjures up Proustian images of nougat from Montélimar, dark red plums from Agen and *calissons* (diamond-shaped, almond-flavored sweets) from Aix-en-Provence. House classics include the *mélange Faguais* (a blend of teas from India, China and Sri Lanka), a jam made with three different citrus fruits, and such rareties as its pickled gherkins which have to be ordered in advance!

Not forgetting

■ **Ricci Club Hommes (18)** 17 rue François-Ier, 75008 ☎ 01 49 52 57 39 *Off-the-peg menswear, accessories* ■ **Weston (19)** 114 avenue des Champs-Élysées, 75008 ☎ 01 45 62 26 47 *Men's and women's footwear* ■ **Cartier (20)** 51 rue François-Ier, 75008 ☎ 01 53 93 95 50 *Jewelry, perfume, leather goods.*

to the trilling of mobile phones. ■ Where to stay ➥ 22 ■ Where to eat ➥ 66 ➥ 74 ■ After dark ➥ 86 ➥ 96.

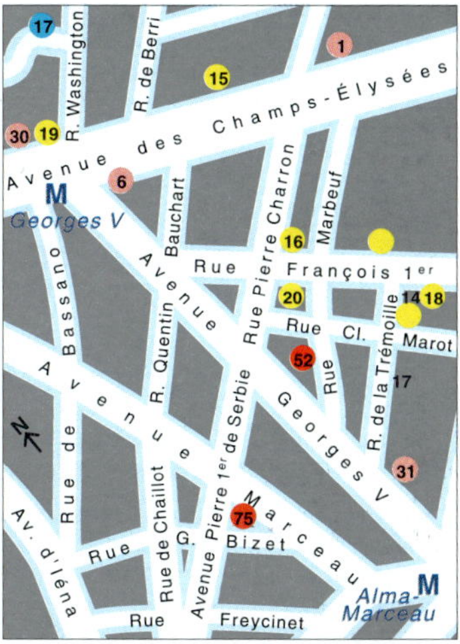

18

17

16

19

7

20

15

In the area

Faubourg Saint-Honoré, bounded by the Palais de l'Élysée, rue Royale and place de la Concorde, has a number of stylish 'historic monuments'. The world-famous and truly unique studio-fashion houses of Hermès, Lanvin, Laroche and Au Nain Bleu combine tradition and expertise with a witty,

Where to shop

Hermès (21)

24 rue du Faubourg Saint-Honoré, 75008 ☎ 01 40 17 47 17

M *Concorde* ***Accessories, perfume*** *Mon. 10am-1pm, 2.15-6.30pm; Tue.–Sat. 10am–6.30pm* *Duty-free for export*

The famous Hermès scarves and animal motif ties still sell like hot cakes. However, the house specialty remains its saddle-stitched leather, made in the Hermès workshops. Other popular items include bags (Bugatti, Kelly) and even shoe-trees and mobile-phone cases.

Au Nain Bleu (22)

406–410 rue Saint-Honoré, 75008 ☎ 01 42 60 39 01 ➠ 01 42 61 75 67

M *Concorde* ***Toys*** *Mon.–Sat. 9.45am–6.30pm* *Duty-free for export, purchases mailed abroad*

The oldest toyshop in Paris remains young at heart and continues to delight young and old alike with its remarkable window displays. From handmade wooden blocks to electric Ferraris, its toys have evolved over the years to keep pace with changing fashions.

Lanvin Hommes (23)

15 rue du Faubourg Saint-Honoré, 75008 ☎ 01 44 71 31 33

M *Concorde* ***Off-the-peg menswear*** *Mon.–Sat 10am–6.45pm* *Café Bleu* ***Lanvin Femme*** *22 rue du Faubourg Saint-Honoré ☎ 01 44 71 31 73*

Jeanne Lanvin has impressed her style on the very walls (decorated by sculptor Albert Rateau) of her fashion houses, where the degree of luxury is directly related to the floor level. From the first-story leisurewear, casuals and accessories, you move up through off-the-peg fashions. By the time you reach the sixth story, made-to-measure suits are made for a clientele who each have a personal dossier of precisely recorded details so that they can place an order from anywhere in the world. Distinctive panamas by Gelot sit alongside more ordinary hats, while the tie collection runs into the hundreds.

Lalique (24)

11 rue Royale, 75008 ☎ 01 53 05 12 12 ➠ 01 42 65 59 06

M *Concorde, Madeleine* ***Home decor*** *Mon. 10am–6.30pm; Tue.–Sat. 9.30am–6.30pm* *Duty-free for export*

Lalique crystal at its dazzling best: classic vases, champagne goblets and flutes. The boutique has been extended to include accessories, from handbags and belts with crystal clasps to colored pendants and Lalique translucent rings.

Not forgetting

■ **Ladurée Royale (25)** 16 rue Royale, 75008 ☎ 01 42 60 21 79 *Patisserie* ■ **Jadis et Gourmande (26)** 27 rue Boissy-d'Anglas, 75008 ☎ 01 42 65 23 23 *Confectionery, chocolates.* ■ **Guy Laroche (27)** 28–30 rue du Fbg Saint-Honoré, 75008 ☎ 01 40 06 01 70 *Haute couture, women's off-the-peg fashion.* ■ **Loft (28)** 12 rue du Fbg St-Honoré, 75008 ☎ 01 42 65 59 65 *Men's and women's off-the-peg fashion.*

modern elegance. ■ Where to stay ➥ 22 ■ Where to eat ➥ 62 ➥ 66

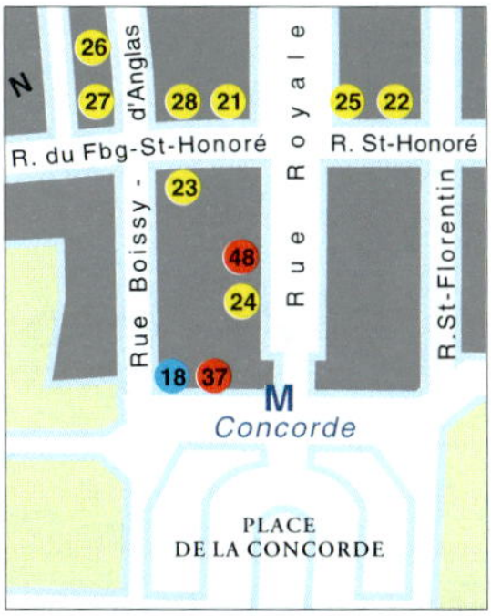

23

27

21

21

26

24

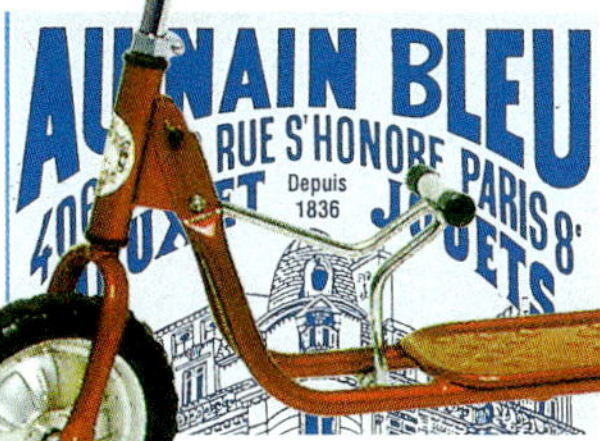

Scooters (from F435) are among the many traditional toys offered by Au Nain Bleu.

22

In the area

The district is dominated by the vast 19th-century church of La Madeleine, intended to echo the Parthenon in Athens. Like the church, the district has more presence than actual charm. However, it does have a remarkable vitality, as well as a number of magnificent shops (mostly

Where to shop

Gien (29)

18 rue de l'Arcade, 75008 ☎ 01 42 66 52 32 ➡ 01 42 65 15 77

Madeleine, Havre-Caumartin **Home decor earthenware** *Tue.–Sat. 10am–7pm* *Duty-free for export, purchases mailed abroad*

A huge wall display presents the dozens of different styles of plate blazoned in blue and white for which Gien has been famous for almost 200 years. On the second floor, tables are set with traditional and modern-style dinner services. A collection of teapots decorated with country motifs adds a touch of rural charm.

Paraboot (30)

13 rue Vignon, 75008 ☎ 01 47 42 55 05 ➡ 01 47 42 55 08

Madeleine ***Men's and women's footwear*** *Mon.–Sat. 10am–7pm* *Duty-free for export* *9 rue de Grenelle, 75007 ☎ 01 45 49 24 26*

Paraboot is renowned for its leisure-sports footwear and for ensuring that the Paris sporting set, from hikers to horse riders, is well-shod. The leather is hand cut from traditionally tanned, top-quality skins, while rubber soles ensure flexibility and durability. If you don't hunt, shoot or fish, Paraboot also offers some superb moccasins and lace-ups.

Hédiard (31)

21 place de la Madeleine, 75008 ☎ 01 43 12 88 88 ➡ 01 42 66 31 97

Madeleine ***Delicatessen*** *Mon.–Sat. 9am–11pm* *Purchases mailed abroad* *Mon.–Sat. 9am–11pm*

Hédiard makes ordinary food look like decorative art, with its rows of colored jams, mustards and other preserves. Fruits for all seasons, from all over the world, are arranged in still lifes that would do credit to Giuseppe Arcimboldo (1530–93). Here, lovers of fine foods find that their vice becomes an esthetic pleasure to be indulged unrestrainedly. Hédiard also offers an unlimited choice of wines and champagnes.

Fauchon (32)

26–30 place de la Madeleine, 75008
☎ 01 47 42 96 00 ➡ 01 47 42 83 75

Madeleine ***Delicatessen, wine cellar, bakery, patisserie, confectionery*** *Mon.–Sat. 9.30am–7pm* *Purchases mailed abroad*

Every week you can taste a new wine here and, on Saturday, the producer will reveal the secrets and characteristics of his wine. Founded in 1886 by Auguste Fauchon, this establishment has acquired an international reputation for the quality and variety of its gastronomic products.

Not forgetting

■ **Blanc Bleu (33)** 5 boulevard Malesherbes, 75008 ☎ 01 47 42 02 18 *Sportswear.* ■ **Pierre Frey (34)** 22 rue Royale, 75008 ☎ 01 49 26 04 77 *A range of magnificent furnishing fabrics.*

devoted to home decor and gastronomic pleasures) in a relatively small area. ■ Where to stay ➥ 26
■ Where to eat ➥ 62

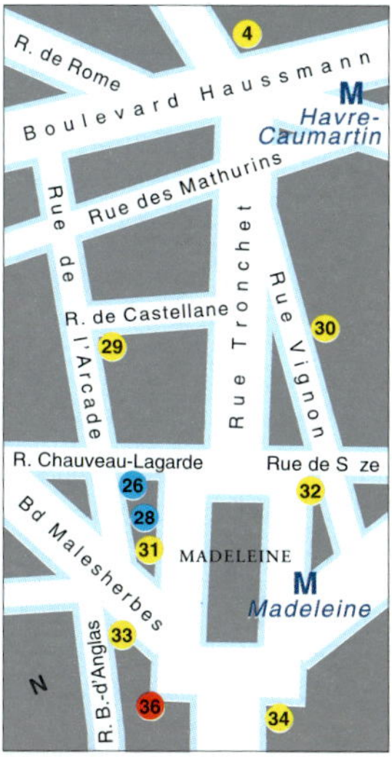

32

30

29

La Madeleine, where exquisite flavors and sophisticated tableware go hand in hand.

1

32

In the area

The most dazzling names in the jewelry world are found in a relatively small but impressive area around the legendary Ritz Hotel ➡ 28. Place Vendôme is an appropriate setting for the some of the world's most beautiful stones. ■ Where to stay ➡ 24 ➡ 28 ➡ 30 ■ Where to

Where to shop

Colette (35)

213 rue Saint-Honoré, 75001 ☎ 0155 35 33 90 ➡ 01 55 35 33 99

M *Tuileries, Pyramides* ***Home décor, off-the-peg fashions, sportswear, groceries, beauty products, bookshop*** 🕒 *Mon.–Sat. 10.30am–7.30pm* ▭ *Duty-free for export, purchases mailed abroad*

A social phenomenon – definitely the in-place to shop. The inspired whims of its creators have filled this emporium with items from around the world – from China tea to the latest young designer fashions. Try the amazing selection of more than 50 different mineral waters at the bar!

Philippe Model (36)

33 place du Marché Saint-Honoré, 75001 ☎ 01 42 96 89 02

M *Tuileries, Opéra* ***Hats, women's footwear, accessories*** 🕒 *Mon. 10am–6pm; Tue.–Fri. 10am–7pm; Sat. noon–7pm* ▭ *Duty-free for export*

The season's creative designs are premiered at the spring race meetings, especially the *Prix de Diane-Hermès* at Chantilly, where the extravagant hats are on show. Designs for everyday wear are up-to-the-minute but more restrained.

Maria Luisa (37)

2–4 rue Cambon, 75001 ☎ 01 47 03 96 15 ➡ 01 47 03 94 17

M *Concorde* ***Women's off-the-peg fashion, footwear, accessories***
🕒 *Mon.–Sat. 10.30am–7pm* ▭ *Duty-free for export*

This young Venezuelan uses personal taste and intuition to choose the very best of the very latest in French fashion design. Ranges include designs by Eric Bergère – elegant, simple and witty.

Meyrowitz (38)

5 rue de Castiglione, 75001 ☎ 01 42 60 63 64 ➡ 01 42 61 36 30

M *Concorde* ***Opticians, optical instruments*** 🕒 *Mon.–Sat. 9.30–6pm*
▭ *Duty-free for export*

Alfonso XIII of Spain, Edward VIII of England and the Aga Khan are just three of the prestigious 'regulars' whose favorite styles are now available in exclusive gold and tortoiseshell designs. In the 1930s Meyrowitz produced the goggles worn by early aviators. Today, it offers a range of binoculars, barometers and prescription spectacles.

Not forgetting

■ **Dinh Van (39)** 16 rue de la Paix, 75002 ☎ 01 42 61 74 49 *Jewelry.*
■ **Poiray (40)** 1 rue de la Paix, 75002 ☎ 01 42 61 70 58 *Jewelry.*
■ **Daum (41)** 4 rue de la Paix, 75002 ☎ 01 42 61 25 25 *Home decor.*
■ **Charvet (42)** 28 place Vendôme, 75001 ☎ 01 42 60 30 70 *Men's and women's made-to measure shirts, off-the-peg women's suits* ■ **Chanel (43)** 31 rue Cambon, 75001 ☎ 01 42 86 28 00 *Haute couture, off-the-peg fashion, perfume, accessories, jewelry and watches.* ■ **Bob Shop (44)** 20 rue Cambon, 75001 ☎ 01 40 15 96 55 *Women's trousers.* ■ **Longchamp (45)** 404 rue Saint-Honoré, 75001 ☎ 01 43 16 00 16 *Accessories.*

eat ➡ 62 ➡ 64 ➡ 74
After dark ➡ 88 ➡ 90
What to see ➡ 104

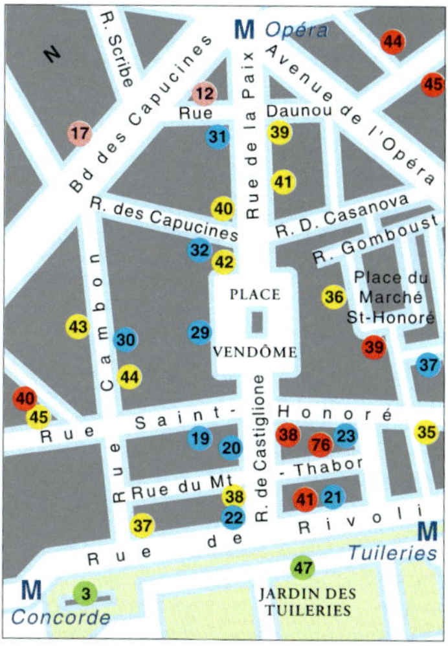

36

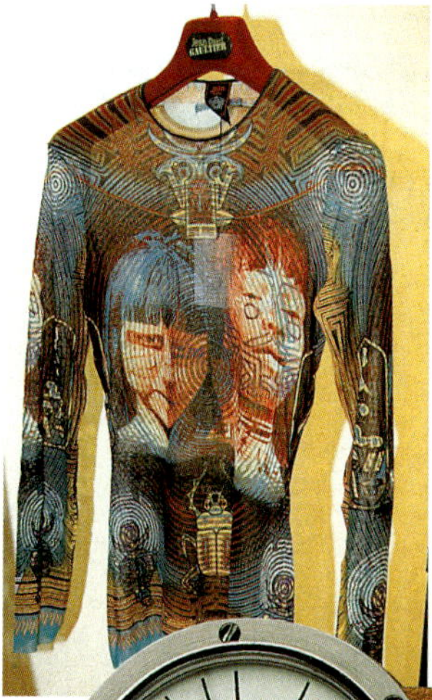
37

39

7

43

43

43

In the area

Until the 17th century, the Palais-Royal was the Paris residence of the kings of France. For a long time after that, it remained the exclusive venue of the capital's most elegant women, and a secret garden visited by writers and children. Today, priceless treasures are concealed beneath its arcades.

Where to shop

Legrand (46)

1 rue de la Banque, 75002 ☎ 01 42 60 07 12 ➠ 01 42 61 25 51

M *Bourse* ***Delicatessen, wine cellar, articles for service of wine*** *Tue.–Fri. 9am–7.30pm; Sat. 8.30am–1pm, 3–7pm* *Purchases mailed abroad* *119 rue de Dessous-des-Berges, 75013 ☎ 01 45 83 58 88*

A must for connoisseurs of regional wines, fine alcohols and chocolates. Ranges include the famous *Ébène* (70% cocoa) from Weiss, makers of chocolate in Saint-Étienne since 1882, and all kinds of great and lesser vintages selected by the third generation of the Legrand family. They have also had the good taste to retain the original storage jars and decor of this traditional grocer's store near the Paris Stock Exchange.

Maison de Vacances (47)

63–64 galerie Montpensier, 75001 ☎ 01 47 03 99 74 ➠ 01 47 03 99 24

M *Palais-Royal* ***Home decor*** *Mon. 2–7pm; Tue.–Sat. 11am–7pm* *Duty-free for export, purchases mailed abroad*

Michèle Fouks bases her 'chamber music' theme on three complementary tones – cream, ecru and celadon – and a perfect contrast of soft and rough textures. Sheets, blankets and pajamas in loosely woven, unbleached linen, cashmere or angora. ★ All items can be individually monogrammed, from the photo album in its linen case to the breakfast set for two in white and gold porcelain, from the table linen to the toweling and lawn bathroom linen.

Les Salons du Palais-Royal Shiseido (48)

142 galerie de Valois, 75001 ☎ 01 49 27 09 09 ➠ 01 49 27 92 12

M *Palais-Royal* ***Perfume, cosmetics*** *Mon.–Sat. 9am–7pm* *Duty-free for export*

A showcase for the perfumes created by Serge Lutens for Shiseido. An experience to delight the senses, from the apothecary's bottles displaying brightly-colored contents – *Iris* (pale mauve), *Fleur d'Oranger* (mandarin), *Myrthe* (bright red), *Ambre* (cognac colored) and *Rose de Nuit* (lemon) – to the veritable symphony of scents. The experience is completed by deliciously fragrant green tea served while your purchases are being expertly and exquisitely gift-wrapped.

Didier Ludot (49)

24 galerie Montpensier, 75001 ☎ 01 42 96 06 56

M *Palais-Royal* ***Antiques, haute couture*** *Mon.–Sat. 10.30am–7pm*

Second-hand clothes, shoes, handbags and luggage by Chanel, Hermès, Balenciaga, Ciurrèges, Balmain, Givenchy, Dior and Vuitton. A collector's boutique that could compete with the fashion museum ➡ 106. A must for devotees of Dior's 'little black dress'.

Not forgetting

■ **Jean-Paul Gaultier (50)** 6 rue Vivienne, 75002 ☎ 01 42 86 05 05
Off-the-peg men's and women's wear as well as the designer's celebrated jeans.

■ Where to eat ➥ 70 ■ After dark ➥ 90 ■ What to see ➥104 ➥ 106

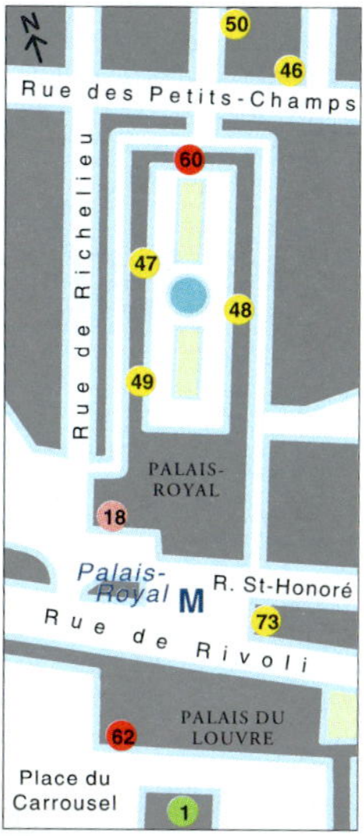

48

48

47

50

In the area

The place des Victoires provides a link between what was once the intellectual center of Paris (Palais-Royal) and the so-called *ventre de Paris* (belly of Paris), Les Halles food market before it was transferred to Rungis. In the wake of such pioneers as Kenzo and Victoire, established

Where to shop

Bonpoint (51)

50 rue Étienne-Marcel, 75002 ☎ 01 40 26 20 90

M *Les Halles, Bourse* ***Children's off-the-peg fashion*** *Mon.–Sat. 10am–7pm* *Duty-free for export* *67 rue de l'Université, 75007 ☎ 01 45 55 63 70*

A paradise for spoiled children, with everything you need to dress them from top to toe in coordinated outfits in a wide range of colors: dream-like dresses for a princess and beautiful gifts for new arrivals. Modern and classic, and always good taste.

Ventilo (52)

27bis rue du Louvre, 75001 ☎ 01 42 33 18 67 ➠ 01 44 76 83 03

M *Les Halles* ***Women's off-the-peg fashion, home décor*** *Mon.–Sat. 10.30am–7.30pm* *Mon.–Sat. 11am–6pm ☎ 01 44 76 82 97* *59, rue Bonaparte 75006 ☎ 01 43 26 64 84*

Three floors of casual and easy-to-wear summer and winter fashions in natural materials and fabrics, presented in a natural wood setting. The home decor department is on the top floor, next to the restaurant-*salon de thé*, a favorite meeting place for the journalists and fashion set of the place des Victoires.

Kenzo (53)

3 place des Victoires, 75001 ☎ 01 40 39 72 03 ➠ 01 40 39 79 40

M Palais-Royal ***Off-the-peg menswear and women's fashion*** *Mon. 11am–7pm; Tue.–Sat. 10am–7pm* *Duty-free for export* *16–17 boulevard Raspail, 75007 ☎ 01 42 22 09 38 / 01 45 49 33 75*

Bright colors, unusual prints and beautiful tailoring by this most Parisian of Japanese fashion boutiques. Sophisticated fashions, dresses in lightweight fabrics and rich brocades for women; dark suits, shirts in every color and extravagant ties for men; ★ and a reasonably priced 'Jungle' range for the younger generation.

Victoire Femme (54)

12 place des Victoires, 75001 ☎ 01 42 61 09 02 ➠ 01 42 33 35 49

M *Palais-Royal* ***Women's off-the-peg fashion*** *Mon.–Sat. 10am–7pm* *Duty-free for export* *1 rue Madame, 75006 ☎ 01 45 44 28 14*

The latest designs and accessories for a clientele that, for the past 20 years, has become accustomed to the best in modern fashion. Next door, a sister boutique offers easy-to-wear fashion at affordable prices.

Not forgetting

■ **Piétrement Lambert et Cie (55)** 58 rue Jean-Jacques-Rousseau, 75001 ☎ 01 42 33 30 50 *Pâté de foie gras, game, capons, truffles.* ■ **Claudie Pierlot (56)** 1 rue Montmartre, 75001 ☎ 01 42 21 38 38 *Women's off-the-peg fashion.* ■ **Agnès B. (57)** 2, 3, 6, 10, rue du Jour, 75001 ☎ 01 45 08 56 56 *Off-the-peg fashion for men, women and children, cosmetics, accessories.*

in the 1970s, other designers moved into and gradually transformed the district.

■ Where to eat ➥ 70

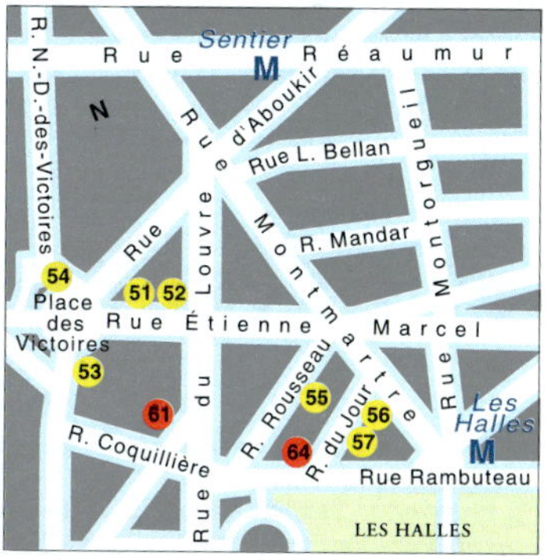

54

51

53

52

54

51

51

In the area

For a long time, Saint-Germain-des-Prés was a village combining provincial charm with intellectual sophistication. Today, fashion boutiques have replaced the old bookstores and shops selling objets d'art.

■ Where to stay ➡ 38 ➡ 40 ➡ 42 ■ Where to eat ➡ 78

Where to shop

Deyrolle (58)

46 rue du Bac, 75007 ☎ 01 42 22 30 07

Ⓜ *Rue-du-Bac* ***Stuffed animals, natural science supplies, educational posters*** 🕒 *Mon.–Sat. 10am–6.45pm* ▭

Established in 1831, Deyrolle is more like the Natural History Museum ➡ 120 than a shop that sells stuffed animals. An avid clientele of interior designers. One of the most extraordinary shops in Europe – well worth a look.

Debauve & Gallais (59)

30 rue des Saint-Pères, 75007 ☎ 01 45 48 54 67 ➠ 01 45 48 21 78

Ⓜ *Saint-Germain-des-Prés* ***Chocolates*** 🕒 *Mon.–Sat. 9am–7pm* ▭

In the 18th century, this store supplied royalty with fine chocolate: double-vanilla flavored chocolate for the king and chocolate drops flavored with almond oil for the queen. It acquired a new dimension when a pharmacist extended the range with 'healthy' (sugar-free) chocolate and coffee-flavored chocolate for 'addicts'. Specialties include *Théobroma*, the world's darkest chocolate (99% cocoa), and *Grains d'Arabica*, coffee beans in dark chocolate.

L'Artisan Parfumeur (60)

24 boulevard Raspail, 75007 ☎ 01 42 22 23 32

Ⓜ *Rue-du-Bac, Sèvres-Babylone* ***Perfume*** 🕒 *Mon.–Sat. 10.30am–7pm* ▭ *Duty-free for export*

'Alternative' perfumes, with variations on a theme (fig, mimosa, leaf), in subtly different blends for your skin or for use in the home. For example, the silk sachets with winter and summer blends to scent your closets and chests.

Arnys (61)

14 rue de Sèvres, 75007 ☎ 01 45 48 76 99 ➠ 01 45 48 84 72

Ⓜ *Sèvres-Babylone* ***Off-the-peg menswear*** 🕒 *Mon. 10am–1pm, 2–7pm; Tue.–Sat. 10am–7.30pm* ▭ *Duty-free for export, purchases mailed abroad*
@ *arnysparis@aol.com*

The quintessence of Rive-Gauche fashion encapsulated in a range of traditional styles 'revisited': from the corded-velvet lumber jacket with its colored wool lining to the high-waisted trousers with suspenders (as worn by the Duke of Windsor) that conceal the stomach. Each new suit is made to measure before being brought out in an off-the-peg version. Shirts have 26 different styles of collar and 7 different styles of cuff.

Not forgetting

■ **Corinne Zaquine (62)** 38 rue de Grenelle, 75007 ☎ 01 45 48 93 03 *Women's hats, formal suits.* ■ **Rodika Zanian (63)** 8 rue de la Chaise, 75007 ☎ 01 45 49 25 73 *Women's off-the-peg fashion.* ■ **Martine Sitbon (64)** 13 rue de Grenelle, 75007 ☎ 01 44 39 84 44 *Women's off-the-peg fashion.* ■ **C.F.O.C. (65)** 163 boulevard Saint-Germain, 75006 ☎ 01 45 48 00 18 *Asian textiles.*

After dark ➥ 86 ➥ 88
➥ 98 What to see ➥ 116

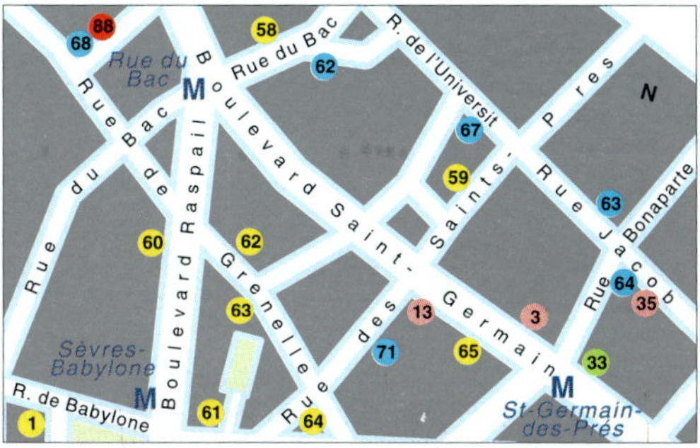

61

64

58

59

58

60

62

64

In the area

Place Saint-Sulpice is only a stone's throw from the busy district of Saint-Germain-des-Prés. For a long time it was a peaceful oasis, bounded by the church and fountain of Saint-Sulpice, near the Jardin du Luxembourg ➡ 122. The 1980s saw the arrival of the first of the boutiques that today

Where to shop

Erès (66)

4bis rue du Cherche-Midi, 75006 ☎ 01 45 44 95 54 ➡ 01 42 22 34 83

Saint-Sulpice ***Women's swimwear, lingerie*** *Mon.–Sat. 10am–7pm* *Duty-free for export*

Unrivaled for its beautiful swimwear. Every season sees around 100 new designs by Irène Leroux. Since 1965, she has continued to find new materials and colors while maintaining the athletic yet sophisticated elegance for which the label is renowned.

Poilâne (67)

8 rue du Cherche-Midi, 75006 ☎ 01 45 48 42 59 ➡ 01 45 44 99 80

Sèvres-Babylone, Saint-Sulpice ***Bread, Viennese bread and patisserie*** *Mon.–Sat. 7.15am–8.15pm*

The pictures hanging on the walls and a unique library trace Poilâne's history through three generations of bread-making. Today, Lionel Poilâne perpetuates the art of traditional bread-making, leaving his dough to rise in wicker baskets lined with linen. The shop is always full and, at certain times of the day, customers queue for brioches and apple tarts.

Delage (68)

6 rue Mézières, 75006 ☎ 01 42 84 15 24 ➡ 01 42 84 15 26

Saint-Sulpice ***Women's footwear*** *Mon., Sat. 10am–1pm, 2–6.45pm; Tue.–Fri. 10am–6.45pm* *Duty-free for export, purchases mailed abroad*

Sheer luxury in the form of simply designed, leather footwear weighing only a few ounces and available in a wide range of unusual colors. Made from wild animal skins: crocodile (30 shades), ostrich, shagreen, lizard (60 shades) and sharkskin for court shoes, moccasins and boots of varying widths, styles and heel-heights. Routine repairs are carried out using the original last in the boutique's own workshops.

A.P.C. (69)

3–4 rue de Fleurus, 75006 ☎ 01 42 22 12 77 ➡ 01 45 49 19 15

Saint-Placide ***Off-the-peg menswear and women's fashion*** *Mon.–Sat. 10.30am–7pm* *Duty-free for export* ***Surplus*** *32 rue Cassette, 75006 ☎ 01 45 48 43 71;* ***General store*** *(accessories, jeans) 45 rue Madame, 75006 ☎ 01 45 48 72 42*

In less than ten years, this label has achieved worldwide acclaim. Its success lies in its exclusive range of materials and colors, traditional expertise and the 'revolutionary normality' of a basic and extremely versatile wardrobe. Off-the-peg menswear and women's fashion have been extended by a range of accessories from two new nearby boutiques.

Not forgetting

■ **Robert Clergerie (70)** 5 rue du Cherche-Midi, 75006 ☎ 01 45 48 75 47 *A must for women's footwear: elegant, fashionable and comfortable.*

crowd the area, devoted to fashion and interiors. ■ Where to stay ➥ 42 ■ Where to eat ➥ 78 ➥ 82 ■ What to see ➥ 122 ■ What to buy ➥ 140

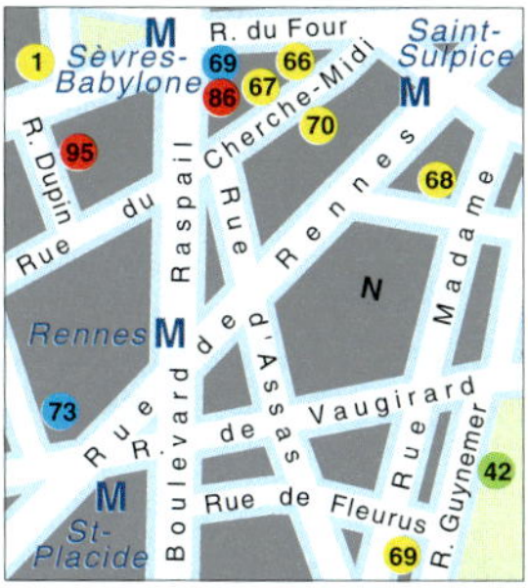

66

67

67

68

68

Basic facts

Apart from its sale rooms, Paris is full of art galleries, antiques galleries, second-hand stores, flea markets ➥ 162 and world famous craftsmen. They tend to be grouped in streets or blocks, forming 'little villages'. Parisians like nothing better than to go there to stroll or to look for

Where to shop

Le Village Suisse (71)
78 avenue de Suffren, 75015

M *La Motte-Picquet-Grenelle* **Second-hand shops** 🕒 *Thu.–Mon. 10.30am–7pm*

There is nothing remotely Swiss about this friendly 'village' near the Eiffel Tower, where local families take their Sunday stroll. Dozens of tiny shops offer an eclectic range of good-quality merchandise, from traditional English-style items, rustic furniture, and curios from Africa to light fittings and ornaments.

Carré Rive Gauche (72)
Rues des Saints-Pères, du Bac, de l'Université and quai Voltaire, 75007

M *Rue-du-Bac* P ***Antiques, art galleries*** 🕒 *Mon.–Sat. 10am–6pm*

A host of art galleries and antiques shops have turned one of the oldest and quietest districts in Paris into a vast and fascinating showcase – furniture, paintings, porcelain and valuable carpets – that combines past and present. ★ In May, the Carré holds a five-day event known as the 'Objet Extraordinaire' (unusual object). During this period, every window becomes a curiosity shop, and the district a regular Aladdin's cave as it turns the spotlight on its most extravagant and unusual pieces.

72

73

74

collectors' items, or both. As well as reflecting past and present cultures, these 'villages' are also excellent indicators of fashion.

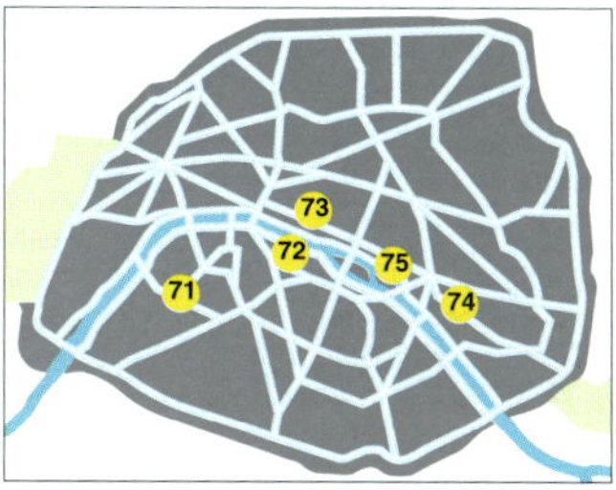

Le Louvre des Antiquaires (73)

2 place du Palais-Royal, 75001
☎ 01 42 97 27 00

M *Palais-Royal* P ***Antiques*** *Sep.–June: Tue.–Sun. 11am–7pm / July–Aug.: Tue.–Sat. 11am–7pm* *Expert advice by appointment*

The Louvre des Antiquaires is a vast three-story gallery that stands almost next door to the Louvre Museum ➡ 104. It houses some 250 top antique shops selling jewelry, paintings, tapestries and porcelain. Although this indoor gallery is warm and cozy in winter, the open-air markets are much more fun in summer.

Le Viaduc des Arts (74)

9–129 avenue Daumesnil, 75012

M *Gare-de-Lyon, Bastille* ***Traditional crafts*** *daily 9am–7pm (variable depending on craft workers)*

A disused railway viaduct has been converted into an impressive series of traditional craft workshops and galleries that stretch for a mile. Its arches house stonecutters, cabinet-makers, glass artists, embroiderers, feather dealers, calligraphers, costumiers, stringed-instrument makers, confectioners, artists and photographers, as well as restaurants and bistros. Along the top of the old viaduct, the tree-lined avenue of the 'Coulée verte' stretches from the Bastille to Reuilly.

Not forgetting

■ **Village Saint-Paul (75)** rues Saint-Paul and Charlemagne, 75004 *Antiques* *Thu.–Mon. 11am–7pm*

73

72

73

Basic facts

The many second-hand shops and stalls of Saint-Ouen (76), the noisy flea markets (*marchés aux puces*) of Montreuil (77) and the charming pavement 'stalls' of Vanves (78) are full of idle onlookers, dedicated sightseers and buyers looking for bargains.

Where to shop

Puces de Saint-Ouen

Porte-de-Clignancourt
Sat.–Mon. 7.30am–7pm
This world famous market is the oldest and largest of the Paris flea markets. It was established in the 19th century and today covers 8.6 acres, with 9 miles of aisles, 2,000 stalls and 150,000 visitors per week. The Saint-Ouen (or more precisely Clignancourt) flea market in fact consists of ten or so smaller markets, each defined by the quality, price and style of its merchandise.

Marché Vernaison
Sat.–Mon.
01 40 12 10 14
Furniture and knick-knacks. The oldest and most charming of the Saint-Ouen flea markets. It was named after Romain Vernaison who used to rent his land to rag-and-bone merchants so they could sell china vases at the foot of the city's fortifications, where traders were exempt from the city toll. By 1920, the land was occupied by second-hand dealers. Édith Piaf made her debut at Chez Louisette, the bistro at aisle 10.

Marché Biron
Antiques and other items of value. Beautiful and well-restored, but expensive furniture.

Marché Malik
This is the 'in' place for hard-up trendies. Enter via rue Jules Vallès whose stalls are piled high with second-hand clothes, kitchen utensils and records.

Marché Malassis
A fine selection of antiques and furniture in a modern building.

Marché Dauphine
Contemporary art and old furniture displayed over two stories.

Marché Serpette
Stallholders here undertake to sell only old items. Goods on sale include quality leather armchairs, old-fashioned knick-knacks and beautiful wood furniture.

Marché Paul-Bert
Second-hand goods, pewter, bronze statues, porcelain, Chinese ornaments, ironware and other items that seem to have come straight out of people's attics: a truly uplifting experience!

Marché Jules-Vallès
Toys, crafts, accessories and rustic furniture.

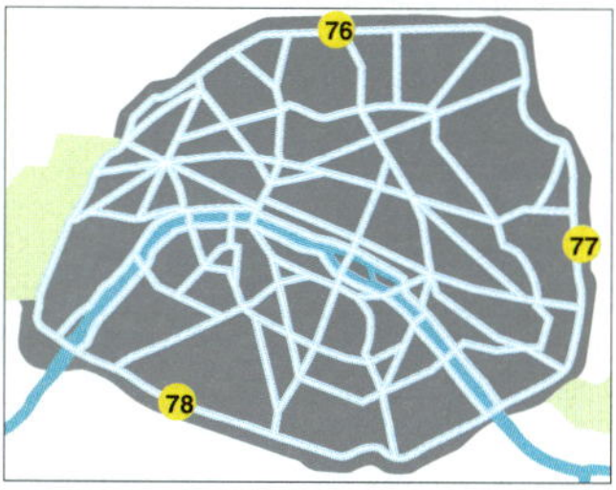

Puces de Montreuil

Porte-de-Montreuil
Sat.–Mon. 7am–7pm

This noisy and popular flea market is situated on the Périphérique (Paris ring road). Although not the place to go if you want to enjoy a quiet stroll, it is the most amazing of the Paris flea markets. You have to fight your way past rolls of fabrics at F10 per meter (yard), piles of bicycles for under F900 each, batteries for every kind of vehicle, charming knick-knacks that once belonged to a set, piles of second-hand clothes…

Puces de Vanves

Porte-de-Vanves (avenue Georges-Lafenestre)
Sat.–Sun. 7am–7.30pm

Smaller than Saint-Ouen and more civilized than Montreuil. The merchandise is laid at your feet… on the pavement. The antiques are neat and tidy, the knick-knacks charming and the wood furniture (although not always period) reasonable. It is advisable to get there early, as this is a small market and the bargains don't last long. For second-hand clothes and kitchen utensils, rue Marc Sangnier is a real bargain basement.

A word or two of advice…

- Travel to the markets by subway. It is impossible to park near the markets and incorrectly parked cars are soon towed away by the police.
- Don't be put off buying larger items of furniture. Stallholders will deliver within the Paris area when the market closes.
- Get there early so as not to miss the best bargains. Alternatively, it can sometimes be easier to negotiate a price at closing time.
- Bear in mind that stallholders do not willingly discuss business at lunchtime!
- Bargain by all means, but not indiscriminately. It is better to find a fault that enables you to reasonably offer a lower price rather than automatically asking for a 50% reduction.
- Make sure you take cash with you. It is easier to strike a bargain with cash, and there are always long queues at the cash machines.
- The Saint-Ouen and Montreuil flea markets are open on Mondays (only a few stalls are closed). It is easier to strike a deal on a Monday when the markets are less crowded and stallholders are more readily available.

You are here...
At bus stops and in metro stations, signs and maps enable you to find out exactly where you are.

Finding your way

Arrondissements
Paris has 20 *arrondissements* (districts), numbered in a spiral from the center (Ile de la Cité) outward. They correspond to the capital's historic boundaries.

10 Maps

Rive Droite and Rive Gauche
The River Seine divides Paris both geographically and culturally. The Rive Droite (Right Bank) is linked with business and commerce, while the Rive Gauche (Left Bank) is synonymous with culture. This division dates from the 12th century and reached its height in the 1930s, when Saint-Germain-des-Prés claimed to be the intellectual center of the world. Today the terms Rive Droite and Rive Gauche are still more closely associated with a particular lifestyle than a geographical location.

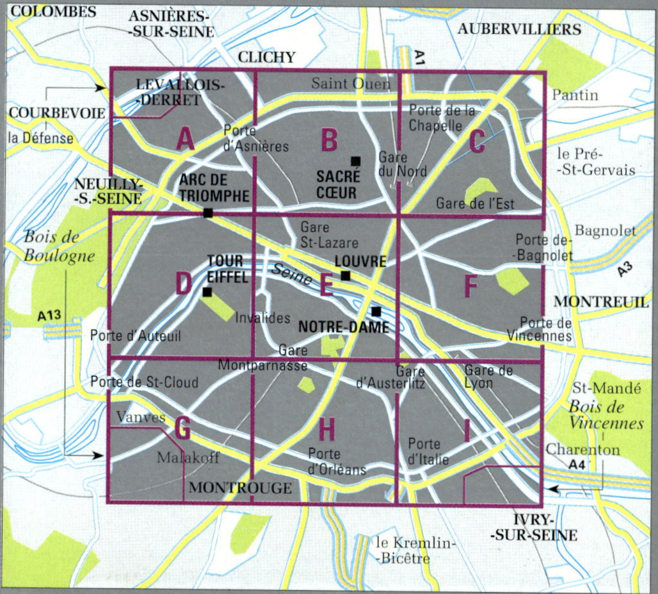

Street index

Each street name is followed by a bold letter indicating which map to refer to, and a grid reference.

Index

Abbreviations

Av. = avenue
bd = boulevard
m. = métro
pl. = place
pte = porte
r. = rue
sq. = square

Métro map

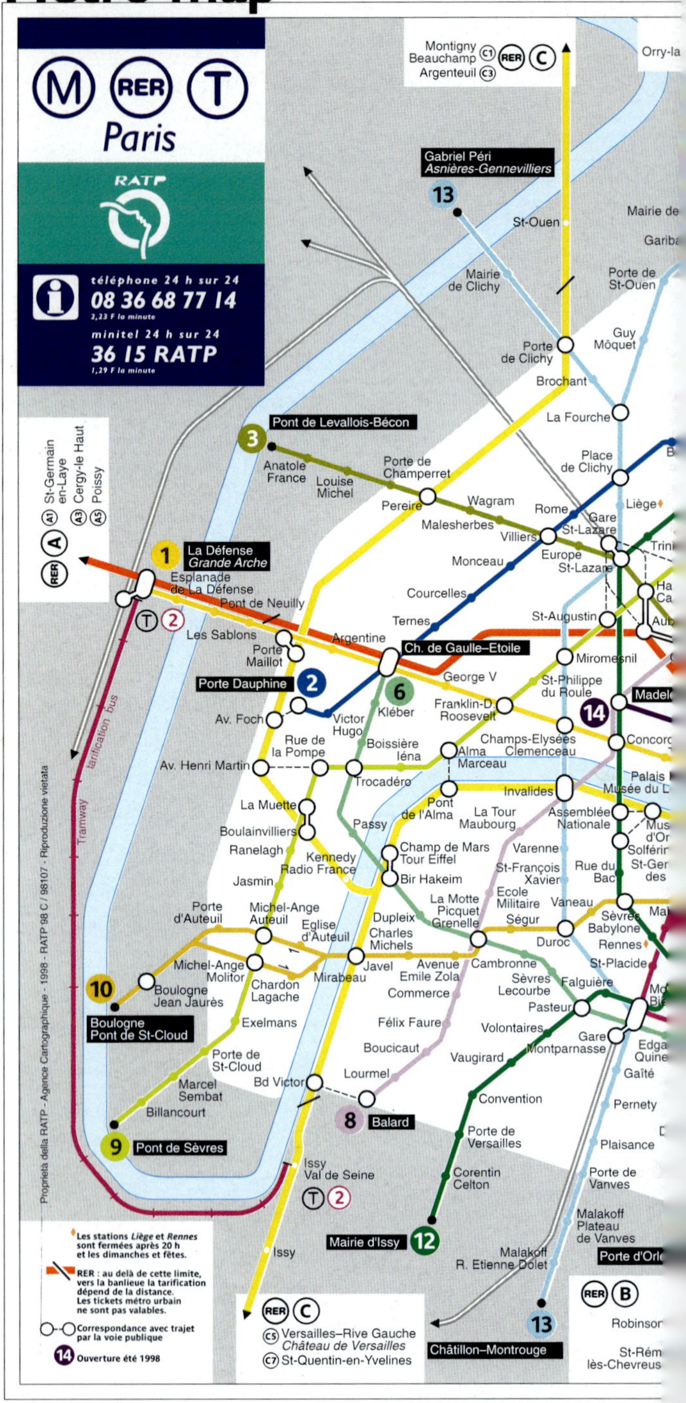

M RER T
Paris
RATP
téléphone 24 h sur 24
08 36 68 77 14
2,23 F la minute
minitel 24 h sur 24
36 15 RATP
1,29 F la minute
Montigny Beauchamp C1
Argenteuil C3
RER C
Gabriel Péri
Asnières-Gennevilliers
13
St-Ouen
Mairie de Clichy
Porte de St-Ouen
Guy Môquet
Porte de Clichy
Brochant
La Fourche
Pont de Levallois-Bécon
3
Anatole France
Louise Michel
Porte de Champerret
Pereire
Wagram
Malesherbes
Villiers
Rome
Place de Clichy
Liège
Gare St-Lazare
Europe
St-Lazare
Monceau
Courcelles
Ternes
St-Augustin
RER A
A1 St-Germain en-Laye
A3 Cergy-le Haut
A5 Poissy
1
La Défense
Grande Arche
Esplanade de La Défense
Pont de Neuilly
T 2
Les Sablons
Porte Maillot
Argentine
Ch. de Gaulle–Etoile
Miromesnil
George V
St-Philippe du Roule
Porte Dauphine
2
6
Kléber
Franklin-D. Roosevelt
14
Av. Foch
Victor Hugo
Rue de la Pompe
Boissière
Iéna
Champs-Elysées Clemenceau
Concorde
Alma Marceau
Av. Henri Martin
Trocadéro
Invalides
Pont de l'Alma
La Muette
La Tour Maubourg
Assemblée Nationale
Boulainvilliers
Passy
Ranelagh
Kennedy Radio France
Champ de Mars Tour Eiffel
Varenne
Bir Hakeim
St-François Xavier
Rue du Bac
Jasmin
La Motte Picquet Grenelle
Ecole Militaire
Vaneau
Porte d'Auteuil
Michel-Ange Auteuil
Eglise d'Auteuil
Dupleix
Ségur
Sèvres Babylone
Charles Michels
Duroc
Rennes
Michel-Ange Molitor
Javel
Avenue Emile Zola
Cambronne
St-Placide
Chardon Lagache
Mirabeau
Sèvres Lecourbe
Falguière
10
Boulogne Jean Jaurès
Commerce
Pasteur
Boulogne
Pont de St-Cloud
Exelmans
Félix Faure
Volontaires
Gare Montparnasse
Tarification bus
Tramway
Porte de St-Cloud
Boucicaut
Vaugirard
Gaîté
Marcel Sembat
Bd Victor
Lourmel
Billancourt
Convention
Pernety
8
Balard
9
Pont de Sèvres
Porte de Versailles
Plaisance
Issy Val de Seine
T 2
Corentin Celton
Porte de Vanves
Malakoff Plateau de Vanves
Issy
Mairie d'Issy
12
Malakoff R. Etienne Dolet
RER B
RER C
C5 Versailles–Rive Gauche
Château de Versailles
C7 St-Quentin-en-Yvelines
13
Châtillon–Montrouge
Les stations Liège et Rennes sont fermées après 20 h et les dimanches et fêtes.
RER : au delà de cette limite, vers la banlieue la tarification dépend de la distance. Les tickets métro urbain ne sont pas valables.
Correspondance avec trajet par la voie publique
14 Ouverture été 1998
Proprietà della RATP - Agence Cartographique - 1998 - RATP 98 C / 98107 - Riproduzione vietata

13 St-Denis–Université
RER B (B3) Aéroport Ch. de Gaulle CDG
(B5) Mitry–Claye
Basilique de St-Denis
St-Denis Porte de Paris
Tramway tarification bus
7 La Courneuve–8 Mai 1945
La Courneuve Aubervilliers
La Plaine Stade de France
Fort d'Aubervilliers
Bobigny–Pablo Picasso
T 1
5
Aubervilliers–Pantin 4 Chemins
4
12 Porte de La Chapelle
Porte de La Villette
Bobigny–Pantin R. Queneau
Simplon
Jules Joffrin
Marx Dormoy
Corentin Cariou
Eglise de Pantin
Marcadet Poissonniers
Crimée
Hoche
Château Rouge
La Chapelle
Riquet
Porte de Pantin
Ourcq
Barbès
Gare du Nord
Stalingrad
Laumière
Jaurès
Danube
7bis Pré-St-Gervais
Lorette
Poissonnière
7bis
Bolivar
Botzaris
Louis Blanc
Buttes Chaumont
Télégraphe
3bis Porte des Lilas
Gare de l'Est
Château Landon
Colonel Fabien
Jourdain
Place des Fêtes
11 Mairie des Lilas
Rue Montmartre
Château d'Eau
Pyrénées
Jacques Bonsergent
Belleville
St-Fargeau
Bonne Nouvelle
Goncourt
Pelleport
Gallieni
Strasbourg St-Denis
Couronnes
Porte de Bagnolet
3
République
Ménilmontant
Temple
Parmentier
Arts et Métiers
Réaumur Sébastopol
St-Maur
3bis Gambetta
Mairie de Montreuil
Filles du Calvaire
Etienne Marcel
Oberkampf
Père Lachaise
Croix de Chavaux
9
Les Halles
Rambuteau
St-Ambroise
Philippe Auguste
St-Sébastien Froissart
Châtelet Les Halles
Voltaire
Richard Lenoir
Alexandre Dumas
Robespierre
Chemin Vert
Charonne
Porte de Montreuil
Hôtel de Ville
Bréguet Sabin
Boulets Montreuil
St-Paul
Avron
Maraîchers
11
Pont Marie
Ledru Rollin
2
Buzenval
Bastille
Sully Morland
Nation
RER A (A2) Boissy-St-Léger (A4) Marne-la-Vallée Parc Disneyland
St-Michel Notre-Dame
Faidherbe Chaligny
Porte de Vincennes
Maubert Mutualité
Reuilly-Diderot
6
Picpus
St-Mandé Tourelle
Quai de la Rapée
Montgallet
Cardinal Lemoine
Gare de Lyon
Bel Air
Bérault
1
Jussieu
Daumesnil
10
Gare d'Austerlitz
Place Monge
Michel Bizot
Château de Vincennes
Bercy
Dugommier
Censier Daubenton
St-Marcel
Porte Dorée
Campo Formio
Quai de la Gare
Porte de Charenton
Cour St-Emilion
Les Gobelins
Chevaleret
Liberté
Bd Masséna
14 Bibliothèque
Charenton-Ecoles
Corvisart
Ecole vétérinaire de Maisons Alfort
Nationale
Maisons-Alfort Stade
Place d'Italie 5
Porte d'Ivry
Tolbiac
Ivry sur-Seine
Pierre Curie
Maisons-Alfort Les Juilliottes
Maison Blanche
Porte de Choisy
Créteil-L'Echat
Maisons-Alfort Alfortville
Créteil Université
Le Kremlin-Bicêtre
Porte d'Italie
7
Villejuif Léo Lagrange
Mairie d'Ivry
Créteil–Préfecture
8
Villejuif P. Vaillant-Couturier
Orly Sud
RER C (C2) Massy-Palaiseau
(C4) Dourdan-la-Forêt
(C6) St-Martin d'Etampes
(C8) Versailles–Chantiers
RER D (D2) Melun
(D4) Malesherbes
7
Villejuif–Louis Aragon

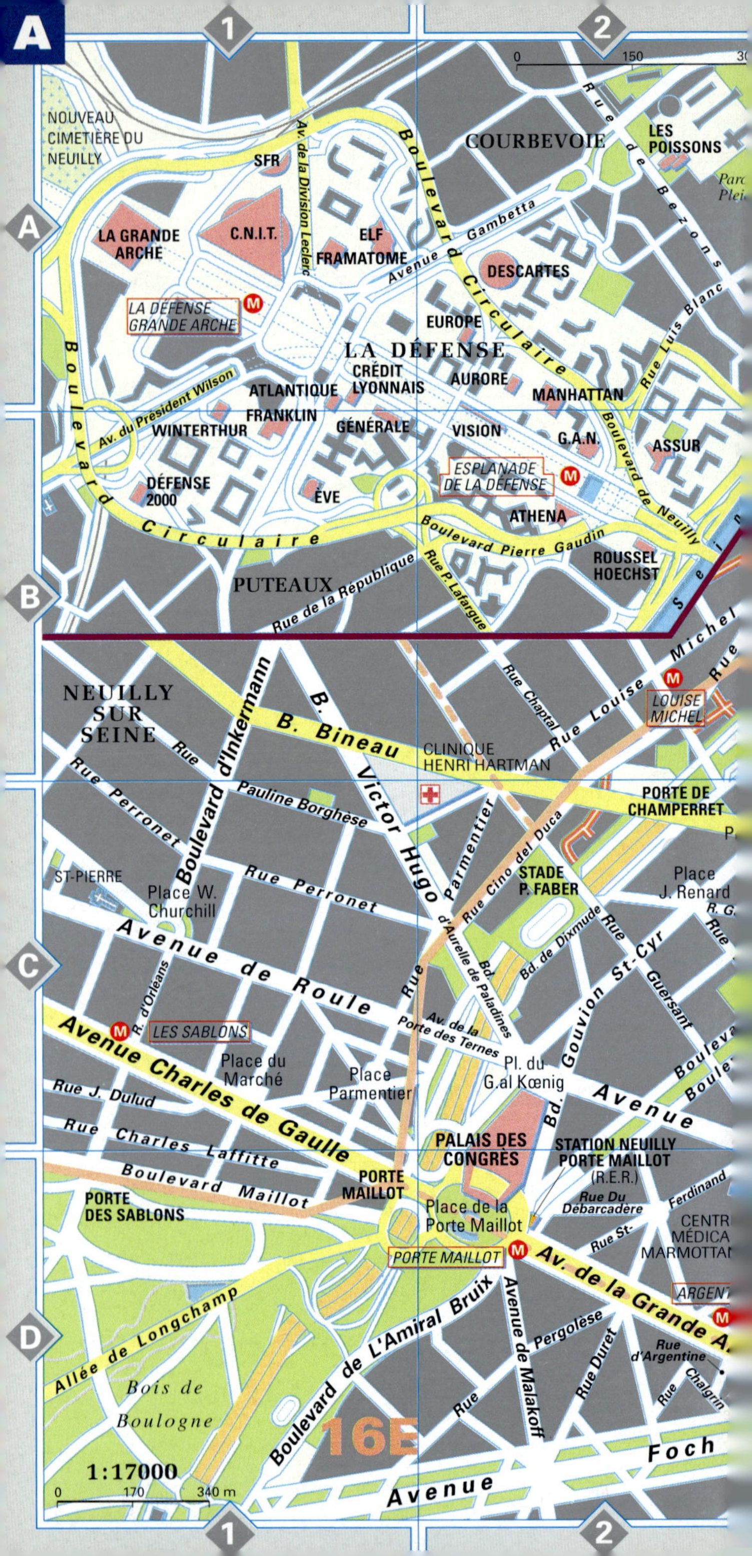
A
1
2
0
150
COURBEVOIE
LES POISSONS
Rue de Bezons
NOUVEAU CIMETIÈRE DU NEUILLY
SFR
Av. de la Division Leclerc
Boulevard Circulaire
LA GRANDE ARCHE
C.N.I.T.
ELF
FRAMATOME
Avenue Gambetta
DESCARTES
Rue Louis Blanc
LA DÉFENSE GRANDE ARCHE
EUROPE
LA DÉFENSE
CRÉDIT LYONNAIS
ATLANTIQUE
AURORE
MANHATTAN
Av. du Président Wilson
FRANKLIN
WINTERTHUR
GÉNÉRALE
VISION
G.A.N.
ASSUR
Boulevard de Neuilly
ESPLANADE DE LA DÉFENSE
DÉFENSE 2000
ÈVE
ATHENA
Boulevard Pierre Gaudin
ROUSSEL HOECHST
PUTEAUX
Rue de la République
Rue P. Lafargue
B
NEUILLY SUR SEINE
Boulevard d'Inkermann
B. Bineau
Rue Chaptal
Rue Louise Michel
LOUISE MICHEL
CLINIQUE HENRI HARTMAN
PORTE DE CHAMPERRET
Rue Perronet
Rue Pauline Borghèse
Victor Hugo
Parmentier
Rue Cino del Duca
STADE P. FABER
Place J. Renard
ST-PIERRE
Place W. Churchill
Rue Perronet
Bd. de Dixmude
C
Avenue de Roule
Rue d'Aurelle de Paladines
Bd. Gouvion St-Cyr
Rue Guersant
R. d'Orleans
LES SABLONS
Av. de la Porte des Ternes
Avenue Charles de Gaulle
Place du Marché
Place Parmentier
Pl. du G.al Kœnig
Avenue
Rue J. Dulud
Rue Charles Laffitte
PALAIS DES CONGRÈS
STATION NEUILLY PORTE MAILLOT (R.E.R.)
Boulevard Maillot
PORTE MAILLOT
PORTE DES SABLONS
Place de la Porte Maillot
Rue Du Débarcadère
Ferdinand
Rue St-
PORTE MAILLOT
Av. de la Grande A.
Boulevard de L'Amiral Bruix
Avenue de Malakoff
D
Allée de Longchamp
Pergolèse
Rue Duret
Rue d'Argentine
Chalgrin
Bois de Boulogne
16E
Rue
Avenue Foch
1:17000
0
170
340 m

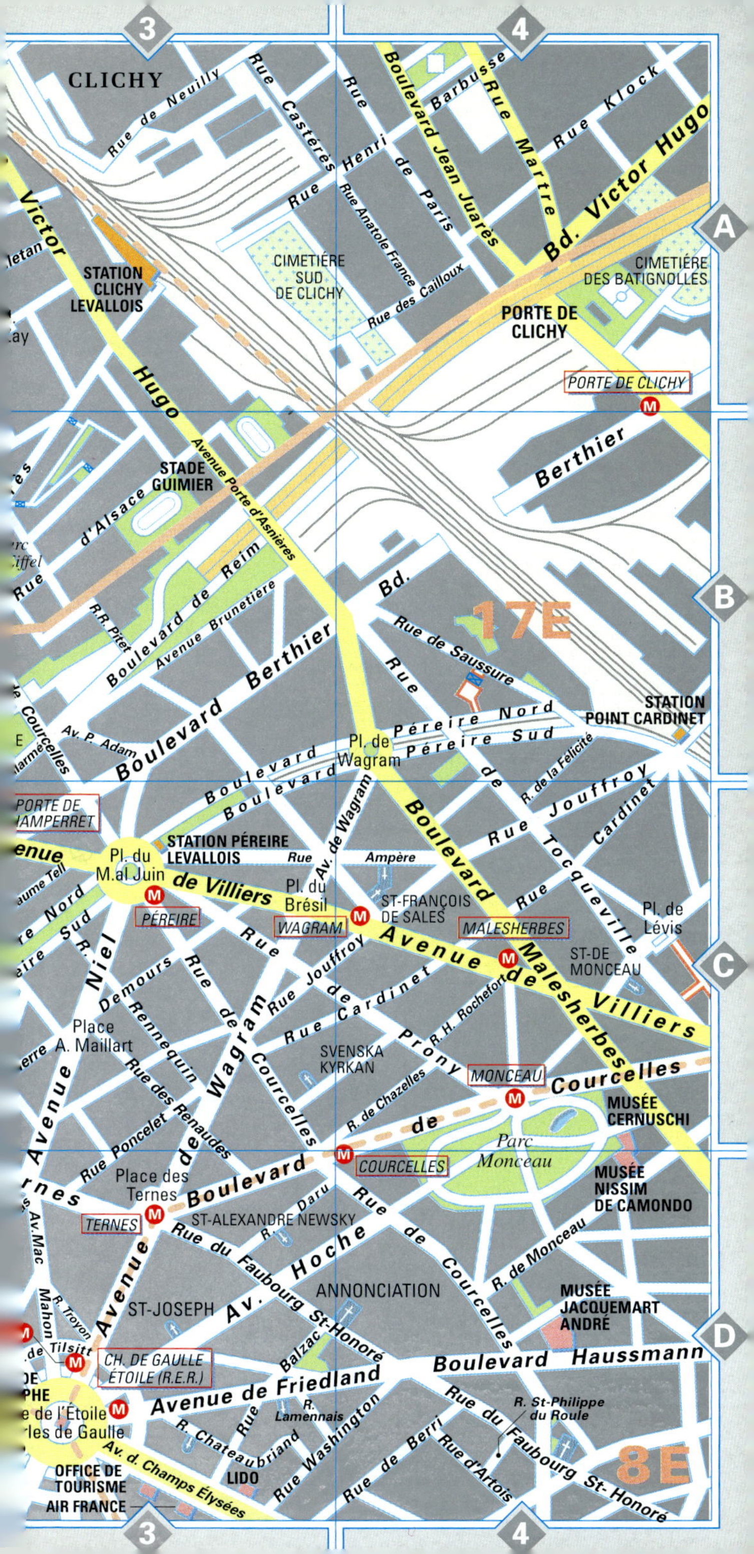
3
4
CLICHY
Rue de Neuilly
Rue Castérès
Rue Henri Barbusse
Boulevard Jean Jaurès
Rue Martre
Rue Klock
Bd. Victor Hugo
Rue Anatole France
Rue de Paris
Victor Hugo
STATION CLICHY LEVALLOIS
CIMETIÉRE SUD DE CLICHY
Rue des Cailloux
CIMETIÉRE DES BATIGNOLLES
PORTE DE CLICHY
PORTE DE CLICHY
A
Berthier
STADE GUIMIER
Avenue Porte d'Asnières
Rue d'Alsace
Boulevard de Reims
R.R. Pitet
Avenue Brunetière
Boulevard Berthier
Bd.
17E
B
Rue de Saussure
STATION POINT CARDINET
Courcelles
Av. P. Adam
Boulevard
Boulevard Péreire Nord
Boulevard Péreire Sud
Pl. de Wagram
R. de la Félicité
Rue Jouffroy
Rue Cardinet
PORTE DE CHAMPERRET
STATION PÉREIRE LEVALLOIS
Pl. du M.al Juin
Avenue de Villiers
Rue Ampère
Av. de Wagram
Boulevard Malesherbes
Rue Tocqueville
Pl. du Brésil
ST-FRANÇOIS DE SALES
PÉREIRE
WAGRAM
MALESHERBES
Pl. de Lévis
ST-DE MONCEAU
C
R. Niel
Rue Demours
Rue Rennequin
Place A. Maillart
Avenue de Wagram
Rue de Courcelles
Rue Jouffroy
Rue de Prony
Rue Cardinet
R. H. Rochefort
SVENSKA KYRKAN
R. de Chazelles
MONCEAU
Courcelles
MUSÉE CERNUSCHI
Rue des Renaudes
Rue Poncelet
Boulevard de Courcelles
COURCELLES
Parc Monceau
MUSÉE NISSIM DE CAMONDO
Place des Ternes
TERNES
Ternes
ST-ALEXANDRE NEWSKY
R. Daru
Rue de Courcelles
Rue du Faubourg St-Honoré
Av. Hoche
Av. Mac Mahon
R. Troyon
Avenue
ST-JOSEPH
ANNONCIATION
R. de Monceau
MUSÉE JACQUEMART ANDRÉ
D
R. de Tilsitt
CH. DE GAULLE ÉTOILE (R.E.R.)
Balzac
Boulevard Haussmann
Avenue de Friedland
R. Lamennais
Rue Washington
R. Chateaubriand
Rue de Berri
Rue d'Artois
R. St-Philippe du Roule
Rue du Faubourg St-Honoré
8E
Place de l'Étoile Charles de Gaulle
Av. d. Champs Élysées
OFFICE DE TOURISME
LIDO
AIR FRANCE

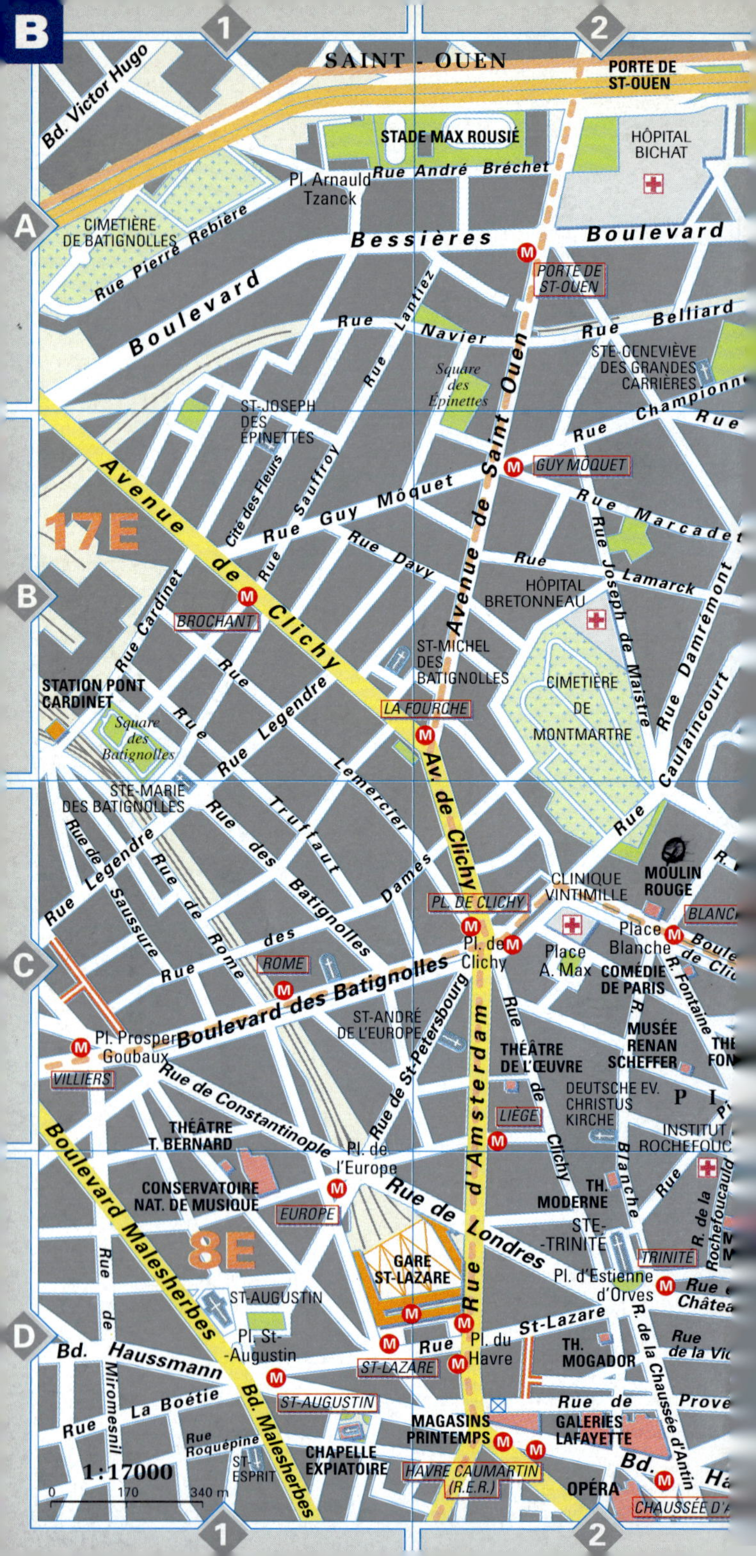

B
1
2
A
B
C
D
SAINT - OUEN
PORTE DE ST-OUEN
Bd. Victor Hugo
STADE MAX ROUSIÉ
HÔPITAL BICHAT
Pl. Arnauld Tzanck
Rue André Bréchet
CIMETIÈRE DE BATIGNOLLES
Rue Pierre Rebière
Boulevard Bessières
PORTE DE ST-OUEN
Boulevard
Rue Lantiez
Rue Navier
Rue Belliard
STE-GENEVIÈVE DES GRANDES CARRIÈRES
Square des Épinettes
Avenue de Saint Ouen
ST-JOSEPH DES ÉPINETTES
Rue Championnet
Rue Sauffroy
GUY MOQUET
Rue Guy Môquet
Rue Marcadet
17E
Cité des Fleurs
Rue Davy
Rue Lamarck
Avenue de Clichy
HÔPITAL BRETONNEAU
Rue Joseph de Maistre
Rue Damrémont
Rue Cardinet
BROCHANT
ST-MICHEL DES BATIGNOLLES
STATION PONT CARDINET
Rue Legendre
CIMETIÈRE DE MONTMARTRE
LA FOURCHE
Square des Batignolles
Rue Caulaincourt
Lemercier
STE-MARIE DES BATIGNOLLES
Av. de Clichy
Rue Truffaut
Rue des Dames
Rue de Saussure
Rue de Rome
Rue des Batignolles
CLINIQUE VINTIMILLE
MOULIN ROUGE
PL. DE CLICHY
BLANCHE
Place Blanche
Pl. de Clichy
Place A. Max
ROME
COMÉDIE DE PARIS
Boulevard des Batignolles
R. Fontaine
ST-ANDRÉ DE L'EUROPE
Rue de St-Petersbourg
MUSÉE RENAN SCHEFFER
Pl. Prosper Goubaux
VILLIERS
THÉÂTRE DE L'ŒUVRE
Rue de Clichy
Rue d'Amsterdam
Rue de Constantinople
DEUTSCHE EV. CHRISTUS KIRCHE
LIÈGE
THÉÂTRE T. BERNARD
Pl. de l'Europe
INSTITUT ROCHEFOUC
Boulevard Malesherbes
CONSERVATOIRE NAT. DE MUSIQUE
Rue de Londres
TH. MODERNE
Rue Blanche
EUROPE
R. de la Rochefoucauld
STE-TRINITÉ
8E
GARE ST-LAZARE
TRINITÉ
Pl. d'Estienne d'Orves
Rue de Miromesnil
ST-AUGUSTIN
Pl. St-Augustin
Rue St-Lazare
Pl. du Havre
TH. MOGADOR
R. de la Chaussée d'Antin
Rue de la Vic
Bd. Haussmann
ST-LAZARE
ST-AUGUSTIN
Rue La Boétie
Bd. Malesherbes
Rue de Provence
MAGASINS PRINTEMPS
GALERIES LAFAYETTE
Rue Roquépine
ST-ESPRIT
CHAPELLE EXPIATOIRE
HAVRE CAUMARTIN (R.E.R.)
Bd.
OPÉRA
CHAUSSÉE D'A
1:17000
0
170
340 m

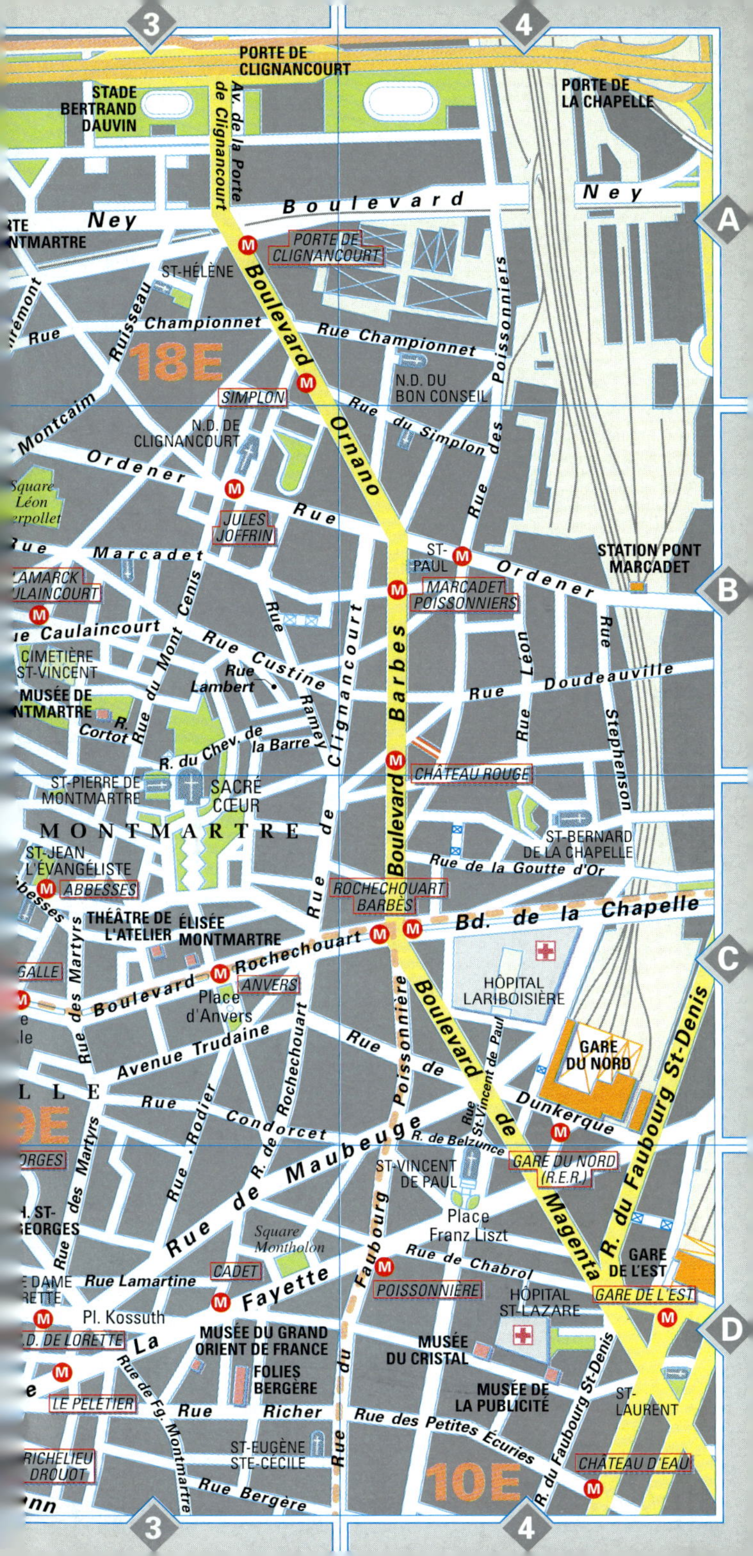

3
4
PORTE DE CLIGNANCOURT
STADE BERTRAND DAUVIN
Av. de la Porte de Clignancourt
PORTE DE LA CHAPELLE
Boulevard
Ney
Ney
A
PORTE DE CLIGNANCOURT
ST-HÉLÈNE
Boulevard
Ornano
Championnet
Rue Championnet
Rue
Ruisseau
18E
SIMPLON
N.D. DU BON CONSEIL
Poissonniers
Rue du Simplon
Rue des
Montcalm
N.D. DE CLIGNANCOURT
Ordener
Square Léon Serpollet
JULES JOFFRIN
Rue
Marcadet
ST-PAUL
Ordener
STATION PONT MARCADET
B
LAMARCK CAULAINCOURT
MARCADET POISSONNIERS
Rue Caulaincourt
Rue du Mont Cenis
Rue Custine
Rue
Clignancourt
Barbès
Léon
Rue
CIMETIÈRE ST-VINCENT
Rue Lambert
Rue Doudeauville
MUSÉE DE MONTMARTRE
R. Cortot
Rue du Chev. de la Barre
Ramey
Stephenson
Boulevard
CHÂTEAU ROUGE
ST-PIERRE DE MONTMARTRE
SACRÉ CŒUR
MONTMARTRE
Rue de
ST-BERNARD DE LA CHAPELLE
ST-JEAN L'ÉVANGÉLISTE
Rue de la Goutte d'Or
ABBESSES
ROCHECHOUART BARBÈS
Bd. de la Chapelle
THÉATRE DE L'ATELIER
ÉLISÉE MONTMARTRE
Boulevard Rochechouart
C
PIGALLE
ANVERS
HÔPITAL LARIBOISIÈRE
Rue des Martyrs
Place d'Anvers
Boulevard
Poissonnière
Rue St-Vincent de Paul
GARE DU NORD
Avenue Trudaine
Rue de Dunkerque
R. du Faubourg St-Denis
Rue Condorcet
Rue Rodier
Rue de R. de Rochechouart
Rue de Maubeuge
R. de Belzunce
de
GARE DU NORD (R.E.R.)
9E
ST-GEORGES
Rue des Martyrs
ST-VINCENT DE PAUL
Magenta
N.-D. ST-GEORGES
Square Montholon
Place Franz Liszt
Rue de Chabrol
GARE DE L'EST
CADET
Rue Lamartine
Fayette
POISSONNIÈRE
HÔPITAL ST-LAZARE
GARE DE L'EST
NOTRE DAME DE LORETTE
Pl. Kossuth
D
N.D. DE LORETTE
La
MUSÉE DU GRAND ORIENT DE FRANCE
MUSÉE DU CRISTAL
FOLIES BERGÈRE
Faubourg
Rue du
MUSÉE DE LA PUBLICITÉ
R. du Faubourg St-Denis
ST-LAURENT
LE PELETIER
Rue de Fg. Montmartre
Rue Richer
Rue des Petites Écuries
ST-EUGÈNE STE-CÉCILE
RICHELIEU DROUOT
CHÂTEAU D'EAU
10E
Rue Bergère

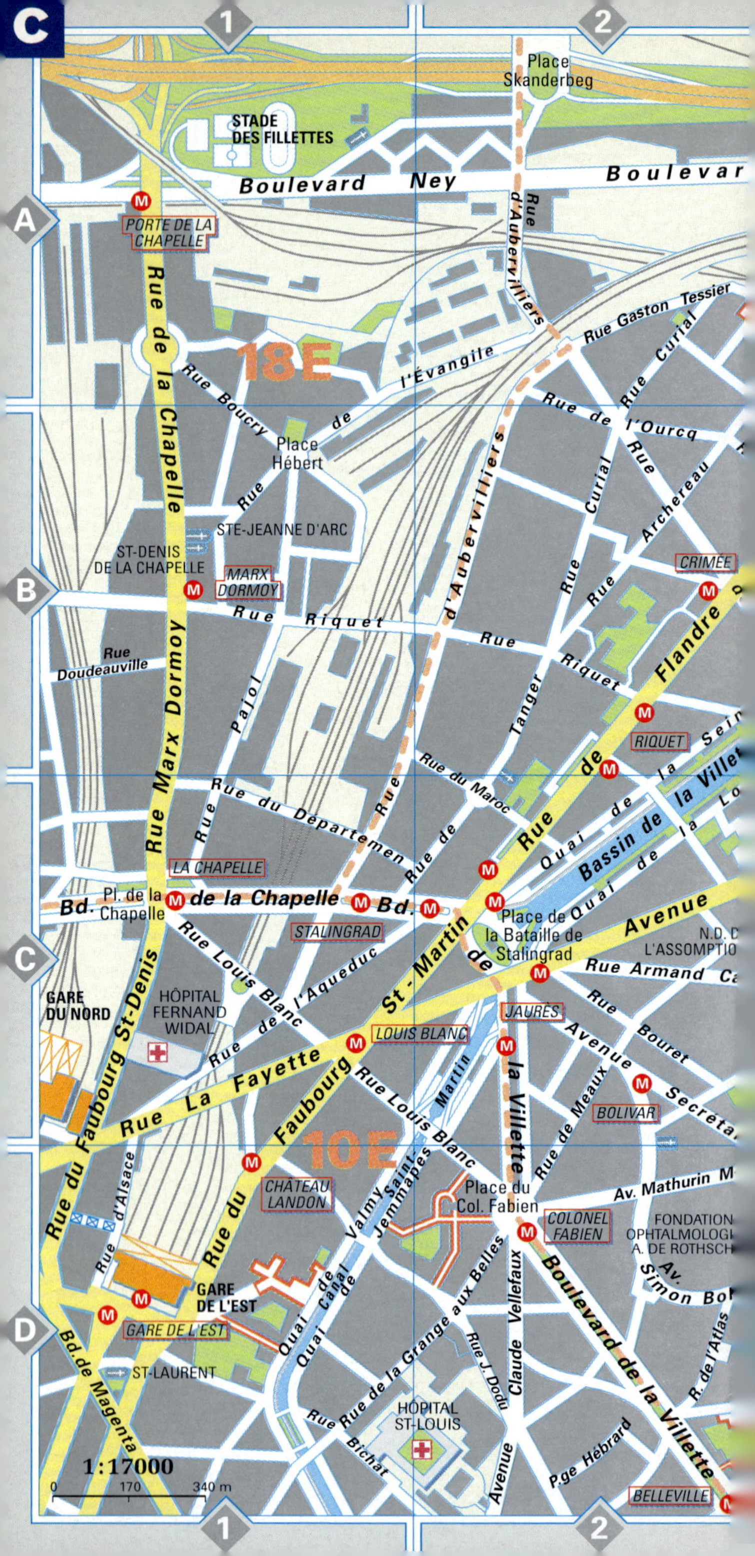

C
1
2
A
B
C
D
Place Skanderbeg
STADE DES FILLETTES
Boulevard Ney
Boulevar
PORTE DE LA CHAPELLE
Rue d'Aubervilliers
Rue Gaston Tessier
18E
Rue de l'Évangile
Rue Curial
Rue Boucry
Rue de l'Ourcq
Place Hébert
Rue Archereau
Rue de la Chapelle
STE-JEANNE D'ARC
ST-DENIS DE LA CHAPELLE
MARX DORMOY
CRIMÉE
Rue Riquet
Rue Doudeauville
Rue Tanger
Rue de Flandre
Rue Pajol
RIQUET
Rue Marx Dormoy
Rue du Maroc
Rue du Département
Rue de la Seine
Quai de la Seine
Bassin de la Villette
Quai de la Loire
LA CHAPELLE
Bd. de la Chapelle
Pl. de la Chapelle
STALINGRAD
Place de la Bataille de Stalingrad
Avenue
N.D. D L'ASSOMPTIO
Rue Armand Ca
Rue Louis Blanc
Rue de l'Aqueduc
Rue du Faubourg St-Martin
Avenue Jean Jaurès
JAURÈS
GARE DU NORD
HÔPITAL FERNAND WIDAL
Rue Bouret
LOUIS BLANC
Avenue Secrétan
Rue La Fayette
Rue de Meaux
BOLIVAR
Rue du Faubourg St-Denis
Quai de Valmy
Quai de Jemmapes
Canal Saint Martin
Rue de la Villette
10E
Rue d'Alsace
CHÂTEAU LANDON
Place du Col. Fabien
Av. Mathurin M
COLONEL FABIEN
FONDATION OPHTALMOLOGI A. DE ROTHSCH
Av. Simon Bo
GARE DE L'EST
Rue de la Grange aux Belles
Avenue Claude Vellefaux
Boulevard de la Villette
R. de l'Atlas
GARE DE L'EST
Bd. de Magenta
ST-LAURENT
Rue J. Dodu
HÔPITAL ST-LOUIS
Rue Bichat
P.ge Hébrard
1:17000
0
170
340 m
BELLEVILLE
1
2

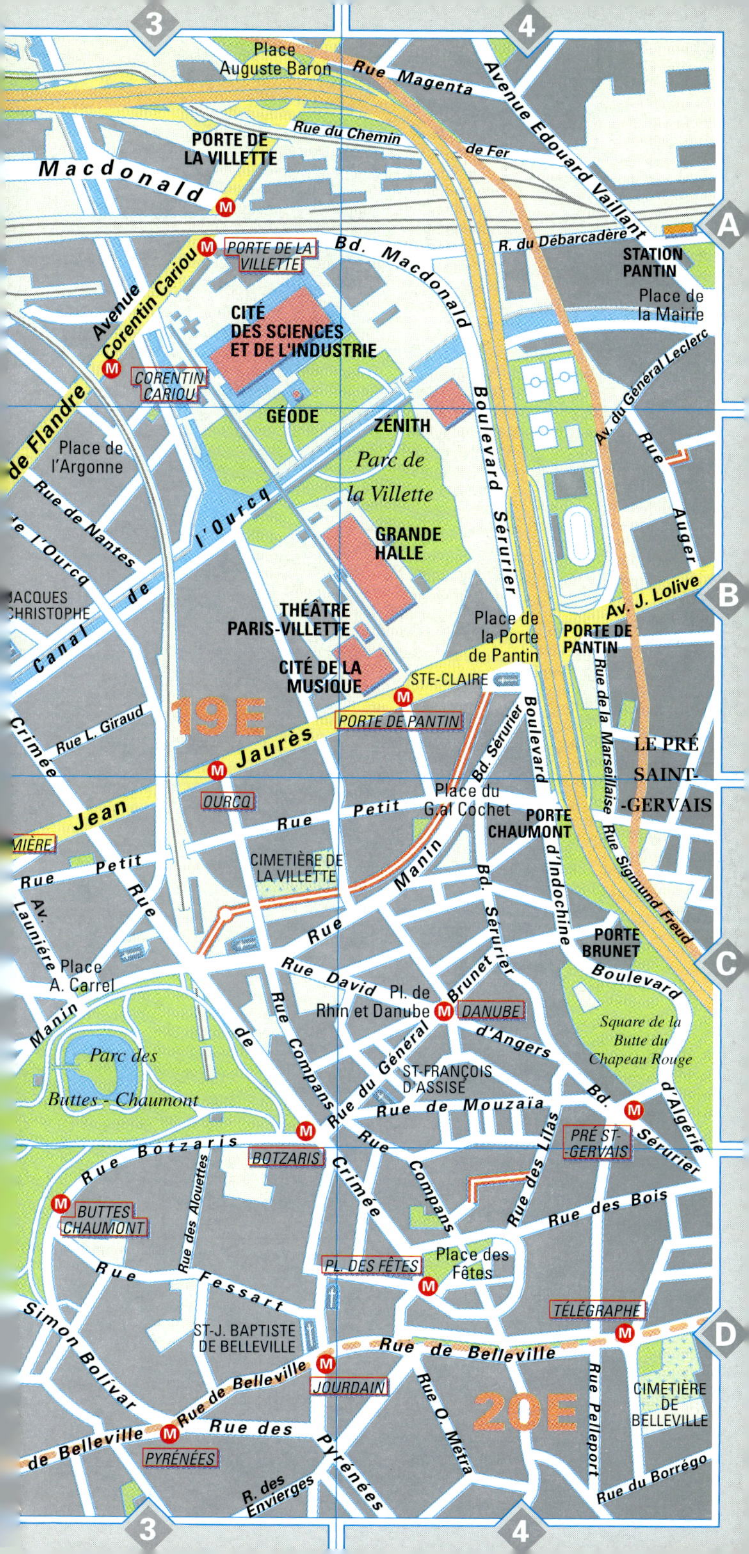

3
4
A
B
C
D
Place Auguste Baron
Rue Magenta
Avenue Edouard Vaillant
Rue du Chemin de Fer
PORTE DE LA VILLETTE
Macdonald
R. du Débarcadère
STATION PANTIN
Place de la Mairie
PORTE DE LA VILLETTE
Bd. Macdonald
Avenue Corentin Cariou
CITÉ DES SCIENCES ET DE L'INDUSTRIE
CORENTIN CARIOU
Av. du Général Leclerc
de Flandre
GÉODE
ZÉNITH
Parc de la Villette
Boulevard Sérurier
Rue Auger
Place de l'Argonne
Rue de Nantes
de l'Ourcq
l'Ourcq
GRANDE HALLE
Canal de
JACQUES CHRISTOPHE
THÉATRE PARIS-VILLETTE
Place de la Porte de Pantin
Av. J. Lolive
PORTE DE PANTIN
CITÉ DE LA MUSIQUE
STE-CLAIRE
19E
PORTE DE PANTIN
Rue de la Marseillaise
Crimée
Rue L. Giraud
Jaurès
Bd. Sérurier
Boulevard
LE PRÉ SAINT-GERVAIS
Jean
OURCQ
Place du G.al Cochet
Rue Petit
PORTE CHAUMONT
MIÈRE
Rue Petit
CIMETIÈRE DE LA VILLETTE
Rue Sigmund Freud
Av. Laumière
Rue
Manin
d'Indochine
Bd. Sérurier
Rue
PORTE BRUNET
Place A. Carrel
Rue David
Pl. de Rhin et Danube
Brunet
DANUBE
Boulevard
Manin
Rue de
d'Angers
Square de la Butte du Chapeau Rouge
Parc des Buttes - Chaumont
Rue Compans
Rue du Général
ST-FRANÇOIS D'ASSISE
Rue de Mouzaïa
Bd. Sérurier
d'Algérie
PRÉ ST-GERVAIS
Rue Botzaris
BOTZARIS
Crimée
Rue Compans
Rue des Lilas
Rue des Alouettes
BUTTES CHAUMONT
Rue des Bois
Rue Fessart
PL. DES FÊTES
Place des Fêtes
TÉLÉGRAPHE
Simon Bolívar
ST-J. BAPTISTE DE BELLEVILLE
Rue de Belleville
Rue de Belleville
JOURDAIN
Rue O. Métra
20E
Rue Pelleport
CIMETIÈRE DE BELLEVILLE
de Belleville
Rue des
PYRÉNÉES
Pyrénées
R. des Envierges
Rue du Borrégo

D
1
2
A
B
C
D
Avenue Foch
Place du M.al de Lattre de Tassigny
MUSÉE ARMÉNIEN
MUSÉE D'ENNERY
PORTE DAUPHINE
Route de Suresnes
STATION FOCH PORTE DAUPHINE (R.E.R.)
Avenue Bugeaud
Avenue Raymond Poincaré
Av. Victor Hugo
VICTOR HUGO
Place Victor Hugo
Rue Copernic
Rue Lauriston
MUSÉE DE LA CONTREFAÇON
UNIVERSITÉ PARIS IX
Rue des Belles Feuilles
Rue de la Pompe
ST-ALBERT LE GRAND
Rue Flandrin
Rue de la Faisanderie
Rue Spontini
ST-HONORÉ D'EYLAU
NOUVELLE ÉGLISE ST-HONORÉ D'EYLAU
Avenue Kléber
BOISSIÈRE
Boulevard Lannes
Boulevard Flandrin
Avenue Victor Hugo
Rue de Longchamp
Rue Saint Didier
R. L. Delibes
Rue Dufrénoy
Place de Mexico
Villa Longchamp
Avenue Henri Martin
STATION H. MARTIN (R.E.R.)
Rue de Longchamp
Avenue d'Eylau
POMPE
Place Tattegrain
N.D. DE CHALDÉE
TROCADÉRO
Avenue Georges Mandel
Place du Trocadéro et du 11 Novembre
CŒUR IMMACULÉ DE MARIE
16E
Rue Cortambert
CIMETIÈRE DE PASSY
Jardins du Trocadéro
Rue Octave Feuillet
Boulevard Émile Augier
ANNONCIATION
Avenue Paul Doumer
Rue Franklin
PALAIS DE CHAILLOT
Place Varsovie
Rue de la Tour
Av. des
STATION PASSY LA MUETTE
MUETTE
Rue Massenet
Rue Nicolo
Place de Costa Rica
Avenue
Rue de Passy
MUSÉE DU VIN
CHAMP DE MARS (R.E.R.)
R. Bois le Vent
BOULAINVILLIERS (R.E.R.)
N.D. DE GRÂCE DE PASSY
PASSY
Av. Mozart
Rue de Boulainvilliers
Place Chopin
Rue Singer
Rue Raynouard
Quai
Rue des Vignes
RANELAGH
Av. de Lamballa
Avenue du Président Kennedy
PONT DE BIR HAKEIM
BIR HAKEIM
Rue du Ranelagh
AV. DU PRES. KENNEDY MAISON DE RADIO-FRANCE (R.E.R.)
Rue de l'Assomption
Place Rodin
Allée des Cygnes
MAISON DE RADIO-FRANCE
Rue La Fontaine
Quai de Grenelle
Rue Charles
Rue Émeriau
PONT DE GRENELLE
Rue Théophile Gautier
Rue Félicien David
Avenue de Versailles
Rue Rouelle
STATUE DE LA LIBERTÉ
Place St-Charles
Avenue
Rue Linois
Rue St-
Rue de Lourmel
ST-TRINITÉ
Place de Barcelone
15E
Quai André Citroën
MIRABEAU
JAVEL (R.E.R.)
Rue
Place Ch. Michels
Rue Émile Zola
PONT MIRABEAU
JAVEL
Avenue de Javel
CHARLES MICHELS
Av.
Rond Point du Pt. Mirabeau
1:17000
0
170
340 m
ST-CHRISTOPHE DE JAVEL
Place Violet

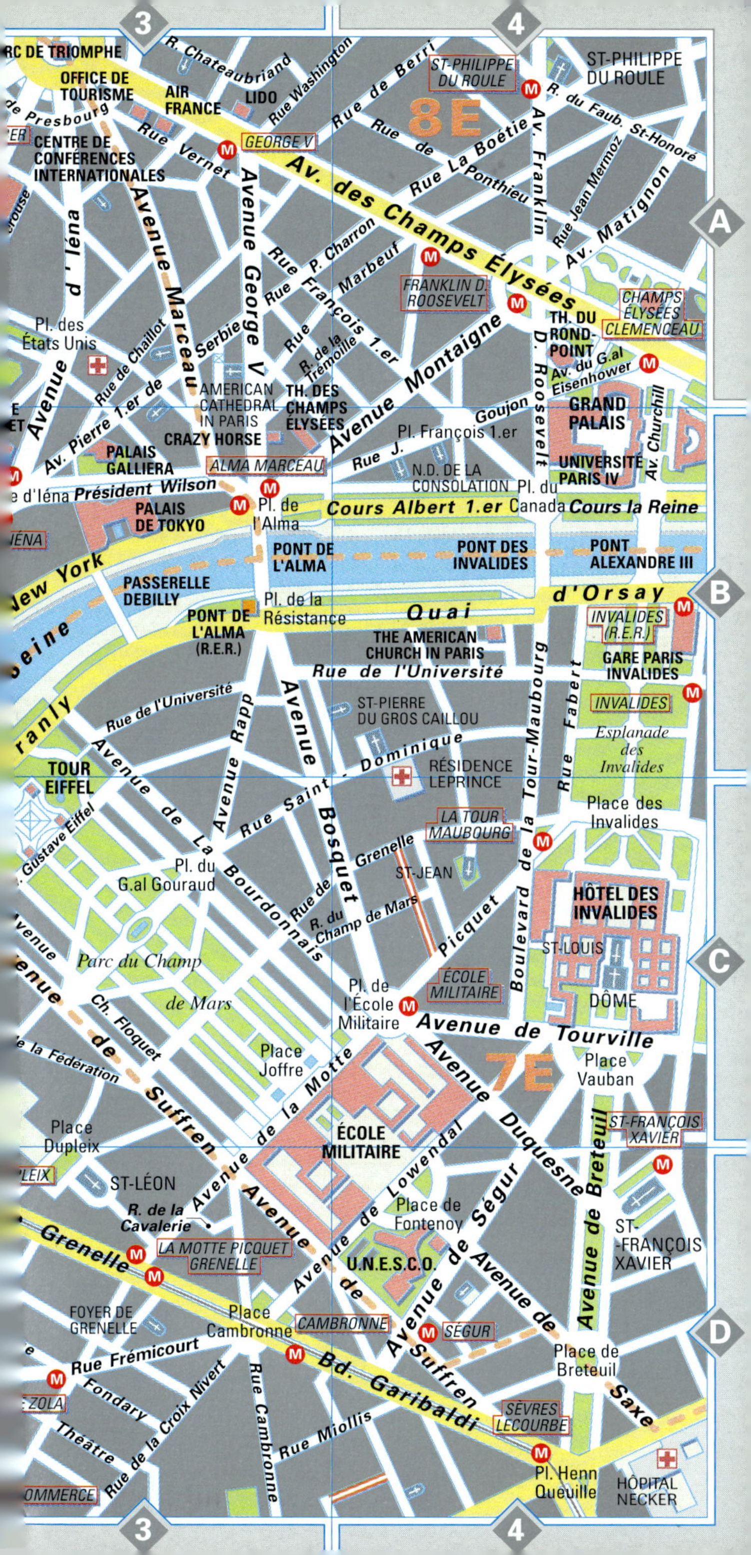
3
4
RC DE TRIOMPHE
OFFICE DE TOURISME
AIR FRANCE
LIDO
R. Chateaubriand
Rue Washington
Rue de Berri
ST-PHILIPPE DU ROULE
ST-PHILIPPE DU ROULE
R. du Faub. St-Honoré
8E
de Presbourg
Rue Vernet
GEORGE V
CENTRE DE CONFÉRENCES INTERNATIONALES
Rue de Ponthieu
Rue La Boétie
Av. Franklin
Rue Jean Mermoz
Av. Matignon
Av. des Champs Élysées
A
Avenue d'Iéna
Avenue Marceau
Avenue George V
Rue P. Charron
Rue Marbeuf
Rue François 1.er
FRANKLIN D. ROOSEVELT
CHAMPS ÉLYSÉES CLEMENCEAU
TH. DU ROND-POINT
Pl. des États Unis
Rue de Chaillot
Rue de Serbie
R. de la Trémoille
Avenue Montaigne
D. Roosevelt
Av. du G.al Eisenhower
Av. Churchill
Av. Pierre 1.er de Serbie
AMERICAN CATHEDRAL IN PARIS
TH. DES CHAMPS ÉLYSÉES
Goujon
GRAND PALAIS
Pl. François 1.er
CRAZY HORSE
PALAIS GALLIERA
ALMA MARCEAU
Rue J.
N.D. DE LA CONSOLATION
Pl. du Canada
UNIVERSITÉ PARIS IV
Président Wilson
PALAIS DE TOKYO
Pl. de l'Alma
Cours Albert 1.er
Cours la Reine
IÉNA
PONT DE L'ALMA
PONT DES INVALIDES
PONT ALEXANDRE III
New York
PASSERELLE DEBILLY
Pl. de la Résistance
Quai d'Orsay
B
Seine
PONT DE L'ALMA (R.E.R.)
INVALIDES (R.E.R.)
THE AMERICAN CHURCH IN PARIS
GARE PARIS INVALIDES
Rue de l'Université
Rue de l'Université
ST-PIERRE DU GROS CAILLOU
INVALIDES
Branly
Avenue Rapp
Avenue Bosquet
Bd. de la Tour-Maubourg
Rue Fabert
Esplanade des Invalides
TOUR EIFFEL
Rue Saint-Dominique
RÉSIDENCE LEPRINCE
Avenue de La Bourdonnais
Place des Invalides
LA TOUR MAUBOURG
Gustave Eiffel
Pl. du G.al Gouraud
Rue de Grenelle
ST-JEAN
HÔTEL DES INVALIDES
R. du Champ de Mars
Picquet
Boulevard de la Tour-Maubourg
ST-LOUIS
Parc du Champ de Mars
C
Pl. de l'École Militaire
ÉCOLE MILITAIRE
DÔME
Avenue de Tourville
Ch. Floquet
la Fédération
Place Joffre
7E
Place Vauban
Avenue Duquesne
Avenue de Suffren
Avenue de la Motte Picquet
ST-FRANÇOIS XAVIER
Place Dupleix
ÉCOLE MILITAIRE
Avenue de Lowendal
UPLEIX
ST-LÉON
Place de Fontenoy
Avenue de Ségur
ST-FRANÇOIS XAVIER
R. de la Cavalerie
Avenue de Breteuil
Grenelle
LA MOTTE PICQUET GRENELLE
U.N.E.S.C.O.
FOYER DE GRENELLE
Place Cambronne
CAMBRONNE
SÉGUR
D
Rue Frémicourt
Bd. Garibaldi
Place de Breteuil
Fondary
Rue de la Croix Nivert
Rue Cambronne
Avenue de Suffren
Avenue de Saxe
ZOLA
Théâtre
Rue Miollis
SÈVRES LECOURBE
Pl. Henri Queuille
HÔPITAL NECKER
OMMERCE
3
4

E
1
2
A
B
C
D
CHAPELLE EXPIATOIRE
ST-ESPRIT
ARCHEVÊCHÉ DE PARIS
Bd. Malesherbes
R. Pasquier
R. de l'Arcade
Rue Tronchet
R. Vignon
HAVRE CAUMARTIN (R.E.R.)
GALERIES LAFAYETTE
Rue Auber
Boulevard
OPÉRA
CHAUSSÉE D'ANTIN
AUBER (R.E.R.)
TH. ÉDOUARD VII
Place de l'Opéra
Rue Place Beauvau
TH. DE LA MADELEINE
A.
Place de la Madeleine
OLYMPIA
Bd. des Capucines
QUA SEPTE
du Faubourg St-Honoré
STE-MARIE MADELEINE
Bd. de la Madeleine
OPÉRA
PALAIS DE L'ÉLYSÉE
8E
MADELEINE
R. des Capucines
Rue de la P
TH. DANOU
B
Pl. Gaillo
R. Duphot
Rue Cambon
Rue Royale
Rue Boissy d'Anglas
Avenue Gabriel
PLACE VENDÔME
TH. DE LA POTINIÈRE
Avenue de l'Opé
Pl. du Marché St-Honoré
N.D. DE L'ASSOMPTION
Rue
PETIT PALAIS
Av. des Champs Élysées
CONCORDE
R. du Mont Thabor
R. de Castiglione
C.
PYRAMIDES
Av. Dutuit
Place de la Concorde
JEU DE PAUME
Rue de Rivoli
St-Honoré
ST-ROCH
Cours la Reine
1ER
ORANGERIE
Place des Pyramides
Jardin des Tuileries
TUILERIES
PONT DE LA CONCORDE
Quai d'Orsay
Quai des Tuileries
MUSÉE DES ARTS DÉCORATIFS
PALAIS RO
Seine
Quai Anatole France
Jardin du Carrousel
INVALIDES (R.E.R.)
PALAIS BOURBON
Bd. St-Germain
ARC DE TRIOMPHE DU CARROUSEL
MUSÉE D'ORSAY (R.E.R.)
PONT SOLFÉRINO
ASSEMBLÉE NATIONALE
PONT ROYAL
Quai
MUSÉE LOUV
PALAIS DE LA LÉGION D'HONNEUR
MINISTÈRE DE LA DÉFENSE
PONT DU CARROUSEL
INSTITUT GÉOGRAPHIQUE NATIONAL
MUSÉE D'ORSAY
R. du Bac
Quai Voltaire
SOLFÉRINO
Rue de Lille
Rue de Verneuil
Quai Malaquai
STE-CLOTILDE
Rue de Bellechasse
Rue de Grenelle
MINISTÈRE DU TRAVAIL
MINISTÈRE DES TRANSPORTS
Rue de l'Université
INS DE FR
Rue Montalembert
PENTEMONT
ST-THOMAS D'AQUIN
ÉCOLE DES BEAUX ARTS
Rue des Saints Pères
VARENNE
7E
Boulevard des Invalides
Boulevard Saint-Germain
Rue Jac
RUE DU BAC
UNIVERSITÉ PARIS V
Rue de Varenne
Rue de Vaneau
MUSÉE RODIN
MUSÉE DINA VIERNY
ST-GERMAIN DES PRÉS
HÔTEL MATIGNON
Rue du Bac
Boulevard Raspail
Rue de la Chaise
ST-GERMAIN DES PRÉS
Rue des
Rue Récamier
Rue de Babylone
Rue du Four
Rue des Canettes
MAB
R. P
SÈVRES BABYLONE
ST-FRANÇOIS XAVIER
ST-SULPICE
Place St-Sulpice
HÔPITAL LAENNEC
ST-SUL
Rue Oudinot
Bd. des Invalides
ST-IGNACE
R. Dupin
Rue de Rennes
CLINIQUE ST-JEAN DE DIEU
Rue de Sèvres
Rue du Cherche Midi
6E
ST-JOSEPH DES CARMES
Rue Madame
Rue de Vaugira
RENNES
PAL LUXEM
VANEAU
Rue de l'Abbé Grégoire
Rue Vaneau
MUSÉE HÉBERT
DUROC
15E
Rue de Fleurus
R. de Fleurus
Jardin du Luxemb
Rue d'Assas
Rue de Vaugirard
ST-PLACIDE
HÔPITAL NECKER
1:17000
0
170
340 m
N.D. DES CHAMPS

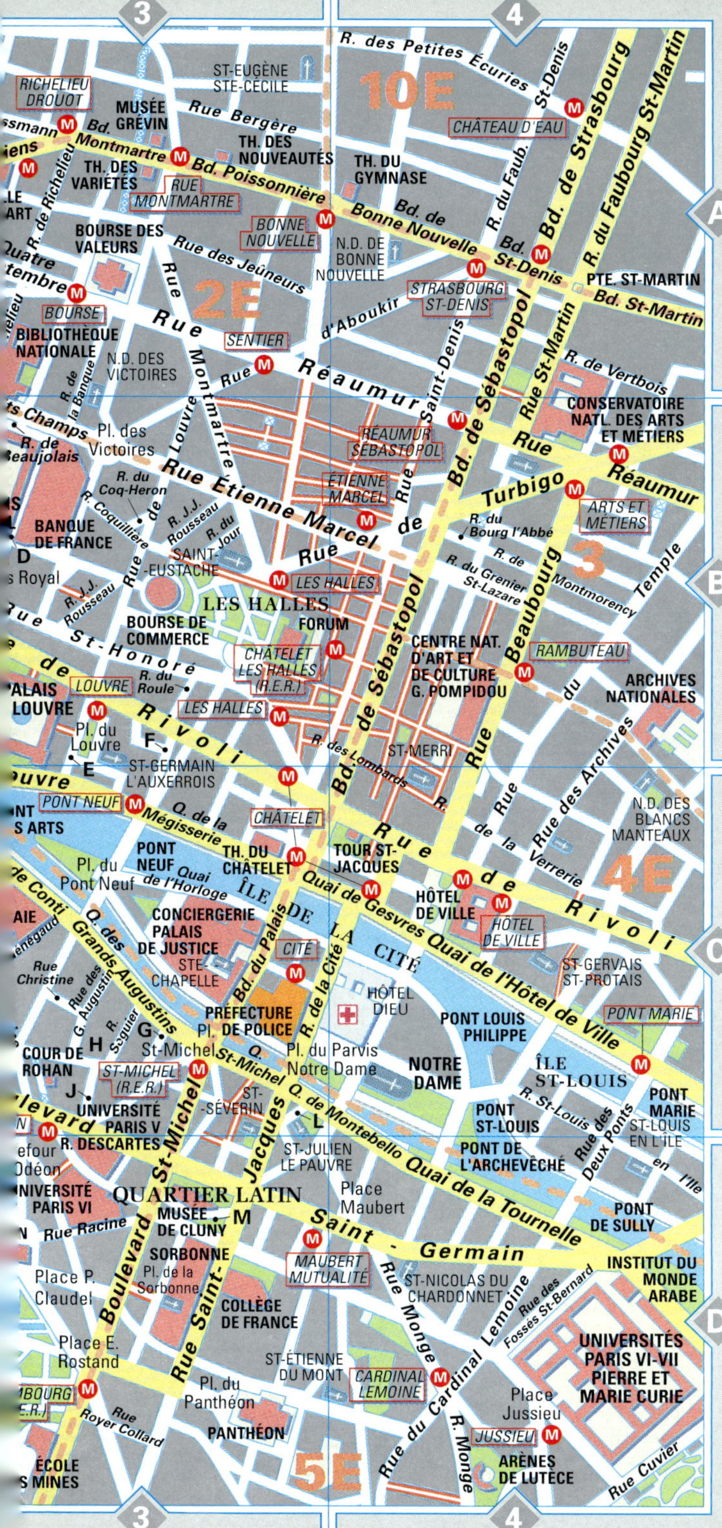
3
4
R. des Petites Écuries
ST-EUGÈNE STE-CÉCILE
10E
RICHELIEU DROUOT
MUSÉE GRÉVIN
Rue Bergère
St-Denis
CHÂTEAU D'EAU
Bd. Montmartre
TH. DES NOUVEAUTÉS
TH. DU GYMNASE
TH. DES VARIÉTÉS
Bd. Poissonnière
RUE MONTMARTRE
R. de Richelieu
Bd. de Strasbourg
R. du Faubourg St-Martin
R. du Faub.
A
BOURSE DES VALEURS
BONNE NOUVELLE
Bd. de Bonne Nouvelle
N.D. DE BONNE NOUVELLE
Rue des Jeûneurs
Bd. St-Denis
PTE. ST-MARTIN
Bd. St-Martin
2E
STRASBOURG ST-DENIS
BOURSE
BIBLIOTHÈQUE NATIONALE
d'Aboukir
SENTIER
Rue Montmartre
Rue Réaumur
Saint-Denis
Bd. de Sébastopol
Rue St-Martin
R. de Verbois
N.D. DES VICTOIRES
R. de la Banque
CONSERVATOIRE NATL. DES ARTS ET MÉTIERS
Pl. des Victoires
R. de Beaujolais
RÉAUMUR SÉBASTOPOL
Rue Réaumur
Rue du Louvre
Rue Étienne Marcel
ÉTIENNE MARCEL
Turbigo
ARTS ET MÉTIERS
R. du Coq-Heron
R. Coquillière
R. J.J. Rousseau
R. du Jour
R. du Bourg l'Abbé
BANQUE DE FRANCE
3
SAINT-EUSTACHE
R. de Montmorency
R. du Grenier St-Lazare
Temple
B
LES HALLES
R. J.J. Rousseau
Rue St-Honoré
BOURSE DE COMMERCE
FORUM
Beaubourg
CENTRE NAT. D'ART ET DE CULTURE G. POMPIDOU
CHÂTELET LES HALLES (R.E.R.)
RAMBUTEAU
ARCHIVES NATIONALES
LOUVRE
R. du Roule
Rue de Rivoli
LES HALLES
Pl. du Louvre
R. des Lombards
ST-MERRI
Rue du Temple
Rue des Archives
ST-GERMAIN L'AUXERROIS
N.D. DES BLANCS MANTEAUX
PONT NEUF
Q. de la Mégisserie
CHÂTELET
Rue de la Verrerie
PONT NEUF
TH. DU CHÂTELET
TOUR ST-JACQUES
Pl. du Pont Neuf
Quai de l'Horloge
ÎLE DE LA CITÉ
Quai de Gesvres
HÔTEL DE VILLE
Rue de Rivoli
4E
CONCIERGERIE PALAIS DE JUSTICE
HÔTEL DE VILLE
Quai de l'Hôtel de Ville
C
Q. des Grands Augustins
STE-CHAPELLE
CITÉ
ST-GERVAIS ST-PROTAIS
Rue Christine
Rue des G. Augustins
Bd. du Palais
R. de la Cité
HÔTEL DIEU
PRÉFECTURE DE POLICE
PONT LOUIS PHILIPPE
PONT MARIE
R. Séguier
Pl. St-Michel
Pl. du Parvis Notre Dame
COUR DE ROHAN
NOTRE DAME
ÎLE ST-LOUIS
ST-MICHEL (R.E.R.)
Q. St-Michel
R. St-Louis en l'Île
PONT MARIE
UNIVERSITÉ PARIS V
ST-SÉVERIN
Q. de Montebello
PONT ST-LOUIS
Rue des Deux Ponts
ST-LOUIS EN L'ÎLE
R. DESCARTES
Boulevard St-Michel
Rue St-Jacques
ST-JULIEN LE PAUVRE
PONT DE L'ARCHEVÊCHÉ
Quai de la Tournelle
UNIVERSITÉ PARIS VI
QUARTIER LATIN
Place Maubert
PONT DE SULLY
Rue Racine
MUSÉE DE CLUNY
Saint-Germain
INSTITUT DU MONDE ARABE
SORBONNE
MAUBERT MUTUALITÉ
Place P. Claudel
Pl. de la Sorbonne
ST-NICOLAS DU CHARDONNET
Rue Monge
Rue des Fossés St-Bernard
COLLÈGE DE FRANCE
Rue du Cardinal Lemoine
D
Place E. Rostand
UNIVERSITÉS PARIS VI-VII PIERRE ET MARIE CURIE
ST-ÉTIENNE DU MONT
CARDINAL LEMOINE
Pl. du Panthéon
Place Jussieu
Rue Royer Collard
PANTHÉON
JUSSIEU
R. Monge
ARÈNES DE LUTÈCE
Rue Cuvier
ÉCOLE DES MINES
5E
3
4

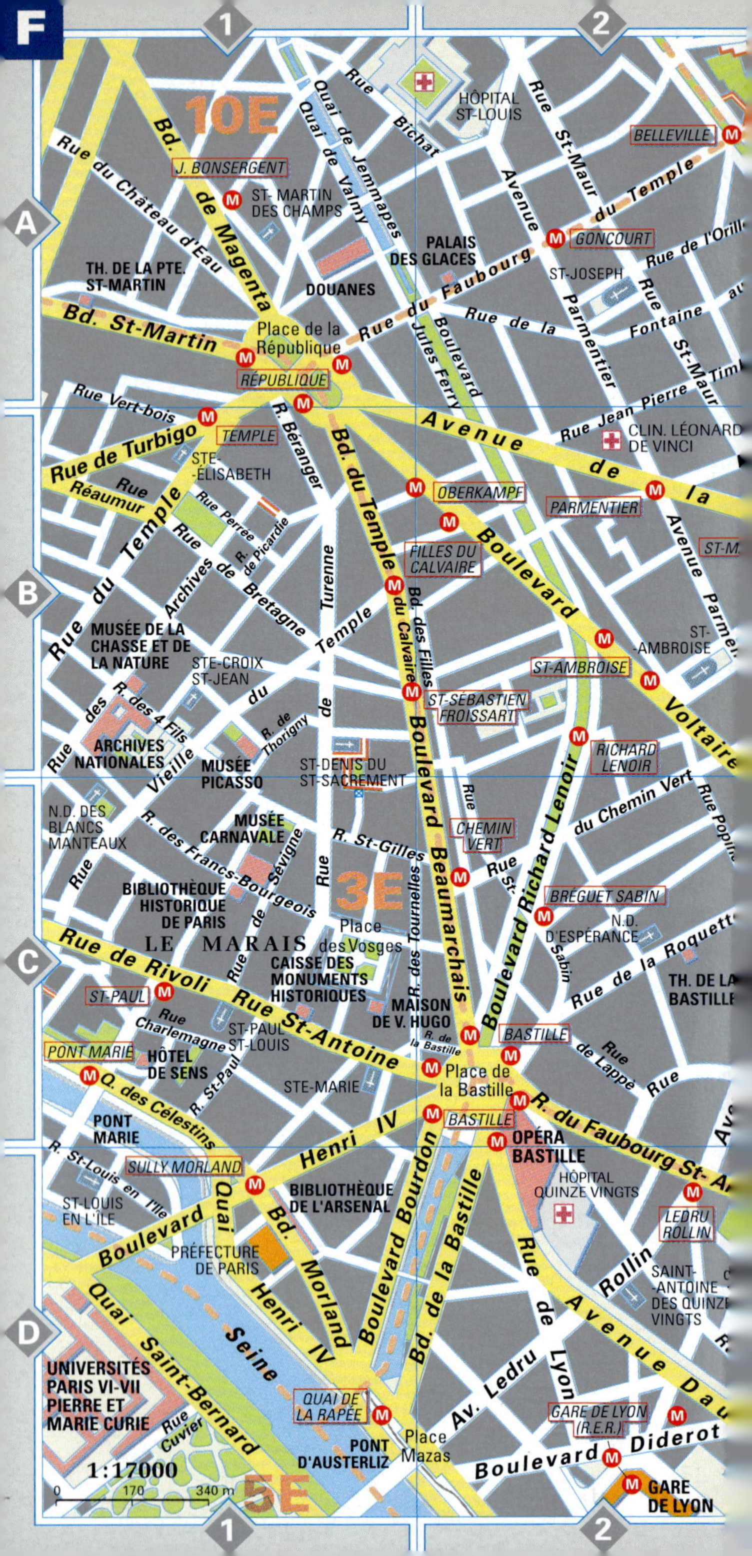
F
1
2
A
B
C
D
10E
3E
5E
HÔPITAL ST-LOUIS
Rue Bichat
Quai de Jemmapes
Quai de Valmy
Rue St-Maur
BELLEVILLE
Rue du Château d'Eau
Bd. de Magenta
J. BONSERGENT
ST-MARTIN DES CHAMPS
Avenue Parmentier
Rue du Faubourg du Temple
GONCOURT
PALAIS DES GLACES
DOUANES
TH. DE LA PTE. ST-MARTIN
Rue de l'Orillon
ST-JOSEPH
Rue de la Fontaine au Roi
Bd. St-Martin
Place de la République
RÉPUBLIQUE
Boulevard Jules Ferry
Rue St-Maur
Rue Jean Pierre Timbaud
Rue Vert-bois
Rue de Turbigo
TEMPLE
R. Béranger
Bd. du Temple
Avenue de la République
CLIN. LÉONARD DE VINCI
STE-ÉLISABETH
Rue Réaumur
OBERKAMPF
PARMENTIER
Rue Perrée
R. de Picardie
Rue des Archives
Rue de Bretagne
Boulevard Voltaire
FILLES DU CALVAIRE
ST-M.
Rue du Temple
Turenne
Bd. des Filles du Calvaire
Avenue Parmentier
MUSÉE DE LA CHASSE ET DE LA NATURE
STE-CROIX ST-JEAN
ST-AMBROISE
ST-AMBROISE
R. des 4 Fils
Rue de Turenne
ST-SÉBASTIEN FROISSART
R. de Thorigny
Boulevard Beaumarchais
RICHARD LENOIR
Boulevard Richard Lenoir
ARCHIVES NATIONALES
Rue Vieille du Temple
MUSÉE PICASSO
ST-DENIS DU ST-SACREMENT
Rue du Chemin Vert
Rue Popincourt
N.D. DES BLANCS MANTEAUX
MUSÉE CARNAVALE
R. St-Gilles
CHEMIN VERT
R. des Francs-Bourgeois
Rue de Sévigné
Rue St-Sabin
BRÉGUET SABIN
BIBLIOTHÈQUE HISTORIQUE DE PARIS
Place des Vosges
N.D. D'ESPÉRANCE
LE MARAIS
R. des Tournelles
Rue de la Roquette
Rue de Rivoli
CAISSE DES MONUMENTS HISTORIQUES
TH. DE LA BASTILLE
ST-PAUL
Rue St-Antoine
MAISON DE V. HUGO
Rue Charlemagne
ST-PAUL ST-LOUIS
R. de la Bastille
BASTILLE
PONT MARIE
HÔTEL DE SENS
Place de la Bastille
Rue de Lappe
Q. des Célestins
R. St-Paul
STE-MARIE
R. du Faubourg St-Antoine
PONT MARIE
BASTILLE
Henri IV
OPÉRA BASTILLE
R. St-Louis en l'Ile
SULLY MORLAND
HÔPITAL QUINZE VINGTS
ST-LOUIS EN L'ÎLE
BIBLIOTHÈQUE DE L'ARSENAL
LEDRU ROLLIN
Boulevard Henri IV
Quai Henri IV
PRÉFECTURE DE PARIS
Bd. Morland
Boulevard Bourdon
Bd. de la Bastille
Rue de Lyon
Rollin
SAINT-ANTOINE DES QUINZE VINGTS
Avenue Daumesnil
Quai Saint-Bernard
Seine
UNIVERSITÉS PARIS VI-VII PIERRE ET MARIE CURIE
Rue Cuvier
QUAI DE LA RAPÉE
Av. Ledru
GARE DE LYON (R.E.R.)
Place Mazas
PONT D'AUSTERLIZ
Boulevard Diderot
1:17000
0
170
340 m
GARE DE LYON

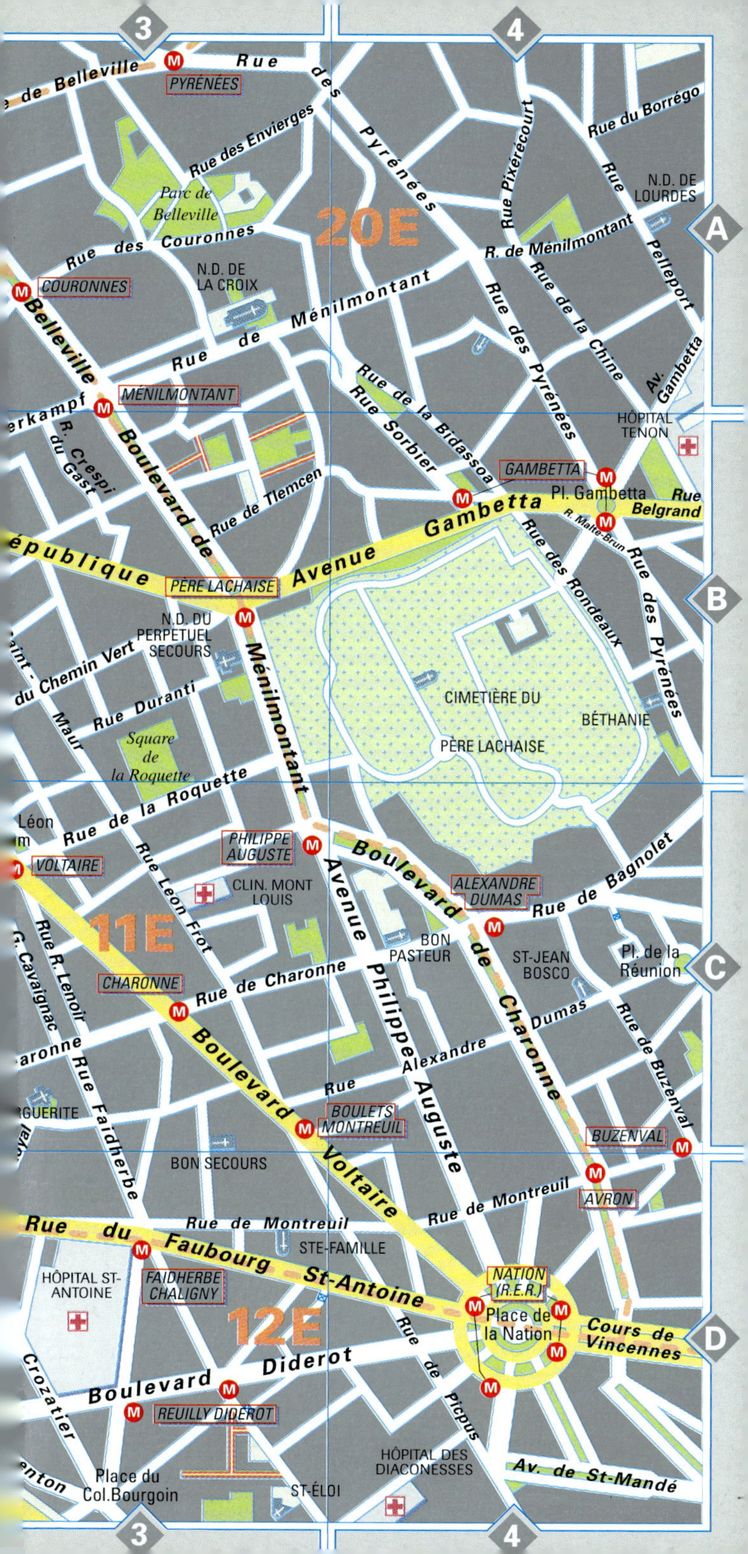
3
4
A
B
C
D
20E
11E
12E
Rue de Belleville
PYRÉNÉES
Rue des Pyrénées
Rue des Envierges
Parc de Belleville
Rue des Couronnes
COURONNES
N.D. DE LA CROIX
Rue de Ménilmontant
Boulevard de Belleville
MÉNILMONTANT
R. Crespi du Gast
Rue de Tlemcen
Rue Pixérécourt
Rue du Borrégo
Rue Pelleport
N.D. DE LOURDES
R. de Ménilmontant
Rue de la Chine
Av. Gambetta
Rue de la Bidassoa
Rue Sorbier
HÔPITAL TENON
GAMBETTA
Pl. Gambetta
Rue Belgrand
R. Malte-Brun
Avenue Gambetta
Avenue de la République
PÈRE LACHAISE
Boulevard de Ménilmontant
Rue des Rondeaux
N.D. DU PERPETUEL SECOURS
Rue du Chemin Vert
Rue St-Maur
Rue Duranti
Square de la Roquette
CIMETIÈRE DU PÈRE LACHAISE
BÉTHANIE
Rue de la Roquette
Rue Léon Frot
PHILIPPE AUGUSTE
VOLTAIRE
CLIN. MONT LOUIS
Boulevard de Charonne
ALEXANDRE DUMAS
Rue de Bagnolet
BON PASTEUR
ST-JEAN BOSCO
Pl. de la Réunion
Rue R. Lenoir
G. Cavaignac
CHARONNE
Rue de Charonne
Avenue Philippe Auguste
Rue Alexandre Dumas
Rue de Buzenval
Rue Faidherbe
Boulevard Voltaire
BOULETS MONTREUIL
BON SECOURS
BUZENVAL
AVRON
Rue de Montreuil
Rue du Faubourg St-Antoine
STE-FAMILLE
HÔPITAL ST-ANTOINE
FAIDHERBE CHALIGNY
NATION (R.E.R.)
Place de la Nation
Cours de Vincennes
Rue de Picpus
Boulevard Diderot
REUILLY DIDEROT
Rue Crozatier
HÔPITAL DES DIACONESSES
Av. de St-Mandé
Place du Col.Bourgoin
ST-ÉLOI

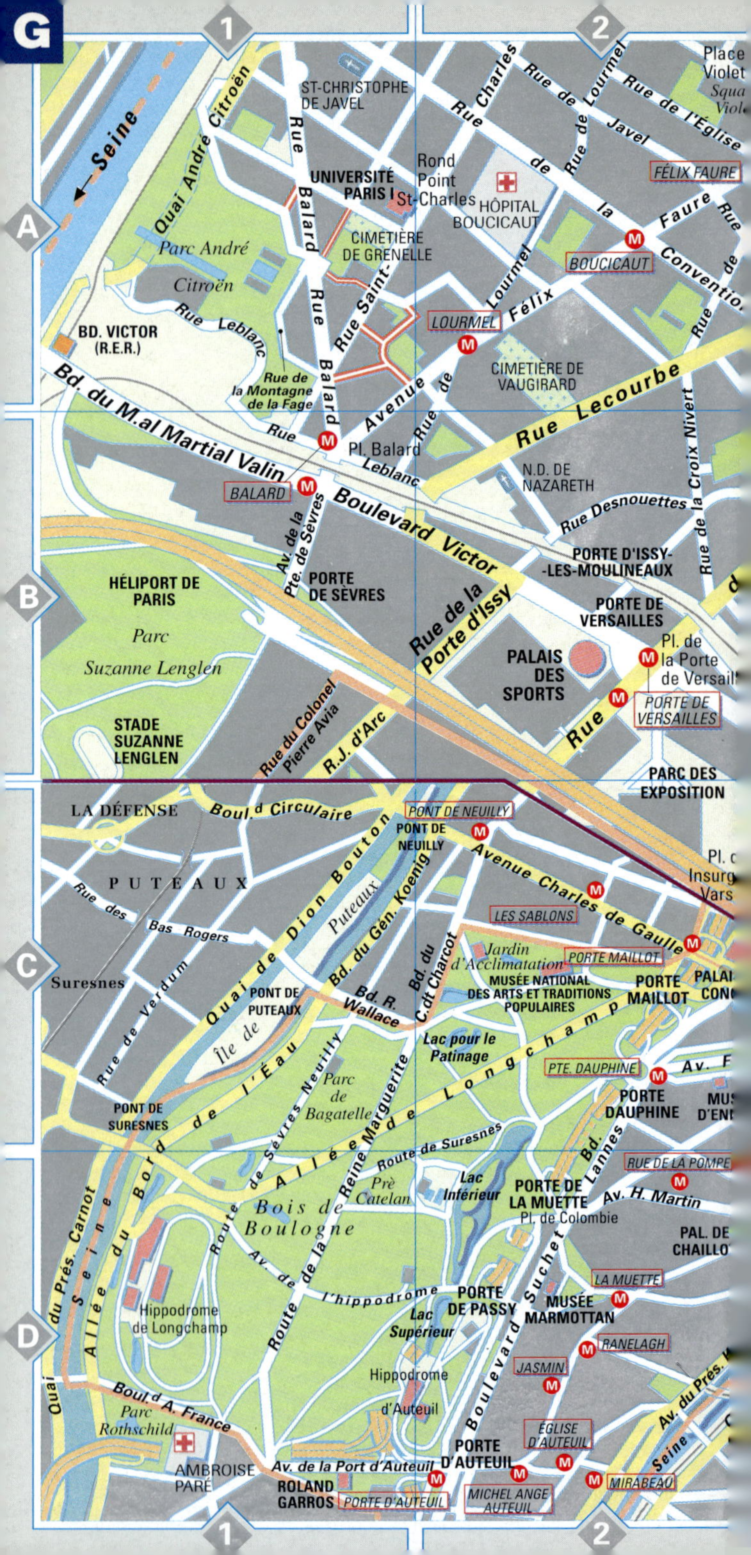

G
1
2
A
B
C
D
Seine
Quai André Citroën
Parc André Citroën
Rue Leblanc
BD. VICTOR (R.E.R.)
Rue de la Montagne de la Fage
ST-CHRISTOPHE DE JAVEL
Rue Balard
UNIVERSITÉ PARIS I
Rond Point St-Charles
HÔPITAL BOUCICAUT
CIMETIÈRE DE GRENELLE
Rue Saint-Charles
Rue Charles
Rue de Lourmel
Rue de Javel
Rue de l'Église
Place Violet
FÉLIX FAURE
Rue de la Convention
Avenue Félix Faure
BOUCICAUT
LOURMEL
CIMETIÈRE DE VAUGIRARD
Avenue de
Rue Lecourbe
Bd. du M.al Martial Valin
Rue Leblanc
Pl. Balard
BALARD
N.D. DE NAZARETH
Rue Desnouettes
Rue de la Croix Nivert
Boulevard Victor
Av. de la Pte. de Sèvres
PORTE DE SÈVRES
PORTE D'ISSY-LES-MOULINEAUX
HÉLIPORT DE PARIS
Parc Suzanne Lenglen
STADE SUZANNE LENGLEN
Rue de la Porte d'Issy
PALAIS DES SPORTS
PORTE DE VERSAILLES
Pl. de la Porte de Versail
PORTE DE VERSAILLES
Rue du Colonel Pierre Avia
R.J. d'Arc
Rue
PARC DES EXPOSITION
LA DÉFENSE
Boul.d Circulaire
PONT DE NEUILLY
PONT DE NEUILLY
Avenue Charles de Gaulle
PUTEAUX
Rue des Bas Rogers
Quai de Dion Bouton
Puteaux
Bd. du Gén. Koenig
LES SABLONS
Jardin d'Acclimatation
PORTE MAILLOT
MUSÉE NATIONAL DES ARTS ET TRADITIONS POPULAIRES
PORTE MAILLOT
Bd. du C.dt Charcot
Suresnes
Rue de Verdun
PONT DE PUTEAUX
Bd. R. Wallace
Île de
Lac pour le Patinage
Allée de Longchamp
PTE. DAUPHINE
PORTE DAUPHINE
Parc de Bagatelle
Route de Sèvres Neuilly
PONT DE SURESNES
Allée du Bord de l'Eau
Route de la Reine Marguerite
Route de Suresnes
Bd. Lannes
RUE DE LA POMPE
Pré Catelan
Lac Inférieur
PORTE DE LA MUETTE
Av. H. Martin
Pl. de Colombie
Bois de Boulogne
Route de Sèvres
PAL. DE CHAILLO
Quai du Prés. Carnot
Allée de la Seine
Av. de l'hippodrome
Boulevard Suchet
LA MUETTE
MUSÉE MARMOTTAN
PORTE DE PASSY
Lac Supérieur
Hippodrome de Longchamp
RANELAGH
JASMIN
Hippodrome d'Auteuil
Boul.d A. France
Parc Rothschild
ÉGLISE D'AUTEUIL
Av. du Prés. K
AMBROISE PARÉ
Av. de la Port d'Auteuil
PORTE D'AUTEUIL
ROLAND GARROS
PORTE D'AUTEUIL
MICHEL ANGE AUTEUIL
MIRABEAU
Seine

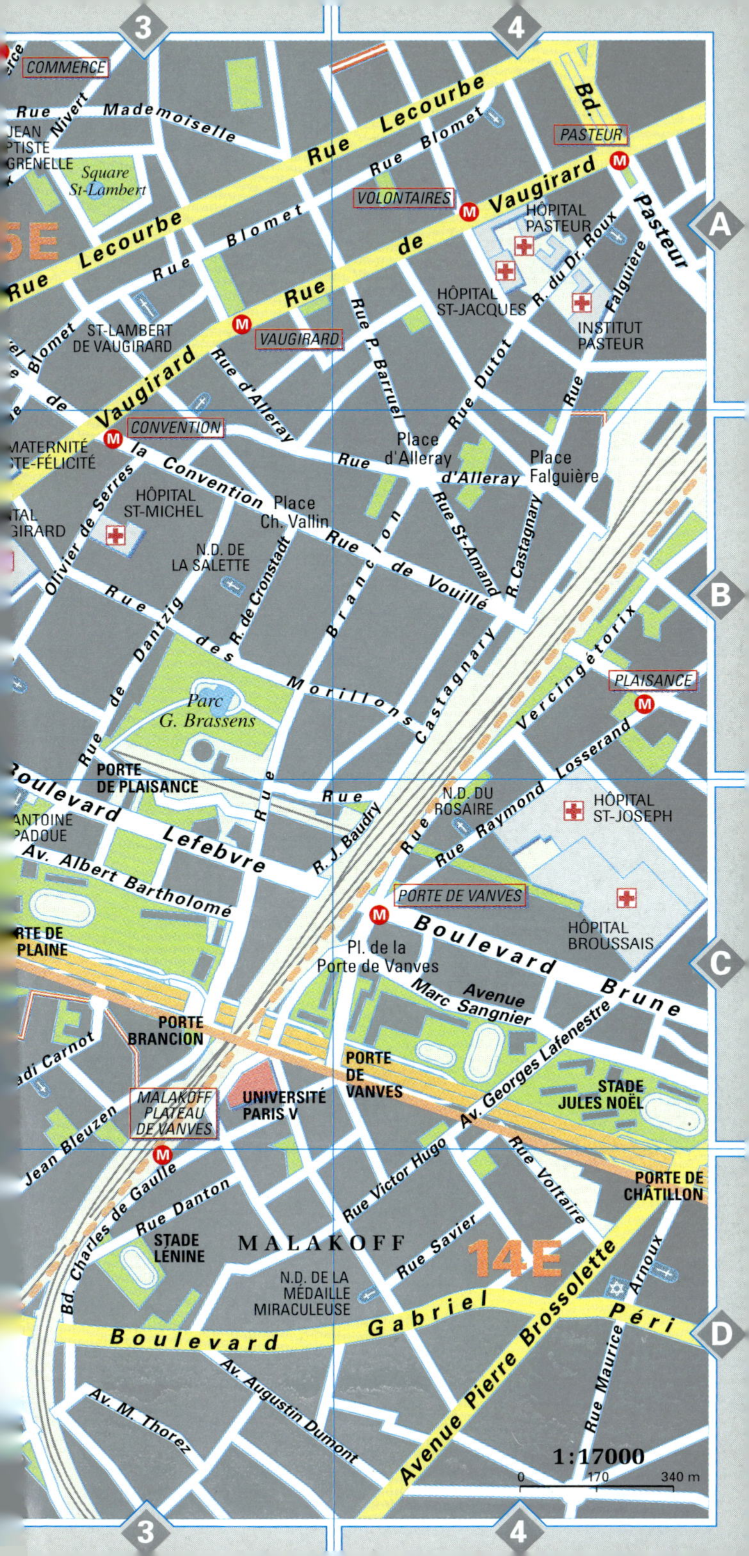

3
4
A
B
C
D
COMMERCE
Rue Mademoiselle
Rue Lecourbe
Rue Blomet
Rue de Vaugirard
Bd. Pasteur
PASTEUR
VOLONTAIRES
HÔPITAL PASTEUR
Square St-Lambert
15E
HÔPITAL ST-JACQUES
R. du Dr. Roux
Rue Falguière
INSTITUT PASTEUR
ST-LAMBERT DE VAUGIRARD
VAUGIRARD
Rue P. Barruel
Rue Dutot
Rue d'Alleray
CONVENTION
Rue de la Convention
MATERNITÉ STE-FÉLICITÉ
Place d'Alleray
Place Falguière
HÔPITAL ST-MICHEL
Place Ch. Vallin
Rue Olivier de Serres
N.D. DE LA SALETTE
R. de Cronstadt
Rue Brancion
Rue de Vouillé
Rue St-Amand
R. Castagnary
Rue de Dantzig
Rue des Morillons
Parc G. Brassens
Rue Castagnary
Rue Vercingétorix
PLAISANCE
PORTE DE PLAISANCE
Boulevard Lefebvre
R. J. Baudry
N.D. DU ROSAIRE
Rue Raymond Losserand
HÔPITAL ST-JOSEPH
Av. Albert Bartholomé
PORTE DE VANVES
HÔPITAL BROUSSAIS
Boulevard Brune
Pl. de la Porte de Vanves
Avenue Marc Sangnier
PORTE BRANCION
PORTE DE VANVES
Av. Georges Lafenestre
STADE JULES NOËL
MALAKOFF PLATEAU DE VANVES
UNIVERSITÉ PARIS V
Jean Bleuzen
Rue Victor Hugo
Rue Voltaire
PORTE DE CHÂTILLON
Bd. Charles de Gaulle
Rue Danton
STADE LÉNINE
MALAKOFF
Rue Savier
14E
N.D. DE LA MÉDAILLE MIRACULEUSE
Rue Arnoux
Boulevard Gabriel Péri
Avenue Pierre Brossolette
Av. Augustin Dumont
Av. M. Thorez
Rue Maurice
1:17000
0
170
340 m

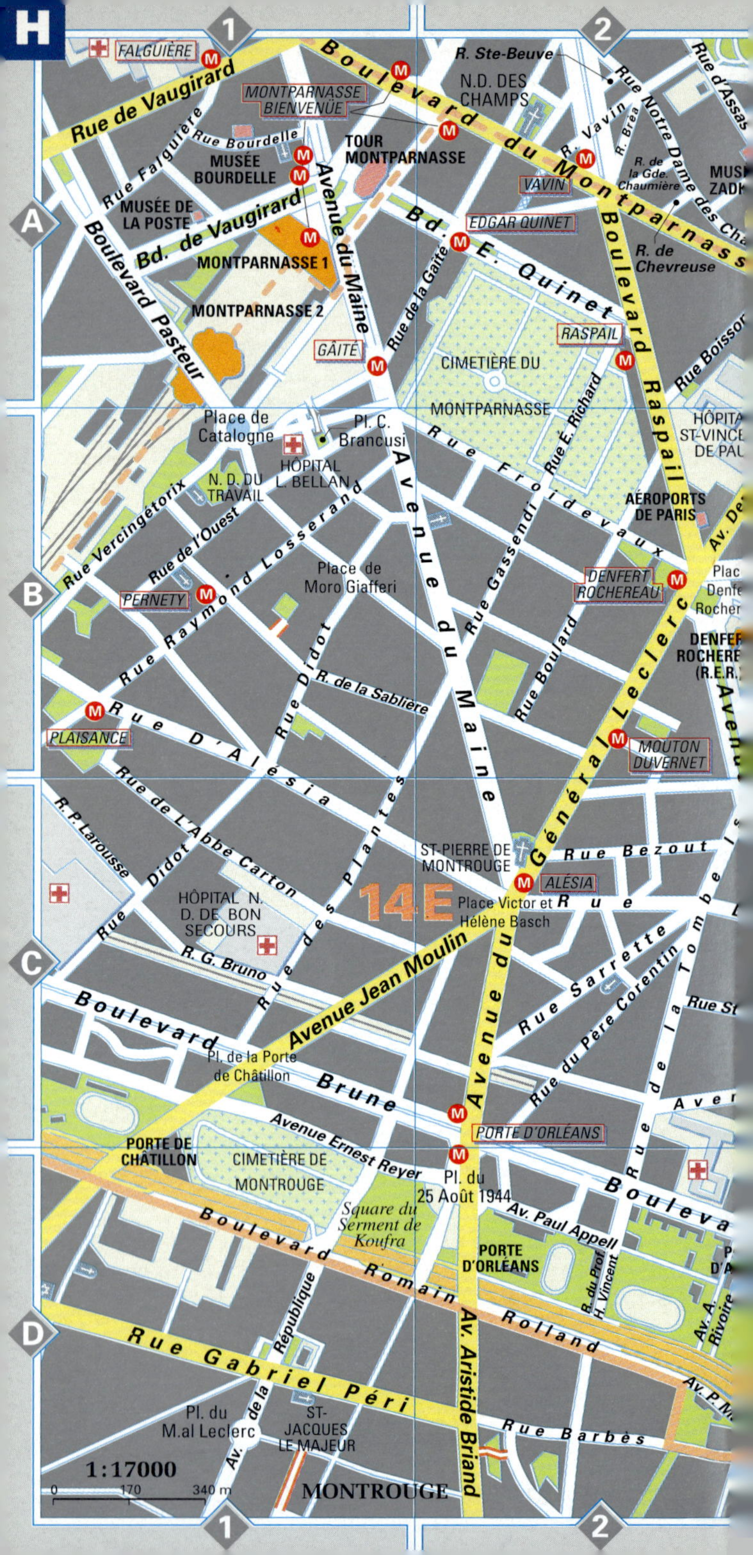
H
1
2
A
B
C
D
FALGUIÈRE
Rue de Vaugirard
Boulevard du Montparnasse
MONTPARNASSE BIENVENÜE
TOUR MONTPARNASSE
R. Ste-Beuve
N.D. DES CHAMPS
Rue Notre Dame des Champs
Rue d'Assas
R. Vavin
R. Bréa
R. de la Gde. Chaumière
R. de Chevreuse
VAVIN
Rue Bourdelle
MUSÉE BOURDELLE
Rue Falguière
MUSÉE DE LA POSTE
Bd. de Vaugirard
Avenue du Maine
MONTPARNASSE 1
MONTPARNASSE 2
Boulevard Pasteur
Bd. E. Quinet
EDGAR QUINET
Rue de la Gaîté
GAÎTÉ
RASPAIL
Boulevard Raspail
CIMETIÈRE DU MONTPARNASSE
Rue Boissonade
Place de Catalogne
Pl. C. Brancusi
HÔPITAL L. BELLAN
N. D. DU TRAVAIL
HÔPITAL ST-VINCENT DE PAUL
Rue Froidevaux
Rue E. Richard
AÉROPORTS DE PARIS
Rue Vercingétorix
Rue de l'Ouest
Rue Raymond Losserand
Place de Moro Giafferi
Rue Gassendi
DENFERT ROCHEREAU
Place Denfert Rochereau
DENFERT ROCHEREAU (R.E.R.)
Av. Denfert-Rochereau
PERNETY
Rue Didot
R. de la Sablière
Rue Boulard
Avenue du Maine
Avenue du Général Leclerc
PLAISANCE
Rue D'Alésia
MOUTON DUVERNET
R. P. Larousse
Rue de L'Abbé Carton
Rue des Plantes
ST-PIERRE DE MONTROUGE
Rue Bezout
ALÉSIA
14E
Place Victor et Hélène Basch
HÔPITAL N. D. DE BON SECOURS
Rue Didot
R. G. Bruno
Avenue Jean Moulin
Rue Sarrette
Rue du Père Corentin
Rue de la Tombe Issoire
Rue St
Boulevard Brune
Pl. de la Porte de Châtillon
Avenue du Maine
Avenue Ernest Reyer
PORTE D'ORLÉANS
PORTE DE CHÂTILLON
CIMETIÈRE DE MONTROUGE
Pl. du 25 Août 1944
Square du Serment de Koufra
Boulevard
Av. Paul Appell
PORTE D'ORLÉANS
R. du Prof. H. Vincent
Av. A. Rivoire
Boulevard Romain Rolland
Av. de la République
Rue Gabriel Péri
Av. Aristide Briand
Av. P. M
Pl. du M.al Leclerc
ST-JACQUES LE MAJEUR
Rue Barbès
1:17000
0
170
340 m
MONTROUGE

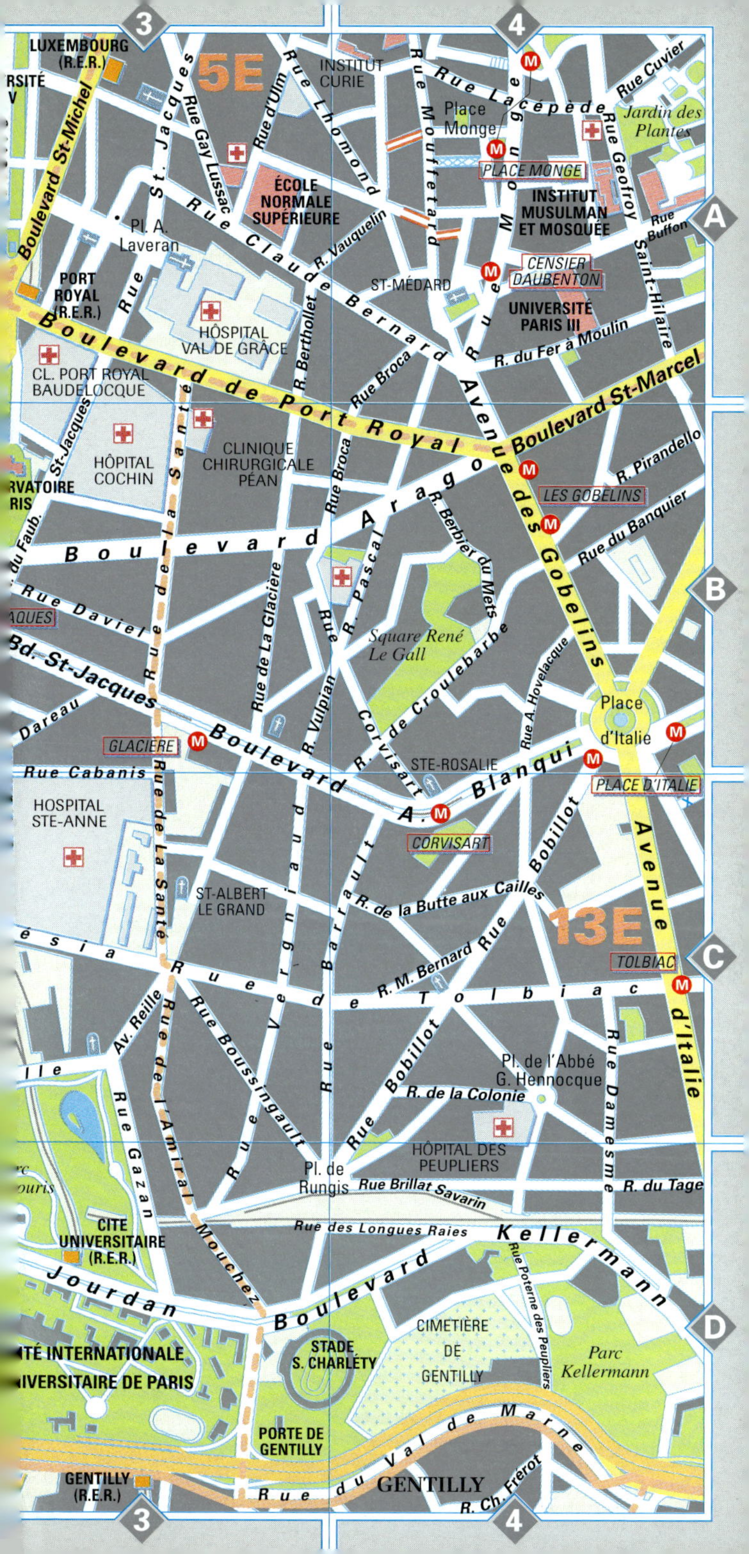

3
4
LUXEMBOURG (R.E.R.)
5E
INSTITUT CURIE
Rue Lacépède
Rue Cuvier
Jardin des Plantes
Place Monge
PLACE MONGE
Rue Monge
Rue Mouffetard
Rue Lhomond
Rue d'Ulm
Rue Gay Lussac
Rue St. Jacques
Boulevard St-Michel
ÉCOLE NORMALE SUPÉRIEURE
INSTITUT MUSULMAN ET MOSQUÉE
Rue Geofroy Saint-Hilaire
Rue Buffon
A
Pl. A. Laveran
Rue Claude Bernard
R. Vauquelin
ST-MÉDARD
CENSIER DAUBENTON
UNIVERSITÉ PARIS III
PORT ROYAL (R.E.R.)
HÔSPITAL VAL DE GRÂCE
R. Berthollet
R. du Fer à Moulin
Boulevard de Port Royal
CL. PORT ROYAL BAUDELOCQUE
Rue Broca
Boulevard St-Marcel
HÔPITAL COCHIN
CLINIQUE CHIRURGICALE PÉAN
R. Pirandello
LES GOBELINS
Avenue des Gobelins
Boulevard Arago
R. Berbier du Mets
Rue du Banquier
Rue du Faub. St-Jacques
Rue de la Santé
B
Rue Daviel
Rue de La Glacière
R. Pascal
Square René Le Gall
Bd. St-Jacques
Dareau
R. de Croulebarbe
Rue A. Hovelacque
Place d'Italie
Rue Vulpian
Rue Corvisart
GLACIÈRE
Boulevard A. Blanqui
STE-ROSALIE
PLACE D'ITALIE
Rue Cabanis
HOSPITAL STE-ANNE
CORVISART
Avenue d'Italie
Rue de La Santé
Rue Vergniaud
Rue Barrault
ST-ALBERT LE GRAND
R. de la Butte aux Cailles
Rue Bobillot
13E
TOLBIAC
C
R. M. Bernard
Rue de Tolbiac
Av. Reille
Rue Boussingault
Rue Damesme
Pl. de l'Abbé G. Hennocque
R. de la Colonie
Rue Gazan
Rue de l'Amiral Mouchez
HÔPITAL DES PEUPLIERS
Pl. de Rungis
Rue Brillat Savarin
R. du Tage
Rue des Longues Raies
CITE UNIVERSITAIRE (R.E.R.)
Boulevard Kellermann
Rue Poterne des Peupliers
Jourdan
D
STADE S. CHARLÉTY
CIMETIÈRE DE GENTILLY
Parc Kellermann
ITÉ INTERNATIONALE
IVERSITAIRE DE PARIS
PORTE DE GENTILLY
Rue du Val de Marne
GENTILLY (R.E.R.)
GENTILLY
R. Ch. Frerot

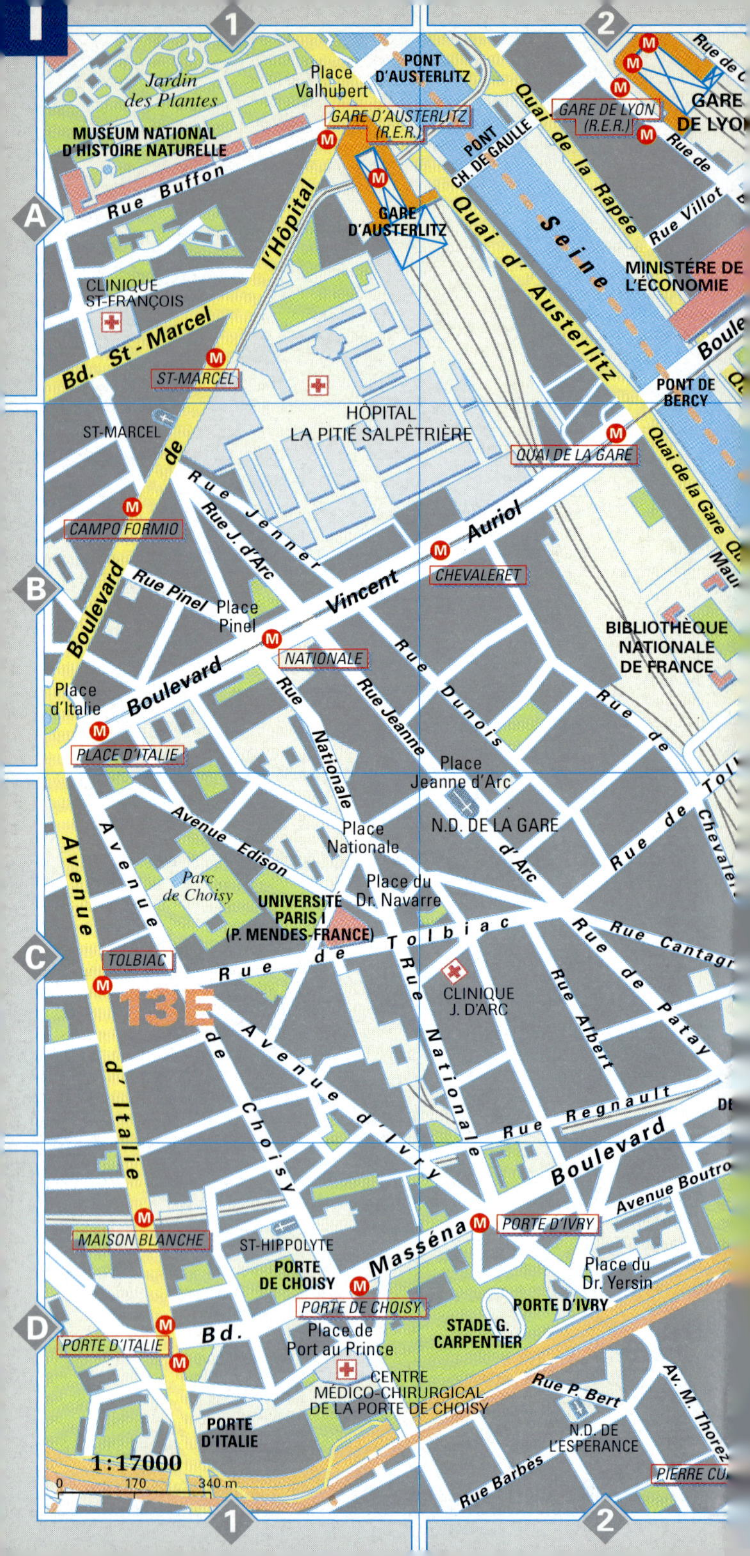
I
1
2
A
B
C
D
Jardin des Plantes
MUSÉUM NATIONAL D'HISTOIRE NATURELLE
Rue Buffon
Place Valhubert
GARE D'AUSTERLITZ (R.E.R.)
PONT D'AUSTERLITZ
PONT CH. DE GAULLE
GARE D'AUSTERLITZ
Quai de la Rapée
GARE DE LYON (R.E.R.)
GARE DE LYON
Rue de
Rue Villot
Quai d'Austerlitz
Seine
MINISTÈRE DE L'ÉCONOMIE
Boule
PONT DE BERCY
CLINIQUE ST-FRANÇOIS
Bd. St - Marcel
l'Hôpital
ST-MARCEL
HÔPITAL LA PITIÉ SALPÊTRIÈRE
QUAI DE LA GARE
Quai de la Gare
de
Rue Jenner
Rue J. d'Arc
CAMPO FORMIO
Auriol
CHEVALERET
Boulevard
Rue Pinel
Place Pinel
Vincent
NATIONALE
BIBLIOTHÈQUE NATIONALE DE FRANCE
Place d'Italie
Boulevard
PLACE D'ITALIE
Rue Nationale
Rue Jeanne
Rue Dunois
Rue de
Place Jeanne d'Arc
Avenue Edison
Place Nationale
N.D. DE LA GARE
d'Arc
Rue de Tol
Chevaleret
Avenue
Avenue
Parc de Choisy
UNIVERSITÉ PARIS I (P. MENDES-FRANCE)
Place du Dr. Navarre
Rue de Tolbiac
Rue Cantagr
TOLBIAC
13E
Rue Nationale
CLINIQUE J. D'ARC
Rue Albert
Rue de Patay
d'Italie
de Choisy
Avenue d'Ivry
Rue Regnault
Boulevard
Avenue Boutro
MAISON BLANCHE
ST-HIPPOLYTE
Masséna
PORTE D'IVRY
PORTE DE CHOISY
PORTE DE CHOISY
Place du Dr. Yersin
PORTE D'IVRY
STADE G. CARPENTIER
PORTE D'ITALIE
Bd.
Place de Port au Prince
CENTRE MÉDICO-CHIRURGICAL DE LA PORTE DE CHOISY
Rue P. Bert
Av. M. Thorez
PORTE D'ITALIE
N.D. DE L'ESPERANCE
1:17000
0 170 340 m
Rue Barbès
PIERRE CU

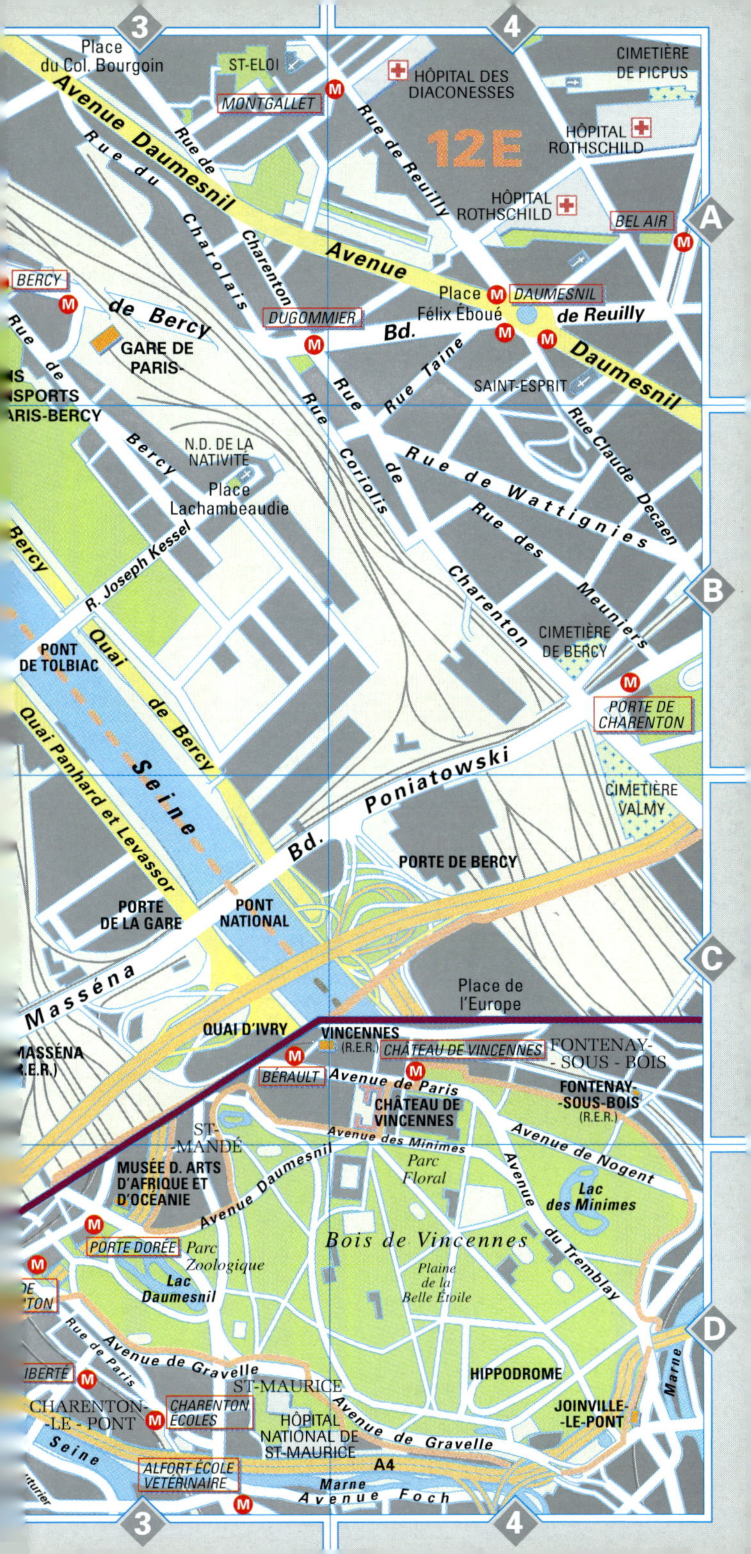
3
4
Place du Col. Bourgoin
ST-ELOI
MONTGALLET
HÔPITAL DES DIACONESSES
CIMETIÈRE DE PICPUS
12E
HÔPITAL ROTHSCHILD
HÔPITAL ROTHSCHILD
BEL AIR
A
Avenue Daumesnil
Rue du Charolais
Rue de Charenton
Rue de Reuilly
Avenue
BERCY
de Bercy
GARE DE PARIS-
DUGOMMIER
Place Félix Éboué
DAUMESNIL
Bd. de Reuilly
Daumesnil
Rue Taine
SAINT-ESPRIT
Rue de Bercy
N.D. DE LA NATIVITÉ
Place Lachambeaudie
Rue Coriolis
Rue de Charenton
Rue de Wattignies
Rue Claude Decaen
Rue des Meuniers
B
R. Joseph Kessel
Bercy
PONT DE TOLBIAC
Quai de Bercy
CIMETIÈRE DE BERCY
PORTE DE CHARENTON
Seine
Quai Panhard et Levassor
Bd. Poniatowski
CIMETIÈRE VALMY
PORTE DE BERCY
PORTE DE LA GARE
PONT NATIONAL
C
Masséna
Place de l'Europe
QUAI D'IVRY
VINCENNES (R.E.R.)
CHÂTEAU DE VINCENNES
FONTENAY- - SOUS - BOIS
MASSÉNA R.E.R.)
BÉRAULT
Avenue de Paris
CHÂTEAU DE VINCENNES
FONTENAY- -SOUS-BOIS (R.E.R.)
ST- -MANDÉ
Avenue des Minimes
Avenue de Nogent
MUSÉE D. ARTS D'AFRIQUE ET D'OCÉANIE
Avenue Daumesnil
Parc Floral
Avenue du Tremblay
Lac des Minimes
PORTE DORÉE
Parc Zoologique
Bois de Vincennes
Lac Daumesnil
Plaine de la Belle Étoile
D
Rue de Paris
Avenue de Gravelle
HIPPODROME
ST-MAURICE
CHARENTON- -LE - PONT
CHARENTON ÉCOLES
HÔPITAL NATIONAL DE ST-MAURICE
Avenue de Gravelle
JOINVILLE- -LE-PONT
Marne
Seine
ALFORT ÉCOLE VÉTÉRINAIRE
A4
Marne
Avenue Foch

General index

See pages 6–15 for practical information about getting there, getting around, and getting by.

Index

The publishers would like to thank Eric Guillemot, Patrick Léger, Roger Gain, Seymourina Cruse, Lionel Monéger, and all the establishments listed in this guide for their help.

Picture Credits

01 *and cover illustration*
Denis Brumaud
6
CAV-J. M. Fabbro
8
Kristof Chemineau (illustrations)
9
Kristof Chemineau (illustrations), Aéroports de Paris (ADP logo)
10
Gallimard-Léonard de Selva (stations), CAV-J. M. Fabbro (TGV), Thalys-SNCF CAV-J. J. d'Angelo (Thalys logo), Eurostar (Eurostar logo)
11
Gallimard-Patrick Léger (boulevard Saint-Germain sign, pedestrian signals, parking meter, parking sign), Gallimard-Xavier Richer (towing sign), Gallimard-Lionel Monéger (pont Charles de Gaulle sign)
12
RATP-Bertrand Chabrol (bus), RATP-Minoli (métro and aerial métro), Didier Lauret (métro, destination sign), Gallimard-E. Guillemot (bus sign), RATP com/Audiovisuel-Chabrol (métro), RATP-Thibaut (logo), RATP-Marguerite (métro tickets)
13
Didier Lauret (bus, bus route, taxis stand, Parisian taxi), Gallimard-Patrick Léger (Batobus sign, métro entrance), RATP com/Audiovisuel-Minoli (Saint-Georges sign)
14
Gallimard-Éric Guillemot (tickets, newspapers), Gallimard-Xavier Richer (police, call box), Gallimard-Patrick Léger (letterbox, advertising pillar, coins),
15
France Télécom (mobile telephone), Gallimard-Xavier Richer (signs), Gallimard-Patrick Léger (church, mosque, synagogue), DR (phone card)
16
Plaza Athénée
19
2 Gallimard-Patrick Léger, 4 Hôtel Raphaël, 5 Gallimard-Patrick Léger, 6 Hôtel Élysée Céramic
21
7 Hôtel Baltimore, 8 Hôtel Le Parc Victor Hugo, 9 K. Palace, 11 Hôtel Garden Élysées
23
12 Hôtel Vigny, 13 Hôtel Vernet, 14 Plaza Athénée, 15 San Régis
25
18 Le Crillon, 19 Marianne Haas, 21 Hôtel Meurice, 23 Royal St-Honoré
27
24 Concortel, 25 Astor Westin Demeure Hôtel, 26 Hôtel Beau Manoir
29
29 Ritz, 30 C. Erwin, 31 Westminster
31
33 Gallimard-Patrick Léger (tiled wall), 33 Gallimard-Éric Guillemot (clocks), 36 Hôtel de la place du Louvre 37 Gallimard-Patrick Léger
33
40 Pavillon Bastille, 42 Hôtel du Jeu de Paume (interiors), 42 Brice Laval (breakfast), 43 Hôtel Saint-Merry, 44 Hôtel Saint-Paul-le-Marais
35
46 Relais Hôtel Vieux Paris, 47 Hôtel Esméralda, 48 Relais Médicis, 49 Select Hôtel (breakfast tray), 49 H.A. Ségalen (atrium), 50 Les Rives de Notre-Dame
37
52 Hôtel des Jardins du Luxembourg, 53 Hôtel des Grands Hommes, 55 Hôtel des Grandes Écoles, 56 Le Clos Médicis
39
58 Relais Christine, 60 Gallimard-Patrick Léger, 61 Buci Latin
41
62 Hôtel Montalembert, 63 Hôtel d'Angleterre, 65 Gallimard-Patrick Léger
43
68 Hôtel Duc de Saint-Simon, 69 Hôtel Lutétia, 71 Hôtel des Saints-Pères
45
74 Hôtel Sainte-Beuve, 75 L'Atelier Montparnasse, 76 Hôtel Raspail-Montparnasse
46
Le Grand Véfour
49
1 P. Mauver, 2 Gallimard-Patrick Léger, 3 Marot-Gaudry, 4 Gallimard-Patrick Léger, 5 La Samaritaine, 6 Gallimard-Roger Gain
53
9 Guy Savoy (plate, kitchen), 9 Gallimard-Roger Gain (interior), 10 Taïra, 12 F. Rambert
55
15 J. Bourboulon et Gallimard-Roger Gain (interior), 17 Gallimard-Patrick Léger 18 Le Petit Colombier
57
22 Alain Ducasse (façade), 22 Gallimard-Gérard Nencioli (plate), 22 DR (bar), 25 Faugeron
59
Gallimard-Patrick Léger, 26 Yachts de Paris, 28 Gallimard-Patrick Léger, 29 Café Six-Huit
61
33 Laurent, 34 Pavillon Ledoyen (façade), 34 Gallimard-Roger Gain (terrace), 35 Gallimard-Roger Gain
63
36 Lucas Carton, 38 Le Carré des Feuillants, 40 Gallimard-Roger Gain, 41 Gallimard-Gérard Nencioli
65
42 L'Œnothèque, 43 Casa Olympe, 44 Guilhaume-Saint-Amour, 45 Drouant (staircase), 45 Gallimard-Gérard Nencioli (Salon Goncourt, sign)
66
47 Gallimard-Roger Gain, 48 Maxim's (Sem drawing), 48 Gallimard-Roger Gain (façade), 50 Gallimard-Roger Gain, 53 Gallimard-Roger Gain
67
49 Gallimard-Roger Gain, 50 Gallimard-Roger Gain, 51 Gallimard-Roger Gain, 53 Gallimard-Gérard Nencioli (ceiling paintings), 53 Gallimard-Roger Gain (room)
69
55 Gallimard-Roger Gain, 56 Table d'Anvers
71
60 Le Grand Véfour (plate), 60 Gallimard-Roger Gain (room), 61 Gérard Besson, 62 Café Marly
73
66 Miravile, 67 Le Monde des Chimères, 68 Gallimard-Roger Gain, 69 Bofinger (dome), 69 Gallimard-Roger Gain (panel, roses)
74
73 Gallimard-Roger Gain, 74 Gallimard-Gilbert Nencioli,

75 Gallimard-
Roger Gain,
76 Gallimard-
Gilbert Nencioli
75
71 Kim Anh,
72 Bertie's,
73 Gallimard-
Patrick Léger,
74 Gallimard-
Gilbert Nencioli,
75 Gallimard-
Roger Gain,
77 Gallimard-
Gilbert Nencioli
77
79 Jacques Cagna,
80 La Timonerie,
81 Bourboulon,
82 Allard (poster),
82 Gallimard-Roger
Gain (kitchen)
79
83 Gallimard-
Roger Gain,
84 L'Arpège,
85 Gallimard-
Patrick Léger,
86 Gallimard-
Gérard Nencioli
81
89 Dominique,
91 G. Ferron,
92 Vin et Marée
83
94 P. Clapot,
95 L'Épi Dupin,
97 La Régalade,
98 La Closerie des Lilas
84
Gaumont
87
2 S. Couturier-
Archipress,
3 Le Flore,
4 Le Café
de l'Industrie,
6 Le Fouquet's
89
8 Le Floridita,
9 P. Tournebœuf,
10 Le China Club
91
14 F. Mei-Tabou
(actors),
14 Théâtre National
de Chaillot (logo),
15 L. Vasconi,
16 Théâtre National
de la Colline
93
19 C. M. Lavrierre,
21 Gallimard-
Patrick Léger
95
24 Gaumont,
25 Gaumont,
26 Gaumont
97
29 Le Bal du
Moulin Rouge,
30 Le Lido,
31 Crazy Horse,
32 Paradis Latin
99
33 Baiser Salé,
34 Gallimard-
Patrick Léger,
36 Le Petit Journal,
37 Hot Brass
100
40 Le Balajo,
41 La Casbah,
42 C. Bamale,
43 Castel
101
39 Les Bains,
40 Le Balajo,
41 La Casbah
102
Gallimard-Roger Violet
104–105
RMN
1 Gallimard-
Patrick Léger,
2 Gallimard-
Patrick Léger
107
7 Gallimard-
Léonard de Selva,
8 Gallimard-
Patrick Léger
10 Gallimard-
Léonard de Selva
109
11 Naucotel-C. Walter,
12 bdic (poster),
12 Gallimard-Patrick
Léger (dome),
13 B. Hatala (Eve)
13 J. Manoukian
(The Thinker)
111
17 Centre Historique
des Archives Nationales,
18 Ville de Paris-
C. Walter,
19 Gallimard-
Patrick Léger
113
22 Gallimard-
Xavier Richer,
23 RMN,
24 Musée Grévin
(Depardieu),
24 Gallimard-Patrick
Léger (waxworks,
entrance, dome)
115
27 Gallimard-Patrick
Léger (Géode, pool at la
Villette),
27 Gallimard-Léonard
de Selva (l'Ourcq canal),
28 DPJ-Mairie de Paris,
29 Musée Édith Piaf,
30 Gallimard-Xavier
Richer
116–117
RMN (paintings,
sculptures),
Gallimard-Patrick Léger
(Musée d'Orsay clock)
119
35 B. Acloque-CNMHS
Paris (stained-glass
windows),
35 Gallimard-Patrick
Léger (Sainte-Chapelle),
36 Gallimard-
Patrick Léger
121
37 RMN-Musée
National du Moyen Âge,
38 IMA,
38 IMA-P. Pitrou,
39 Muséum National
d'histoire Naturelle-
Laurent Bessol
122–123
42 Sénat,
43 DPJ-Ville de Paris,
44 DPJ-Ville de Paris
124
Vaux le Vicomte-
Philippe A. Chastel
126–127
1 RMN,
7 Musée Départemental
du Prieuré-Saint-
Germain-en-Laye,
9 Deshayes,
13 CDT Seine et
Marne-F. Buxin,
15 Parc zoologique
de Thoiry,
16 Parc Astérix
128–129
RMN
131
5 Château de
Malmaison,
6 RMN,
7 Musée Départemental
du Prieuré-St. Germain
133
9 RMN,
10 C. Laroussinie
(riding school),
10 DR (Château de
Chantilly)
135
11 Vaux le Vicomte,
12 Maison du Tourisme
77 (du Val de Marne),
13 CDT de Seine
et Marne-F. Buxin
136–137
14 Disney,
16 Parc Astérix,
17 Golf national
138
Castelbajac
141
1 L. Boegly,
2 Gallimard-
Patrick Léger,
4 Gallimard-
Patrick Léger
143
6 Inès de la Fressange,
7 C. Adjani,
8 Christian Dior,
9 B. Malaisy
(perfume bottle),
9 Nina Ricci
(sweaters),
10 Joseph,
11 L. Vuitton
145
15 Guerlain,
16 Gallimard-
Lionel Monéger,
17 Faguais,
18 Gallimard-
Lionel Monéger,
19 Gallimard-
Patrick Léger,
20 Cartier-G. Panseri
147
21 F. Dumas,
22 Au Nain Bleu,
23 Lanvin-
Boutique Bleue,
24 René Lalique,
26 Jadis et Gourmande,
27 Guy Laroche
149
29 Gien,
30 Paraboot,
31 Gallimard-
Xavier Richer,
32 Hédiard
151
36 Herzog,
37 Gallimard-
Patrick Léger,
39 Dinh Van,
43 Chanel
153
46 Gallimard-
Patrick Léger,
47 L. Dewez,
48 Les Salons du
Palais-Royal Shiseido,
50 Castelbajac (interior),
50 J.P. Peersman (shoes)
155
51 Gallimard-
Lionel Monéger,
52 Ventilo,
53 Gallimard-
Lionel Monéger,
54 Gallimard-
Lionel Monéger
157
58 Gallimard-
Seymourina Cruse,
59 Debauve et Gallais,
60 L'Artisan Parfumeur,
61 Arnys,
62 Corinne Zaquine,
64 Martine Sitbon
(shop),
64 G. Fessy (clothes)
159
66 Erès,
67 Poilâne (façade,
interior)
67 Gallimard-Éric
Guillemot (bread),
68 Gallimard-
Patrick Léger
160
72 Galerie Altero
(mirror),
73 Le Louvre
des Antiquaires,
74 Semaest-F. Jolly
161
72 Gallimard-Patrick
Léger (quai Voltaire),
73 Le Louvre
des Antiquaires
162–163 Gallimard-
Seymourina Cruse
164 Gallimard-
Patrick Léger
165 Gallimard-
Lionel Monéger